BOOKS BY ALAN HARRINGTON

The Revelations of Dr. Modesto
Life in the Crystal Palace
The Secret Swinger
The Immortalist

Psychopaths...

ALAN HARRINGTON

SIMON AND SCHUSTER • NEW YORK

To Bill and Galen Cole

First printing
SBN 671-21192-7
Library of Congress Catalog Card Number: 77-189744
Designed by Irving Perkins
Manufactured in the United States of America

Portions of this book have appeared in *Playboy.*

The author and Simon and Schuster wish to thank the following for permission to reprint certain excerpts:

Basic Books, Inc., New York: for excerpt from *Black Rage* by William H. Grier and Price M. Cobbs, copyright © 1968.

Dial Press, New York: for excerpt from *Revolution for the Hell of It* by Abbie Hoffman, copyright © 1968 by The Dial Press, Inc.

Doubleday & Company, New York: for excerpt from *the lives and times of archy & mehitabel* by Don Marquis, copyright 1927 by Doubleday & Company, Inc.

Grove Press, Inc., New York: for excerpt from *The Autobiography of Malcolm X*, with the assistance of Alex Haley, copyright © 1964 by Alex Haley and Malcolm X, copyright © 1965 by Alex Haley and Betty Shabazz; and for excerpt from *The Wretched of the Earth* by Frantz Fanon, translated from the French by Constance Farrington, copyright © 1963 by Présence Africaine.

Harper & Row, Publishers, Inc., New York: for excerpt from *Psychiatry and the Dilemmas of Crime* by Seymour Halleck, M.D.

Holt, Rinehart and Winston, Inc., New York: for excerpt from *Must You Conform?* by Robert Lindner, copyright © 1956 by Robert Lindner.

The Macmillan Company, New York: for excerpt from *The Informed Heart* by Dr. Bruno Bettelheim, copyright © 1960 by Bruno Bettelheim.

C. V. Mosby Co., St. Louis, Missouri: for excerpt from *The Mask of Sanity*, Dr. Hervey Cleckley, ed., copyright © 1964 by Hervey Cleckley.

Princeton University Press, New Jersey: for excerpt from *The Collected*

Works of C. G. Jung, ed. by G. Adler, M. Fordham, and H. Read, trans. by R. F. C. Hull, Bollingen Series XX, vol. 6, "Psychological Types," copyright © 1971 by Princeton University Press.

G. P. Putnam's Sons for excerpt from The Politics of Ecstasy by Timothy Leary, copyright © 1968 by The League for Spiritual Discovery, Inc.

Scott Meredith Literary Agency, Inc., New York: for excerpt from The White Negro by Norman Mailer, published by City Lights Books. Reprinted by permission of the author and the author's agent, Scott Meredith Literary Agency, Inc., 580 Fifth Avenue, New York, N. Y. 10036.

Straight Arrow Publishers, Inc., San Francisco: for excerpt from an interview by Jann Wenner with John Lennon in Rolling Stone magazine of January 21, 1971, copyright © 1971 by Straight Arrow Publishers, Inc. All rights reserved.

The New York Times Company, New York: for excerpt from "The Devil's Architect," by James P. O'Donnell, in The New York Times Magazine, copyright © 1969 by The New York Times Company.

Viking Press, Inc., New York: for excerpt from On the Road by Jack Kerouac, copyright © 1955, 1957 by Jack Kerouac.

Van Nostrand Reinhold Company, New York: for excerpt from The Psychopath by William and Joan McCord.

The Village Voice, Inc., New York: for excerpt from "The Psychopath: Hero of Our Age" by Michael L. Glenn, M.D., in The Village Voice, September 14, 1967, copyright © 1967 by The Village Voice, Inc.

Grateful acknowledgments to:

Chief psychiatrist Dr. Thomas P. Detre, Drs. David Kupfer, Jerry Maxmen, Thomas Steele and Gary Tucker, social worker Carol Anderson, Yale-New Haven Hospital; Dr. Tomislav Zargaj, director, Danvers State Hospital, Hathorne, Massachusetts; Dan Sakall, adult probation officer, State Superior Court, Tucson, Arizona; Officer Peter Hughart, Police Department, San Mateo, California; Professor Stanley Schachter, Department of Psychology, Columbia University; Luba Petrova Harrington for making available her taped interviews with "Lee Raymond"; and Charles Schmid, Jr., State Penitentiary, Florence, Arizona, for the use of his poem, "Residual Man."

Contents

NOTE: All names of persons directly involved in the "Psychopathic Tales"—psychopaths and victims alike—as well as of those described in illustrative stories, anecdotes and the case histories, are fictional. As exceptions, Dr. Timothy Leary, Richard Alpert (now Baba Ram Dass), Neal Cassady and Jack Kerouac have been identified. Otherwise only men commonly known for having been convicted in court of violent crimes, such as Gary Steven Krist, Charles Manson, "Tex" Watson and Charles Schmid, Jr. (and their victims) are given their correct names.

I

Coming of the Psychopath

"There walk among us men and women who are in but not of our world," wrote the late Robert Lindner. ". . . Often the sign by which they betray themselves is crime, crime of an explosive, impulsive, reckless type. Sometimes the sign is ruthlessness in dealing with others socially, even commercially."

The menacing individuals to whom Dr. Lindner referred in *Must You Conform?* are well known. They have a familiar name. In psychiatric as well as popular literature, in Sunday supplements, in law and sociological studies, at cocktail parties and inquests, in the armed forces, at medical conventions, in employment offices, in clinics and police stations, they are readily identified as psychopaths.

PHARMACIST NABBED
IN NEW SEX DRUGGING

Druggist K.L.S., convicted four years ago of kidnapping and sexually assaulting three young women after giving them knockout drops, was charged yesterday with a similar assault on a shapely housewife.

S. was arrested by the same detective who bagged him in 1964 and his arraignment was handled by Bronx District Attorney Burton Roberts, who was prosecutor at his 1965 trial.

At the conclusion of that trial, S. was sentenced to 40 years to life in prison. He was released from prison in 1967 when the Court of Appeals threw out the kidnapping convictions and ordered a new trial on the other charges of which S. was convicted—attempted rape, assault and attempted assault.

S., 44, was freed in $2,500 bail.

During . . . [his] 1965 trial, three attractive young women testified that he drugged them and drove them to a motel where they were stripped and sexually assaulted.

New York *Daily News*
July 3, 1969

THE WIZARD OF WOO
BY ARTHUR WATSON

To Mathew M., the time he spent romancing lonely, middle-aged women was an investment, one that returned $100,000 in just two years . . .

M. had a way with women . . . a way that led him into at least nine marriages and uncounted romances that paid tidy dividends. So the 1-to-10-year rap he's now doing shouldn't be a total loss. M. is writing his memoirs. Tentative title: "The Computerized Love Bandit."

M. was seized in Memphis . . . and after indicating he would demand a trial, abruptly pleaded guilty here . . .

"It was worse than stealing," he told the court in a handwritten statement. "Promises I had no intention of keeping . . . a past life built on lies. . . . My life revolting even to me . . . I have total obligations of $100,000 and I would like the opportunity to pay them back.

"Let me work to pay them to prove I am no longer a liar . . . I could begin by putting my personal obligations in order, making full restitution and if I can't do this, I'm not fit for society. A man changes, he can change . . . I know I'm at a point of no return in life."

The judge agreed on the point of no return—and sentenced M. to 1 to 10 years in prison.

New York *Sunday News*
August 3, 1969

Whether making headlines like these or living out his days as a troublemaker on the neighborhood level, the traditional psychopath is hardly a new man. We know him as the town drunk, habitual wife-beater, wastrel, swindler, forger, family disgrace, black sheep, the "bad seed" minister's son—or we may recognize *her,* according to perhaps bygone standards, as the loose, man-hungry housewife on the prowl for strangers or as the girl "from a good family" unaccountably gone wrong.

On another level, the psychopath may be a doctor constantly involved in malpractice suits, the businessman whose proposals always appear a little shady and whose ventures somehow fail "through no fault of his own." We have one near-certainty: sooner or later when the classic psychopath comes on stage, things will go wrong.

People associated with him—especially his family and friends —will suffer. And, it so often happens, incomprehensibly. Patterns of temporary success or at least stability are followed by strangely brutal and irresponsible behavior, stupid and unnecessary falls from grace for which there can be no rational explanation. Yet in between these disasters, and sometimes while they are taking place, the offender (it's hard to call him a victim, since he gives little evidence of suffering very much) may remain on the surface an utterly plausible, often attractive individual, lucid and ready with all kinds of explanations. Until he has repeated his destructive routines many times over, his loved ones characteristically long to forgive him, and even blame themselves for having been too harsh. This can be understood because in retrospect his behavior appears in many instances to be simply beyond belief— so much so that the hurt and astonished mate, friend, or business associate who has suffered at the hands of the psychopath may well be persuaded that he or she, not the other, has been temporarily out of his mind.

I am thinking, for example, of a successful mutual-fund salesman who maintained a small mansion, a Rolls-Royce, and his pretty wife in a chic community on Cape Cod during the summers. In addition, he was a writer, and the competition—typing in cottages and hovels nearby—learned that, dismayingly, this new Renaissance man had sold a script to someone like Gregory Peck for $200,000. He had just returned from the Coast. Amusingly enough, the actor found his script in such good shape (it needed only a little polishing) that he had spent the time they had together talking with the writer about mutual funds, and was about to take him on as a financial adviser as well.

Meanwhile Mark, the bluff, hearty Renaissance man, had allowed his friends on the Cape to get in on his growing mutual fund, offering especially advantageous terms. Summer went by, the fall, next year, and the following summer. The script, the deal, were somehow not forthcoming. There was no question that Mark worked hard enough. He had set up his workshop in an old windmill. As early as six in the morning his typewriter could be heard. By eleven his writing stint was over, and he came out on the beach for volleyball. Meanwhile his mutual-fund business grew. A number of merchants in the Cape Cod town put their savings in Mark's enterprise.

A few months later Mark was exposed. There was no script, no deal with Peck or any other star. He had been living high on the moneys he was supposedly investing in his mutual fund. Mark's case may be seen as textbook psychopathy. In a bluff, honest manner, free of strain, he sold whatever he wanted to sell almost without trying. People actually pressed money on him. On the business side there was no "good reason" for the fraud, in that he was in fact a more-than-competent money manager and could have done well without cheating his clients. Typical was the amazing and hardly worthwhile labor that went into maintaining his deceit. Not only did he get up early and tap out something (but not the fake script) on his typewriter, but when his wife expressed uneasiness over the script and the deal with the movie star, Mark one day suddenly produced a copy of a contract with a big film company on that company's true letterhead, with his own, his "agent's," and the actor's signatures at the bottom.

As might have been predicted by anyone having close-in experience with a psychopath, Mark was hospitalized but not prosecuted, and those he defrauded still liked him so much that they declined to testify against him. Soon afterward he was discharged from the mental institution as obviously sane, left his wife, moved to another part of the country, consented to a divorce, married again . . .

Literature on psychopathy goes back 150 years. The newly observed character disorder was described early in the nineteenth century by Dr. J. C. Pritchard in England as "moral insanity."

The French physician Dr. Philippe Pinel, who first freed madmen from dungeons and shackles, called it *"manie sans délire."* Later in the century the Italian Cesare Lombroso saw the lucid, apparently not in the least deranged person who committed violently antisocial acts as a "born criminal" and "moral imbecile."

Today, or until very recently, among students of the psychopath, this much has generally been agreed upon:

.Persons diagnosed as psychopathic begin as rejected, cruelly or indifferently treated children, or may possibly have suffered early brain damage, detected or not. They strike back at the world with aggressive, unrestrained, attention-drawing behavior. (Why one person emerges from a disordered childhood inhibited and neurotic, and another, the psychopath, with the opposite tendencies remains unclear.) Since conscience is instilled by early love, faith in the adults close by, and desire to hold their affection by being good, the child unrewarded with love grows up experiencing no conscience. Uncared for, he doesn't care, can't really love, feels no anxiety to speak of (having experienced little or no love to lose), does not worry about whether he's good or bad, and literally has no idea of guilt.

Psychopathic children can be helped only—and this is debated—by dramatically improved changes in the environment. For adult psychopaths, successful therapy has proved to be all but impossible. For one thing, the therapist's goal must be exactly the opposite of that assumed in treating neurotics: he must try to *instill* guilt and anxiety, rather than alleviate such feelings, in a "patient" who feels fine and believes that there is nothing wrong with him.

The psychopath doesn't suffer so much as he makes others suffer. Since he is free of inhibitions, his impulses are said immediately to spill over into action. He takes what he wants when he wants it. As we have seen, he's supposed to be incapable of loving anyone—but later we will come up against a disturbing mystery: he can sometimes inspire far more devotion than the average person. He may lie glibly and show little if any embarrassment when caught out. The classic psychopath leaves a trail of misery, fighting, fraud, running up debts; he may abandon his wife and children, perhaps returning now and then if he feels like it, or leave a job without notice, or suddenly, for no reason, begin to perform so poorly or dishonestly that the company fires him. If prompted by more vicious impulses, psychopaths will be arraigned as killers, rapists, or molesters of children.* Whether arrested for disturbing the peace, forgery, child abandonment, or murder, the psychopath will react with indifference or, it may be, put on a show of outraged innocence, protesting that he has been framed or misunderstood.

Psychopaths generally go free to create more trouble. They frequently turn on charm that proves hard to resist, time and again deceiving police, judges, juries, hospital authorities, employers, wives and families—and psychiatrists—into accepting their arguments that the latest incident was "all a mistake." If need be, like the "Wizard of Woo," they come on with fake repentance—tearful self-denunciations and the like—which disappears as soon as the immediate objective (freedom or forgiveness) has been attained.

There may follow a quiet period, with every evidence of stability and cautious predictions that the wayward individual has straightened out or learned his lesson. But one thing psychopaths of this kind do not do is learn from painful experience. The prospect of punishment will not keep them from going off the rails again. These men and women don't seem to worry. Ironically, with the Age of Anxiety supposedly oppressing civilized mankind, they have been diagnosed as "deficient in anxiety."

Thus, a quick study of the familiar psychopath, one that most students would accept. But venturing into the literature that attempts to define psychopathy's essential nature (if any), we move into a realm of confusion. Scores of definitions contradict one another. In their "Essay on the Criminal Mind," *The Psychopath,* William and Joan McCord note that "the proliferation of definitions, the tendency to expand the concept to include all deviant behavior, the discrepancies in judgment between different observers—these pitfalls in the history of the concept—are enough to make a systematic diagnostician weep."

---

* But such crimes are not in themselves "psychopathic," and may be committed by persons not in this category.

Adding to this confusion, in 1952 the American Psychiatric Association dropped the designation "psychopath," replacing it with "sociopath." This provoked criticism from many psychiatrists, mainly for the reason given by the McCords: ". . . definition of the 'sociopath' emphasized social maladjustment to the exclusion of other criteria. By lumping together many varied types of criminals, sexual deviants, drunkards, and even unsavory politicians into one mass, such thinking buries the very real differences among them." As of 1971, in another rearrangement, the psychopathic tent covers "antisocial" persons.

The masterwork on the psychopathic mystery is all but universally conceded to be *The Mask of Sanity,* by Hervey Cleckley, M.D., Clinical Professor of Psychiatry at the Medical College of Georgia. Since publication in 1941, the book has gone through four revised editions. Dr. Cleckley was the first to call attention not merely to the seriousness of psychopathy as a nation-wide phenomenon but to its potential for social disaster. "It is urgent and obvious," he wrote, "that we devise more effective means of restraining these people in their persistently destructive careers."

Many other writers have had similar visions of psychopathic menace. For example, Robert Lindner: "Psychopathy represents the most expensive and most destructive of all known forms of errant behavior . . ." And William and Joan McCord: "Psychopathy, possibly more than other mental disorders, threatens the safety, the serenity, and the security of American life."

Much of the literature relating to psychopathy has assumed that the rational but dangerously unstable, erratic people diagnosed as psychopaths are bound to lose: at odds with society, they sooner or later end badly. *The Mask of Sanity* demonstrates this point in one case history after another. But deep into his work, we find Dr. Cleckley disturbed by a kind of person he can't explain. He acknowledges the Successful Psychopath.

This individual's illness, if he is ill, appears circumscribed, and in no way damages his career. Dr. Cleckley never satisfactorily accounts for him, except to distinguish the "partial" from the "full" psychopath, and to note rather lamely that "although they [the successful outlaws] appear on casual inspection as successful members of the community, as able lawyers, executives,

or physicians, they do not, it seems, succeed in the sense of finding satisfaction or fulfillment in their accomplishments." (But it
almost goes without saying that lack of satisfaction or fulfillment
in life can hardly be limited to psychopaths.)

In the late 1940's and early 1950's, the conception of the
part-psychopath began to emerge more clearly in psychiatric
studies. The scheming outlaw inspired a thrill of fear as well as
fascination. There was a sense of menacing strangers in our midst,
brilliant, remorseless people with icy intelligence, incapable of
love or guilt, with aggressive designs on the rest of the world.

The successful psychopath, it was said, could dominate people as he damaged them precisely *because* of his lack of feeling.
Uninvolved with others, he coolly saw into their fears and desires,
and maneuvered them as he wished. Such a man might not, after
all, be doomed to a life of scrapes and escapades ending igno-
miniously in the jailhouse. Instead of murdering others, he might
become a corporate raider and murder companies, firing people
instead of killing them, and chopping up their functions rather
than their bodies. Any vicious needs in him would be carefully
structured and contained, as with the advertising executive beating up girls in obscure hotel rooms, then paying them off in return for silence.

A bold and intimidating figure comes out of the shadows. In
"The Psychopath in Our Society,"* William Krasner drew this
picture:

> He is the world's most consummate actor, since the or-
> dinary passions, scruples, fears or conflicts which affect others
> never confuse him. He is never the bashful lover, the modest,
> unrewarded worker, the pride-bound person who will not ask
> favors. He seems often charming, intelligent, gallant, brave;
> where the timid or conventional fear to tread he plunges;
> even his obvious faults often seem to be only virtues dis-
> guised—restlessness, unreliability, eccentricity, egocentricity.

We now have a disquieting awareness of people among us
who may at the same time be profoundly ill and yet, in many ways,

* *Neurotica II,* 1948.

far more capable than we are. Hints of magic appear: Dr. Cleckley cites, for instance, "the astonishing power that nearly all psychopaths and part-psychopaths have to bind forever the devotion
of women."

The psychopath's special charm is mentioned over and over
again by the people who have been involved with him. To cite
one of many thousand examples, Gary Steven Krist, who kidnapped the heiress Barbara Mackle and hid her in a Georgia
woodland inside a casketlike box of her own design, showed
no remorse whatever for having almost murdered the girl. (Rescuers searching the area for hours following imprecise instructions from the kidnapper had come upon the hiding place by
luck.) "I don't expect to get justice," he told reporters. It would
be the electric chair "or whatever means these barbarian humans
use these days, I suppose." In jail this man received 1,000 letters,
mostly from young girls who believed him innocent, including
one from his abandoned wife—enclosing photos of their two small
sons—who described him in a newspaper interview as "the most
fascinating man I ever met. When he wants to turn it on," she
said, "he can charm the birds right out of the trees. I knew what
he was when I married him; I went into it with my eyes open . . .
He could have been a doctor, even an astronaut."

Evading definition, the psychopath fascinates and draws
emotional responses from the authorities trying to catch him in
their nets. For psychiatrists he resembles the devil in medieval
times, seeming often to incarnate each observer's own devil, the
physician's own obsessions and fears.

In the Middle Ages, churchmen insisted that Satan could
manifest himself in practically any shape or disguise—priest, ped-
dler, or honorable knight. The psychopathic spirit of our time has
been imagined as inhabiting people very different from one another. Crank, obscene phone caller, writer of poison-pen letters;
compulsive, perhaps acid-throwing pursuer of a hated loved one;
lone wolf or, it may be, members of the Florida bike gang who
nailed a girl by her hands to a tree for several hours because she
didn't bring in enough money. But we also have the psychopath

in respectable circles, no longer assumed to be a loser. Or if he loses, he may bring down others with him, in the style of Senator Joseph McCarthy, Dr. Sam Sheppard, or the eventually murdered financier Serge Rubinstein.

William Krasner comments:

> They—psychopath and partpsychopath—do well in the more unscrupulous type of saleswork, because they take such delight in "putting it over on them," getting away with it— and have so little conscience about defrauding their customers. They become private detectives and police, bodyguards, strikebreakers. Many go much higher, to become politicians and industrialists where though often erratic and unreliable their complete lack of scruples overcomes their more or equally able rivals.

Psychopaths have frequently been cited as war heroes. Just the same, according to Lieutenant Colonel Roy R. Grinker and Major John P. Spiegel of the U.S. Marine Corps in *Men Under Stress*, in the armed forces

> psychopathic personalities, among whom we include a heterogeneous group of asocial individuals, are great problems because of their overtly expressed hostilities, alcoholism and aggressive behavior . . . Stockade punishment, loss of rank and pay losses had little deterrent effect. Overseas some of these enlisted men and very few officers were aggressive, fighting and often heroic figures. Here at last their psychopathy was well adapted to their social milieu. Many of them received promotions, decorations and honors. But the return home is a sad sequel, because the aggressive behavior is no longer adaptive and trouble ensues. These psychopaths become worse after combat because they have had aggressions mobilized and approved of by external father figures, and, having corruptible superegos, they have no automatic check on their social behavior.

What links these varied individuals, if they can be so linked? Dr. Cleckley, along with Robert Lindner, likens psychopaths to adolescents driven to extreme behavior by boredom. The author of *The Mask of Sanity* then goes on to a startling though now fashionable conception:

> What he [the psychopath] believes he needs to protest is no small group, no particular institution, set of ideologies, etc., but human life itself. In it he finds nothing deeply meaningful or persistently stimulating, but only some transient and relatively petty pleasant caprices, a terribly repetitious series of minor frustrations, and ennui. Like many teen-agers, SAINTS [all caps mine], history-making statesmen, and other notable LEADERS or GENIUSES, he shows unrest: he wants to do something about the situation.

With the coupling of psychopath and saint—even if the comparison is unfavorable to the former—we have come a long way from the "moral imbecile" of the nineteenth century, the "predatory personality" diagnosed by Dr. Karl Menninger in *A Psychiatrist's World,* or the "hollow, isolated person" identified by Dr. Arnold Buss in his book *Psychopathology.*

The psychopath emerges now as a failed saint. How can this be? We may begin to watch the gradual change-over of an old concept and the birth of a new model in its place, as the psychopath and saint are, by one observer then another, combined into a new kind of person.

Robert Lindner saw this individual as vulgar and fanatic: "I am convinced that the end stages of any given civilization are marked by the appearance of a 'new breed' of men. This breed is always psychopathic, dedicated to action and violence rather than contemplation and compassion." He spoke of "the psychopathic virus" and "a plague of psychopathic behavior." In the 1950's he found that a new kind of youth had come into being: "A profound and terrifying change has overtaken the character of that time of life we call adolescence." More than conventionally rebellious, he stressed, young people were in a state of mutiny against civilization itself.

According to Lindner, psychopathy among the young was expressed not so much in lone-wolf antisocial acts as in conformity. He listed the two principal characteristics of the psychopathic adolescent: (1) acting out in the social theater impulses arising from internal distress, and (2) drifting in crowds. Combined, they produce "a form of disorder that renders its victims essentially anti-social, conscienceless, inclined to violence in behavior and liable to loss of identity in the group, gang, mob or herd."

Lindner did not name but offered evidence for the predominance of another quality in the new man. In contrast to the weariness experienced by many neurotic people, a driving energy possesses the psychopath. Perhaps for this reason and because, in headlong action, such individuals are never weakened by reflection and doubt, "it is characteristic of all movements and crusades that the psychopathic element rises to the top."

Lindner's psychopaths closely resemble Ortega y Gasset's "mass men," described in *The Revolt of the Masses,* who "intervene in everything," and "solely by violence." They also have much in common with Eric Hoffer's true believer. The energies of a psychopath, mass man, or true believer are instantly translated into action. Bourgeois values of moderation, letting the other person speak, respect for the past, gradual change and reform, come under repeated assault. As Hoffer notes in *The True Believer:*

> The superior individual, whether in politics, literature, science, commerce or industry, plays a large role in shaping a nation, but so do individuals at the other extreme—the failures, misfits, outcasts, criminals, and all those who have lost their footing or never had one, in the ranks of respectable humanity. The game of history is usually played by the best and the worst over the heads of the majority in the middle.

Not unexpectedly then, in our own revolutionary or prerevolutionary times, the psychopathic element may, as Lindner predicted, be rising to the top. Shortly before his death, Lindner described the new man as "the harbinger of social and political distress," and suggested that "one of the highest missions a man of our culture can have is this: identify the psychopathic antagonist and to struggle against the conditions that produce him."

We are now far from the conception of the psychopath as a sick man out of phase with a relatively "healthy" society. For perhaps the American way of life has always been a powerful generator of psychopathy. In his *Neurotica* article more than twenty years ago, William Krasner pointed out:

> This is no accident . . . there are very definite aspects to our culture pattern which give them [psychopaths] encouragement. In America we put great value on the acquisition of material gain, prestige, power, personal ascendance, and the competitive massing of goods . . .
>   . . . we have very short memories about the origins of some of our great national fortunes, toward the holders of which we hold so much respect. At the other end, of course, our machine civilization tends to level, and strangle individuality, leaving large groups within our culture fearful, anxious, resentful, and even occasionally openly hostile. In such an atmosphere psychopathy rises, grows and battens.

In 1948 Krasner saw trouble ahead:

> No nation or culture consisting wholly, or even largely, of psychopaths can long survive. The psychopath is a disruptive, parasitic, immoral influence, and any group, while it may for various reasons support and even honor him, must fundamentally rest on a firm economy and a great mass of hardworking responsible people to exist; and, in direct proportion to the extent that he is tolerated, that *his attitudes find support in the culture pattern* [my italics], to that extent it is an unhealthy society.

Yet can resistance—however intemperate and amoral—to an environment that tends to "level, and strangle individuality" necessarily be described in terms of mental illness? Suppose that bourgeois society may in fact be coming to pieces. If the times have grown sick, if middle-class greed and hypocrisy have inflicted on us a mad war, poverty and discrimination, pollution of all kinds—in this society, does the direct-action psychopath become, under certain dramatic circumstances, a relatively well man? The question is whether the psychopathic mode of action can be summed up as destructive and antisocial, which it so often is, and simply left at that. Or could it also be inevitable at the turning point we have reached? Possibly a scene has been set that inescapably calls forth outlaw impulses and reactions.

Against this background, prophesying what may have come upon us, there appeared in the summer of 1957, published in *Dissent* magazine, Norman Mailer's essay "The White Negro." Mailer breaks through to an entirely new conception. The menacing psychopath is embraced. Incredibly (it seems, at first shock), we are urged to turn into an "antithetical" version of the outlaw and find our way to his radical vision of the universe.

"The White Negro" produced the effect of a door suddenly flung open to reveal a frightening jungle just beyond the threshold. In this jungle, "where paranoia is as vital to survival as blood," the new psychopath will be king. Hip is the American existentialist's way to live. The "psychopathic brilliance" of the hipster's style is modeled on the black experience. "The Negro has the simplest of alternatives: live a life of constant humility or ever-threatening danger." To survive, he must remain cool, stay on top of life at every threatening, exciting moment, and live in "the enormous present."

Mailer saw about 10 million Americans as "more or less psychopathic," with (fifteen years ago) only some 100,000 being conscious of what they are. But the hipsters constitute "an elite with the potential ruthlessness of an elite." For the hipster: "His inner experience of the possibilities within death is his logic. So, too, for the existentialist. And the SAINT [my caps] and the bullfighter and the lover."

An absolute and continuing need at every moment to acquit oneself with grace under pressure drives this individual. If he scores, triumphs, gets his way, he grows and lives more intensely. If he fails, allows anyone or any circumstances to put him down, he actually dies a little, his energies weaken, and his soul diminishes: he may even sicken and, Mailer believes, contract cancer.

Psychopathy—hitherto deemed an illness and public menace —is dressed up by Mailer in this remarkable manifesto and presented as an answer to life. What Robert Lindner foresaw with alarm, Mailer celebrates: ". . . the psychopath may indeed be the

perverted and dangerous front-runner of a new kind of personality which could become *the central expression of human nature*
[my italics] before the twentieth century is over. For, *the psychopath is better adapted to dominate* those mutually contradictory
inhibitions upon violence and love which civilization has exacted
of us . . ."

Mailer then suggests that [even in 1957] our cultural direction is already to a marked degree being determined by psychopaths. Not every psychopath is an extreme case, but "the condition of psychopathy is present in a host of people including many
politicians, professional soldiers, newspaper columnists, entertainers, artists, jazz musicians, call-girls, promiscuous homosexuals
and half the executives of Hollywood, television and advertising . . ."

Psychopaths and part-psychopaths, Mailer believes, are trying to create a new nervous system for themselves, one that can
respond to the quickening tempo of our lives as we, perforce,
must live today. (Interestingly, this claim to a new nervous system is also set forth by the psychedelic philosophers, principally
Timothy Leary, who has always believed that the "politics of
the nervous system" will be permanently altered by LSD and
psilocybin trips. After an early trip induced by mushrooms, he
wrote, ". . . we saw ourselves as unwitting agents of a social
process that was far too powerful for us to control or to more than
simply understand. An historical moment that would inevitably
change man at the very center of his nature, his consciousness."
Similarly, Marshall McLuhan finds man's nervous system irrev-
ocably revolutionized by electronics.)

Have we come then to the hour of the psychopath, the
advent of Psychopathic Man? "The only Hip morality," wrote
Mailer in 1957, "is to do what one feels whenever and where it
is possible . . . to be engaged in one primal battle: to open the
limits of the possible for oneself, for oneself alone for that is one's
need," and this involves "adoration of the present."

Again, what was once assumed to be a state of illness is
abruptly declared to be a state of health. For instance, psychopathic time values are invoked. Sixteen years earlier, Dr. Karl
Menninger had noted of psychopaths, as though shaking his head:

"They seem to live only for the moment." And Dr. Arnold Buss: "He [the psychopath] has no sense of time, especially of the future; he senses only the here and now." But to enjoy life, "Here and now, boys!" is the commandment croaked by the mynah bird in Aldous Huxley's last novel, *Island,* which, along with Hesse's *Steppenwolf,* has become scripture for millions. For these young people, Mailer's "enormous present" has arrived, and continuous celebration of the "here and now"; the mind-blowing here and now of all media shows; the thundering walls of music (no longer soft background for talk) that create the stereophonic now in rugless and chairless rooms of the young; the non-negotiable now of student political action.

Are we perhaps arriving at a new style and ideal modeled on psychopathy? According to Mailer, the new man—apparently an advance man heralding the end of softer humanistic values—must above all "find his courage at the moment of violence . . . be cool . . . in control of a situation." Thus, Sharon Tate and her friends might now be alive, according to this concept, had their psychopathic antennae been alert to danger; had they the requisite suspiciousness and trigger alertness to anticipate in the style of James Bond what the wild executioners might be about to do ("liberate them from their affluence"), and at this enormous moment find some way out of their predicament.

As Mailer prophesied, the psychic outlaw among us has the potential to become a storm trooper for the left or right. He may proceed from mystical conviction, or outrage directed against the meaninglessness of life. (We have seen that LSD and other substances can open the road to this frame of mind, releasing latent psychopathy, for example, in formerly innocuous All-American boys.) Whether the revolution of the nervous system is desirable or not, Mailer said a decade and a half ago, it must be gone through. There will be no way around it. "Hip may erupt as a psychically armed rebellion . . . A time of violence, the new hysteria, confusion and rebellion will then be likely to replace the time of conformity."

But can it be true that with the dramatic appearance of the

Psychopathic Ideal a new man has come upon us; that, in order to survive turbulent years ahead, far from seeking to treat the psychopath in clinics, we should rather *emulate* him, learn how to become him? Would it be advisable, for instance, if we adopt a new psychopathic style, for even the nonrevolutionaries among us to honor the present only, and go about annihilating history, past standards, the memory of bygone cultures, eradicate them, for the reason that defunct models of life can only get in our way?

History, we have commonly supposed, teaches that something we like to call "human nature" prevails through the upheavals that take place down through the centuries. Superstructures of behavior come and go but the essential character structure of man endures. But now this has been denied by Mailer, who sees in the late twentieth century the creation of a new nervous system, by Timothy Leary, who describes those of us who have tripped out on LSD as "mutants" whose consciousness will never be the same, and by McLuhan, who envisions new electronic circuitry changing the heads of men and women all over the world.

The idea of a "constant nature underlying history" is rejected also by Dr. Thomas Szasz in *The Myth of Mental Illness.* "Both man and history change," he believes, "and, as they do, 'human nature' changes with them." Like Leary, Dr. Eric Berne, and many others, Dr. Szasz sees the lives we pursue as game-structures of one kind or another. He regards mental disability or malfunction as "more akin to a language problem than to illness," and hysteria, for example, as "sign-using behavior." The patient is reporting that he doesn't understand the game going on. "The analyst seeks to unravel the game of life that the patient plays."

What then is the psychopath signaling? Possibly the breakdown of games that have been sanctioned by Western civilization. Even more important, what are those who have appropriated the term "psychopath" signaling? For in tracking down the psychopath's role we have not so much to determine what he is or may be, but rather to find out why so many people today admire what they *think* he is. We are faced with a revolutionary, hip, but also intellectually chic proposal that Western man is rapidly turning into a person for whom violence, immediate gratification of desire, self-assertion, combat-readiness, and performance are all, while compassion, willingness to wait in line, and refraining from taking advantage have become moral luxuries that growing numbers of us can no longer afford. (Emerson's definition of a gentleman as someone who does not insist on his rights seems now insane.)

We may ask why this model—the view that life must imitate psychopathy, that our scene may, even should, be converted into a playground for psychopaths—has been welcomed and sustained by so many intellectuals. Why have the psychopathic style and ideal become so fashionable?

To be sure, the stage may be filling up with psychopaths of multiple persuasions playing a variety of games. The Mailer psychopath comes across as very different, say, from the Leary psychopath. If you believe existence to be no more or less than games, then the need for Mailer's ferocious ever-alert never-put-me-down competence is relaxed and becomes irrelevant. Street people and black revolutionaries may both live in an enormous present, but in entirely different ways. According to both models, saints and criminals intermingle. Leary, a veteran of the saint's game, has said: "Society has always produced and needed a criminal class. When criminals drop their roles and begin to play a different game incredulous panic can ensue. Can society play its game without having some men acting the part of criminals? If criminals are no longer criminals where do the rest of us stand?"

Possibly then "incredulous panic" may be what an old-fashioned man feels when the saint-psychopath is exalted and turned loose among us as the new man who, for our own protection, we had best try to become. "I'm near-sighted and psychopathic anyway. America I'm putting my queer shoulder to the wheel," proclaimed Allen Ginsberg—as near to a certified American holy man as anyone in our time. Sartre has given us Saint Genet. "Oswald," a psychopathic acquaintance said to me, "was Kennedy's guru."

Dr. Hervey Cleckley notes that a number of his psychopathic subjects have glibly diagnosed their own condition, and yet—even though labeling themselves, employing the right words, and apparently understanding the nature of their disorder (again, if it is absolutely that)—still have no real insight into the element of humanity missing in them. He recalls a psychopathic medical colleague who charmed a women's group with his lecture on the mysterious psychopath. At the trial of a young man accused of planting a bomb on an airplane and blowing up his mother and everyone on board, Dr. Cleckley discovered to his amazement that the prisoner in the dock was, in detached fashion, study-ing . . . *The Mask of Sanity*. (This mass murder became the sub-ject of a routine delivered by Lenny Bruce. "Anyone," he said, "who blows up his mother and forty people *can't be all bad*," and the night club filled with laughter.)

Dr. Cleckley picks out works of J. K. Huysmans *(Against the Grain)*, Sartre *(Nausea)*, and the satirical novels of Evelyn Waugh as projecting in various ways "an unhappy, mutilated and trivial universe." Given such a universe, "if the actual world or man's biological scope were that conveyed in these interesting works, it would not be difficult to account for obsessive illness and for the psychopath's career as *reasonable reactions* [my italics] to a situation where no course is possible except one profoundly pathologic in one way or another."

In *The Naked Lunch* William Burroughs celebrates the New Man also, by sardonically calling for his destruction: "Senators leap up and bray for the Death Penalty with inflexible authority of virus yen . . . Death for dope fiends, death for sex queens (I mean fiends), death for the psychopath who offends the cowed and graceless flesh with broken animal innocence of lithe move-ment . . ." And for Burroughs: "The Planet drifts to random insect doom . . ."

But perhaps this isn't the way things are at all. Can the world really be in such a state? Or have psychopaths through sheer force of brilliance, energy, and obsessiveness impressed a malig-nant dream upon us? In short, are many of the people I have mentioned themselves psychopaths, or touched with psychop-athy, trying to persuade everyone else to join them in one massive aberration, that of free-form anger or disgust, random pleasure-seeking without end, or boredom turned into cruelty? Or as

Shakespeare had one of history's great psychopaths, Richard III, say straight out:

> And therefore—since I cannot prove a lover,
> To entertain these fair well-spoken days—
> I am determined to prove a villain,
> And hate the idle pleasures of these days.
> Plots have I laid, inductions dangerous,
> By drunken prophecies, libels, and dreams . . .

Or may perceptive psychopaths still have something positive to offer? Sweet people don't usually lead uprisings. Conceivably for all their abrasiveness, egocentricity, ill will even, these individuals are right: to heal us some kind of knife is called for. If my surgeon is a sublimated sadist, do I shrink from him?

In "The White Negro," Mailer called attention to the psychic outlaw and predicted that his hour would come. Inevitably, full-blown idealizing of the new man was next. A paean to his prowess came from Michael L. Glenn, M.D., in the "Press of Freedom" column in *The Village Voice* (Sept. 14, 1967). Dr. Glenn entitled his contribution "The Psychopath: Hero of Our Age."

The doctor begins: "The hero of our age is—the psychopath. Free from responsibility, free from guilt, free from anxiety, he pursues his interests without compunction, manipulating others to reach his goals. Corporation president, statesman, educator, physician; his calling is irrelevant: his features are everywhere the same . . ."

Successful psychopaths "find the world's cornucopia open to them as they, without psychiatric label, utilize their psychopathic features for concrete gain. We see them glorified week after week on the covers of *Time, Life* and *Newsweek*. Moreover, every level of our society *seems unwittingly bent on imitating this behavior* [my italics] . . ."

The oncoming psychopath, so feared by Lindner and Krasner, his arrival en masse forecast by Mailer, has already won the day, according to Dr. Glenn. The device of substituting the "sociopathic personality" as a description of the outlaw has, in his words, fixed medical attention on a "disadvantaged group of losers," conveniently ignoring the ones who succeed. "Neither Cleckley nor the APA [American Psychiatric Association] deal with those psychopaths who, with equal endowment but fewer liabilities, *surround us at every turn* [my italics] . . . who shamelessly and guiltlessly, with great charm and 'good intelligence,' manipulate us for their own interests."

This new man puts us through changes, without himself being changed. He "understands The Way Things Are. Making the best of it, he manages to charm, seduce, extort, convince, and hoodwink numbers of people. He sets the tone in politics, art, fashion, etc. He is the price-fixing businessman, the patriot general . . ."

With Mailer, Dr. Glenn finds that the new outlaw, "able to deal coldly with reality, is best fitted for our culture." But while Mailer's psychopath lives on his own frontier, vigilant, alert for whatever may come out of the jungle, determined never to be surprised or to back down, Dr. Glenn's outlaw arrives at his style after traveling a different route—that taken by Timothy Leary, Alan Watts, and thousands of others. He moves with the cool and relaxed wisdom of Asia:

> After all, we all operate in a social labyrinth of roles and rules, talking and giving cues to one another as we seek the easiest route to our goals. Such a social process is game-like . . . The East has for centuries seen social striving as Maya, a playful illusion that all is really serious. The ideal is to laugh at the game while playing it. The social mask is not the same as one's face.
> An adaptive and *essentially psychopathic response* [my italics] is to feel the mask as mask and the face as face, to don the mask when necessary, and to remove it when necessary . . . *A curious sanity rests at the heart of true psychopathy* . . . if one realizes that social interaction is role-playing and appearance, one can play the game without getting lost in it. One enjoys the process itself, and is not chained to Samsara, the endless chain of ups and downs. By refusing to play seriously, one can be anxiety-free, as well as successful. The crucial matter is, does the social mask come

off or does it stick? Is the psychopathic style conscious or hapless? The face beneath the mask, inwardly savoring the outward effect, has the last laugh.

A persistent mystery remains: the potent magic of psychopathy. How can the psychopath—this supposedly cold, predatory individual—inspire such devotion among "normal" people? From the puzzling evidence we have, it seems that, as Lindner believed, outbreaks of extreme psychopathy can be contagious, and that men and women can be led into committing acts of which they would never have dreamed themselves capable, once the psychopathic spell is laid on them.

A civilized man, Albert Speer, Hitler's architect and Armaments Minister, told James P. O'Donnell: *

> . . . Hitler could fascinate, he wallowed in his own charisma, but he could not respond to friendship. Instinctively, he repelled it. The normal sympathies that normal men and women enjoy were just not in him. At the core, in the place where the heart should be, Hitler was a hollow man. He was empty. We who were really close to him, or thought we were, all came to sense this, however slowly. . . . We were all, all of us, simply projections of his own gigantic ego. . . . And yet, Adolf Hitler was my destiny. As long as he was alive he dominated my spirit, at least in part, and to the bitter end. The man's drive—his iron will, his daemonism— fascinated even while it repelled. . . . All the rest of us were spear holders, sycophants—or worse. . . . If at times I could manipulate the Führer's whims in a rational direction, I did so. But, in reality, it was he who was manipulating me. I was enthralled. . . .

Thus, what has been diagnosed as mental illness overpowers what we suppose to be mental health. Perhaps we are going to discover that in times of stress, particularly times of transition when orthodox religions no longer comfort masses of people, mental health rushes toward illness out of a longing for salvation.

We may find also that psychopathy lies waiting, dormant in

* In "The Devil's Architect," *The New York Times Magazine*, Oct. 26, 1969.

millions of nervous systems, holding the possibility of metamor-
phosis into a new kind of human being as soon as the liberating
force comes. Whatever this force—drugs, rock, violence, mystical
experience, or a combination of these—it seems capable of changing an individual, especially a young person, practically overnight. Both for good and evil. A fearsome motorcyclist baptized
in Pat Boone's swimming pool (assuming this to be good) may
embrace Jesus. The YMCA boy one day mounts a hog and starts
turning hairy and savage.

Psychopathic mutants, if they can be so imagined, are often
remembered by friends and neighbors back home as having been
the absolute reverse of their transformed selves. For example,
Charles Watson, disciple of Charles Manson convicted for the
murders of Sharon Tate and her guests, was recalled in his home
town, Copeville, Texas, as a "clean-cut high-school athlete." According to his football coach, Watson had "real good speed." His
brother James: Charles was "a good boy—he never got into
trouble. We always had fun as boys here. We would go to the
lake and go water skiing and used to make go-carts together. He's
a good boy, he's my brother." But the lawyer for the accused who
had known Watson from boyhood observed: "He is thirty pounds
lighter. He looks like a different person. He's very detached and
doesn't seem concerned about anything."

Detached and unconcerned—the mark of clinically diagnosed
psychopaths everywhere, except during brief flare-ups of temper.
But Manson himself, leader of the nomadic family whose members
killed as a means of social protest, for revenge, for pleasure, at
random, and for no reason, may be seen as a spectacular incarna-
tion of destructive psychopathic force—which at times seems
magical, and in a terrible way almost religious—having the outlaw prophet's historic Rasputin-, Savonarola-like gift not merely
for dominating but for bewitching others.

This prompts uneasy questions. First, where does the magic
come from? Manson is described variously as hypnotic, loving,
ingratiating, and terrifying. With a seventh-grade education,
nothing but a record of petty crimes behind him, an amateur's
slight talent with the guitar and soft songs, formed by a childhood
of fear, indifference, and neglect, how does he manage to inspire

such awe and devotion among his followers, particularly the girls
who love him?

"His motions were like magic, it seemed like. The first time I
saw him he was petting a cat. I don't know why that struck me,
but he seemed so kind."

"He gave off a lot of magic. Everyone was so happy around
him."

"The first time I heard him sing it was like an angel. He wrote
songs. Made them up as he went along. Some were beautiful,
happy songs. Others would be sad and moving."

". . . a very beautiful man. We belong to him, not to ourselves. I was told to go [to the Tate home] and I went."

Does such magic as this derive precisely from wretchedness
and deprivation in childhood years? If so, possibly we must acknowledge that since psychopathy may breed psychopathy, we
are now being confronted by increasing numbers of mistreated or
unloved children—from both the slums and the suburbs—who,
having grown up, possess a fearlessness and headlong energy that
we haven't been prepared for.

Gresham's law states that in any monetary exchange bad
currency tends to drive out good. Correspondingly, middle-class
people whose coin is moderation may ask whether psychopathy
tends to drive out sanity, and dominate sanity.

In *The Psychopath,* William and Joan McCord cite a 1933
study:

> Elizabeth Knight, a social worker . . . compared the
> family backgrounds of nine extremely aggressive children
> with those of nine very submissive children. The mothers of
> all the aggressive boys rejected their children; the mothers
> of the submissive lads appeared overprotective. An overtly
> punitive atmosphere dominated the homes of the aggressive
> cases; the homes of the submissive children, on the other
> hand, were "harmonious."

Research of this kind, and there has been a great deal of it,
suggests that neglect or maltreatment of children produces among
the survivors more alert, stronger, belligerent, *predatory* boys and
girls, and that, as the walls of privilege come down, unloved

children may shortly be making a bid to put the advanced society through terrible changes. Put in other terms, have we now a world in which the children of neglect and indifference, those perhaps whipped early and often in anger, are growing up psychopathic from having to deal with unstable, unloving, or exhausted parents, one half-dead parent, or none; have we a world in which these children stand a good chance of dominating and running wild over the children of kindness? Suppose, too, that mystical powers, giving off emanations of either love or hatred, may be distilled *only* from early sorrow. And if these powers can dominate the decency of ordinary people, then is kindness a waste; is giving love to a child bad training? What we can't yet get around is the astonishing fact that lack of love, even cruel treatment, in childhood seems often among psychopaths to produce the power to *inspire* love and fanatical devotion.

Why do supposedly normal people so frequently find themselves bowing down to widely differing kinds of psychopaths, whether Hitler, Charles Manson,* or a fake-inspirational tent-shouter or television preacher? We may discover that we bow down to the psychopath because in times of little faith, seeming to care about the fearful child, he comforts the child in each of us. With the old gods gone, *he* has no doubts, betrays no fear, gives a meaning and authority to life, no matter how twisted, wild, or mysterious it may be.

To look again at our earlier question, can there be something at the very heart of American life that breeds psychopathy? If so, is there anything we can do to change this? Should we? Or will it be best to teach our children the psychopathic style in order that they may survive?

Conceivably religionless man must live in the present, shutting out the past and future, acting out his pleasure and malevolence as he pleases, pursuing his desires without restraint. It may be that now, for him, this has become the only practical way to live, as brilliant individuals among us—basing their own lives on the psychopathic model—have suggested.

* Manson may be diagnosed as paranoid schizophrenic, but in our context he is an inheritor and exponent of the psychopathic style, and a carrier of its virus.

Then, if they are right, what was formerly diagnosed as mental illness has turned into the New Spirit of the Age. Just possibly, too, this need not be so. Perhaps we are being had by sophisticates whose mission it is to universalize their own inability to love, denying the possibilities of warmth and compassion to others. If this is true, assuming the psychopathic spirit to be loose in America, the time may have come to nail down chic, romanticized psychopathy and combat it by every means.

But it is not so easy, not even good enough, to take an overly righteous stand against the psychopath. This kind of person may have infiltrated the society in force; all the same, we have to remind ourselves again that we don't really know him. He may be identified with some success by what he *does,* his impact on others. What he *is* remains something else.

Return to the professional base from which we started. Find a hard definition. That of the McCords, for example: "The psychopath is an asocial, aggressive, highly impulsive person, who feels little or no guilt and is unable to form lasting bonds of affection with other human beings." But then what about a sociopathic group such as Hell's Angels, whose members will be prepared to maim or kill nonbikers who get in their way, yet maintain a fierce all-for-one, one-for-all comradeship with one another, and will risk their lives and manhood to help extricate a fellow Angel from trouble? Such bonds of affection seldom hold middle-class people, who tend carefully to ignore a neighbor in danger. For the McCords, the psychopath "has few values—either those of a society or those of a gang." Yet, as we know, Lindner regards him specifically as a gang member. Eric Berne finds this outlaw obtaining "release from tension" through violence. Dr. Cleckley declares him to be under very little tension. In separate studies, first, David Lykken, and second, Stanley Schachter and Bibb Latané, employing electric shock techniques, demonstrate that psychopaths, lacking anxiety, show little or no "anticipatory emotional response to warning signals"—in direct opposition to Mailer's psychopath, who quivers in response to the remotest warning signal. The British psychiatrist Sir David Henderson makes room for the "creative psychopath," such as (in his view) Lawrence of Arabia. Cleckley finds his psychopaths too impulsive and directionless to be creative. The McCords agree: "Continually searching for a sense of identity, the psychopath often is too preoccupied by his insecurities to permit him to enjoy being creative." Yet elsewhere they contradict this, indicating (as do most other investigators) that the last thing psychopaths worry about is the problem of feeling secure. On the contrary: "The average man wants excitement, but he also wants security. The psychopath, however, often seems willing to sacrifice everything for excitement."

We know that the "psychopath" as a concept, and now ideal, has evolved in startling fashion. What will inform us is precisely the manner in which the term has been *mis*used and glamorized. Hence, in our pursuit, rather than worry about conflicting definitions, it may be more helpful to follow the myth and see where it leads. Misuse is the key—just as it doesn't matter whether Jesus, the actual Jesus, died in the way he did. What matters is the way a sizable portion of the race chose to remember him, and needed to remember him.

Conceivably the times are calling for an idealized version of the Psychopath as Savior. We may see old-fashioned middle-class inhibitory neurosis as obsolete, and abrupt, unrestrained, and conscienceless behavior as a means to mental health. It is also possible to declare irritably that this is all nonsense for the simple reason that psychopathy remains mental illness, and no more, and can't be taken seriously as a world-changing style. So much for the visions of Saul, Mohammed, Marx, Ginsberg . . . Yesterday's madmen *do* wrench history around. But quite apart from this we ought to remember that diagnoses of mental illness have for the most part been made from a bourgeois point of view, with a middle-class bias.

Psychopathy confronts and affronts the bourgeois and all his values, including those held by middle-class psychiatrists and sociologists. This is not to imply that psychopaths are on the right track, and judgments handed down on them by professional people wrong. But the challenge of the outlaw to established struc-

tures should be acknowledged, and the point of view from which
he is declared mentally ill recognized as prejudiced to some degree.

How do we identify a psychopath? He lives *free of form,*
predictable only in his impulsiveness and the probability that if
confined in any sort of routine he will break out of it, bringing
trouble to somebody. He refuses to delay gratification; he will not
yield to the rules of any game but his own. The good of society
doesn't interest him much if at all. According to Lindner, he has
a "completely defective sense of property." Characteristically, he
may steal, "not live up to his family obligations"; he violates time
and duty, wipes out boredom with drugs or drunkenness, blithely
or coldly takes what he wants, grins happily or suddenly explodes
in anger like a baby, *is* one in a sense (a psychiatrist has said that
we are all born psychopaths), hits out, loves, leaves, grasps, ex-
ploits without guilt and regardless of warnings that he's out of
line and subject to punishment.

We have here a revolt against conservative humanism with
its social contracts. For the psychopath, there are no social contracts, such as, for instance, the obligations—assumed by all middle-class authority, including the psychiatric establishment—that
relate to the values of settling down, staying put, rearing a family,
obeying the law (Theodore Roosevelt: "Fear God, and do your
part"), and being productive. In 1941 the U.S. Surgeon General's
Office ascribed to psychopaths the characteristic of being "nomads." This is akin to police classifications of "drifter" or "vagrant"—condemnation enough in many parts of the country to
justify the jailing of shabby-looking people. Another descriptive
tag often used to support a diagnosis of mental illness: "the patient
no longer paid any attention to his personal appearance." For a
number of years now, millions of a rising generation have adopted
a style that provides for deliberately becoming nomads and no
longer paying attention to their personal appearance.

Followers of the style, many, perhaps most, imitation psychopaths (does imitation pursued long enough blend into the actual
condition?), recognize no crime against property. They hold *use*
to be sacred, not ownership. The combination of drugs, evan-
gelical populism, communal living, and readiness for violent

action mingled with an ideal of Buddhist simplicity, going with life from one moment to the next, has created a heady revolutionary brew. The effects, when encountered for the first time, can have a distressing impact on people whose lives have been conventionally ordered.

In Tucson, Arizona, a year ago, a seventy-five-year-old engineer, name him Roger McIntyre, looked out of his back window at dusk, watching, as he loved to do, the pink hollows and shadows made by the setting sun on the Catalina Mountains to the north. He saw to his amazement a gaudily painted hippie bus parked a short distance from the house and a half-dozen young people smoking in his back-yard pagoda. A week earlier the old man had asked some high-school picnickers to get off his property, and then felt ashamed of what he had done. He decided to leave these youngsters alone for a while, hoping that they would soon go away. But they showed no signs of doing so. Instead they brought out a blanket, and several of the young men, whose long filthy hair he had tried not to notice, began to strum guitars.

Mr. McIntyre saw that the members of the group were passing around cigarettes. Through the open window came a familiar burning smell that he recognized (he had traveled in North Africa and many times smelled it there) as kief, or hashish. One of the girls in the party, then another, began acting strangely. They leaped about shrieking, and seemed possessed by devils. The others comforted them a little, but responded for the most part by playing their guitars more wildly. In the twilight then he observed with horror what he took to be a flash of needles.

At this he went out, holding by the collar his harmless old great Dane, and remonstrated with them. What did they think they were doing? Hadn't they better leave now? For a while he was completely ignored. But finally—in an indolent, almost off-hand manner—several of his visitors explained to him that this beautiful pagoda in the middle of the Arizona desert was groovy. It wasn't being used prior to their arrival. Therefore, it was a free dwelling that he had no right to withhold. They weren't doing anyone any harm and intended to stay as long as they wanted. Nobody planned to hurt him. The old man was only hassling himself, and needed to relax. He was then offered a joint to help him change his head.

Although the attitude of the group wasn't menacing in any definable way, Mr. McIntyre felt more frightened than ever before in his life. He felt trapped in another world. For one thing, the two girls were howling like animals and no one did more than pet them now and then. The guitars now seemed to have turned into instruments of aggression. After one more attempt at reasoning, he went back into his house and shamefacedly called the police. The occupiers of his pagoda were more alert than he knew. At the sound of sirens they scrambled, piled into their bus before the law arrived—leaving behind them, as Mr. McIntyre had suspected, butts, loose hemp, a vial—and careened down the dark road.

> America has . . . become a violent, pitiless nation, hard and calculating, whose moments of generosity are only brief intervals in a ferocious narrative of life, bearing a ferocity and an aggression so strange in this tiny world where men die if they do not live together.*

We may now be prepared to distinguish between psychopathy as illness, as means of survival, as deliberately adopted style, and as revolutionary tactic.

In the form of *illness,* we know, psychopathy may be caused by early brain damage. It also commonly arises from some sort of oppression that breaks or warps family life so that the child grows up neglected, abused, or without a stabilizing adult model to guide him. This can happen in the slum or suburb when, for example, to cite only one reason, the slum father has decamped or spends his time drunk, or when the suburban father has run away in his own fashion—commuting to the city, arriving home late and drunk or exhausted, too knocked out to care, after late business sessions.

As *means of survival,* the psychopathic mentality may be formed by very different pressures. In *Black Rage,* Grier and

* From *Black Rage,* by William H. Grier, M.D., and Price M. Cobbs, M.D. Basic Books, New York, 1968.

Cobbs stress that, if life is not to become unbearable, the black man in America must develop a cultural paranoia

> in which every white man is a potential enemy unless proved otherwise, and every social system is set against him unless he personally finds out differently . . .
>
> . . . He can never quite respect laws which have no respect for him, and laws designed to protect white men are viewed as white men's laws. To break another man's law may be inconvenient if one is caught and punished, but it can never have the moral consequences involved in breaking one's own law. The result may be described as *cultural anti-socialism* but it is simply an accurate reading of one's environment . . .
>
> These and related traits are simply adaptive devices developed in response to a peculiar environment. They are no more pathological than the compulsive manner in which a diver checks his equipment before a dive or a pilot his parachute. They represent normal devices for "making it" in America . . .
>
> It is a normal complement of psychological devices, and to find the amount of sickness a black man has, one must first total all that appears to represent illness and then subtract the Black Norm. What remains is illness. To regard the Black Norm as pathological and attempt to remove such traits by treatment would be akin to analyzing away a hunter's cunning or a banker's prudence.

There may be no more precise and chilling description of functional psychopathy than this from *The Autobiography of Malcolm X:*

> . . . actually the most dangerous black man in America was the ghetto hustler . . . the hustler, out there in the ghetto jungles has less respect for the white power structure than any other Negro in North America. The ghetto hustler is internally restrained by nothing. He has no religion, no concept of morality, no civic responsibility, no fear—nothing. To survive, he is out there constantly preying upon others, probing for any human weakness like a ferret. The ghetto hustler is forever frustrated, restless, and anxious for some

"action." Whatever he undertakes, he commits himself to it fully, absolutely.

What makes the ghetto hustler yet more dangerous is his "glamor" image to the school dropout youth in the ghetto. These ghetto teenagers see the hell caught by their parents struggling to get somewhere, or see that they have given up struggling in the prejudiced, intolerant white man's world. The ghetto teenagers make up their own minds they would rather be like the hustlers whom they see dressed "sharp" and flashing money and displaying no respect for anybody or anything. So the ghetto youth become attracted to the hustler worlds of dope, thievery, prostitution and general crime and immorality.

The *psychopathic style* has been modeled in part on the black experience and has risen, in general, from every kind of poverty background—and is now being imitated by middle-class younger people. It has other sources. Everybody can identify them: romantic bravura coming down through Lord Byron, Hemingway, and Mailer; idolizing of cowboys and gangsters in television movies; worship of Humphrey Bogart on screen as the complete psychopath, private detective Sam Spade, and lately infatuation with James Bond; not to forget the fantastic real-life trillion-dollar score of the Mafia, its financiers, arrangers, and enforcers in the George Raft style, corrupting and despoiling cities and towns all over America.

> I've believed for years that we are living in the age of the psychopath, or at least witnessing the start of such an age—for the true psychopath is the hero, the ideal, of the young, the coming generation.
>
> A beautifully amoral egoist, a screaming, stomping temper tantrum, truly and completely guilt free, no strings, baby—hell, yes, this is every child's dream of heaven . . . the violence of these people, that's the truly frightening tale. Incredible.*

But such behavior may not be based on emotional illness at all. Psychopathic action as *revolutionary* tactic has been con-

---

* Patrolman Peter Hughart, Police Department, San Mateo, California.

spicuous for some time in our streets and courtrooms, in student confrontations with harassed deans, and in the form of bombing shooting brick-throwing urine- and feces-hurling hatred of police authority.

Some resisters are making use of a cause to work out childhood furies. But the assault on various structures of authority has come on also because, very simply, the rebel believes that if you obey the rules you will lose. You are shafted, called up in the draft, waste your substance from nine to five in a stupid job, refrain from all kinds of pleasures. You must either join the forces of exploitation, closing your eyes to what seems to be limitless chicanery, or strike back, counterintimidate. You observe that those on the ladder of authority *hardly ever listen* to restrained civilized voices. So the resister goes all out.

Psychopathic tactics that from a bourgeois standpoint have no moral base whatever are employed to combat the evil system. Civilized behavior is seen as a waste of time if civilization itself has grown evil. Thus, Bobby Seale and the Chicago Seven made a shambles of Judge Julius J. Hoffman's court (and possibly his reputation) with wild free-form behavior, and the Black Panthers in a New York pretrial hearing assailed judge and prosecutor with "Faggot!" "Racist Pig!" and all the standard epithets. Before the CBS cameras Jerry Rubin explained calmly that the aim of the Chicago Seven's disruptive courtroom behavior was to give Judge Hoffman a heart attack. Not surprisingly, the judge retaliated with extreme contempt citations and maximum sentences.

As old forms slowly collapse, the display of madness becomes deliberate and turns into a routine. Again, who is to sit in judgment of whom? Today's outlaw refuses to sit still for pious judges he knows have been bought many times by one syndicate or another. Or *any* judge since, say, if charged with murder, he has good reason to believe that proper decorum will lead only to the gas chamber. From his point of view, why show respect for procedures that will surely end your life? Hence, at his Los Angeles trial (October 5, 1970), Charles Manson to Judge Charles H. Older: ". . . Are you going to use this courtroom to kill me? . . .

The minute you say I am guilty, you know what I'm going to do . . ."

"What are you going to do?"

"You know . . ."

"I order you to be quiet, Mr. Manson."

"You order me to be quiet while you kill me in your court. I'm not just going to sit here and let you kill me. I'm a human being and I'm going to fight for my life, one way or the other."

"I'm going to have you removed if you don't stop."

"I'm going to have *you* removed if *you* don't stop. I have a little system of my own . . ." He leaps over the defense table at the judge.

Later, being led away: "In the name of Christian justice, someone should cut your head off!"

In search of justice, we find psychopathy on all sides, including that of law and order. For example, what fairness could Manson expect when he heard that a judge scheduled to try his case had attended a skit performed by members of the bar—based on their hilarious perceptions of Manson's commune—entitled "The Family That Slays Together Stays Together"?

The outlaw's wild and irreverent behavior is often intended, of course, to blow the mind of middle-class authority and pressure it into mistakes. Manson even succeeded in changing President Nixon's head, causing this lawyer to commit an incredible error—his indignant public pronouncement of Manson's guilt while the defendant was still on trial.

Attorney General Mitchell has since seized upon the emotionally loaded epithet, declaring that "psychopaths'" out to destroy American institutions were responsible for a succession of bombings on the West Coast.

The psychopath, points out Dr. Fred Hahn of New York, "invades reality." An already classic example of such an invasion is the skyjacking of commercial airliners for political purposes. The very lives of innocent bourgeois passengers are suddenly threatened in mid-air. Carried out most dramatically by Palestine guerrillas, this tactic—much admired by the sedentary left—helped for a while to foster chic Arabism in intellectual circles and among young revolutionaries everywhere.

We have followed the misuse, mythic development, and the coming to new life of a psychiatric conception originally intended to describe a form of mental illness, and now reach this point:

It's not so much that individuals who may be diagnosed as at least part-psychopaths have risen to eminence and leadership in our country (there's nothing particularly new in this), but that the psychopathic ideal of acting out all desires has become routinely accepted, possibly as supreme—even among people who are not psychopaths.

The ascendancy of the psychopath as a model, so long ago predicted by Mailer, seems close at hand. New violent saints and rapist-prophets appear everywhere. Readiness with fist, brick, knife, and gun may define the new holy orders. But since the violent will always be the most noticeable, violent psychopathy may distract attention from other manifestations of the new style, not all of them necessarily destructive.

May there not be a sweet side to psychopathy, as there is to babies? Has psychopathy perhaps "a good twin"? To say so would be to recognize "psychopathic" as neither good nor bad, or rather to call it a state of being with both good and bad attributes. The outlaw—in uninhibited, free-form action—would then set new standards of sanity, with good and evil quite irrelevant, thus fulfilling the commandment that we become as little children.

We are now confronted by a band of psychopaths in motley, in their various ways evil and sometimes beneficent, headlong and magical, louts and schemers, children unrestrained and charged with energy . . . drunkards and forgers, addicts, flower children, Mafia loan shark battering his victim who can't pay up, charming actor who makes crippled little boys and girls laugh, charming orator, murderer, the prophet who makes us love life again, gentle, nomadic guitarist, hustling politician, hustling judge, writers and preachers coming back with a vengeance to visit retribution on the middle classes that rejected them, whore and pimp, cop on the take, chanters filling the multitudes with joy, prancing Adonis of rock concerts, the saint who lies down in front of tractors, a student rebel, icily dominating Nobel Prize

winner stealing credit from laboratory assistants, the businessman
who then steals the scientist's perception, turning it into millions
. . . all, all doing their thing, which is the psychopathic commandment.

Now to pull back from sentimentality, avoid premature ap-
peasement of the new man. Return to the clinic. Remember what
Dr. Cleckley told us. And Karl Menninger, the McCords, Robert
Lindner: the psychopath is a sick human being and "the harbinger of distress." Possibly then those who glorify the psychopathic way of life—and the others, no matter how brilliant and
forceful, who serve as heroes and models of the new man—are
in varying degrees *all crazy,* and leading us to destruction.

The inquiry seems as much philosophical as clinical. Have
we a plague (Lindner's "psychopathic virus") that will pass or
the revolution of consciousness hailed by so many prophets?
From now on, perhaps the race will indeed require a new
nervous system in order to survive. In a godless universe, the
anxiety-free psychopathic style may be the antidote to mass
suicide. Just the same we should watch out for those who say so.
What games are they playing? How can we be sure they are
not Judas goats? And how many of the authorities we consult
about all this will themselves be psychopaths?

Putting aside for the moment the charming, exciting outlaw,
consider that at one time or another, perhaps without understanding the nature of the assault, most of us have been the
targets of psychopathic aggression. The encounters will in all
likelihood have been distressing, sometimes shocking, beyond
our understanding. We can't imagine why the perverse individual
—the one we married, the troublemaker once thought to be a
friend, malignant neighbor, addict, philanderer, the petty tyrant
placed over us at work—finds it satisfying to bring down so much
grief on others.

It will be helpful to remind ourselves more than once that
the psychopath, and his style, did not come out of nowhere for no
reason. The changing quality of American life has given birth
to him in ever-growing numbers. One result of his drive toward

ascendancy has been that the country is now accustomed to madness of an everyday sort. We accept without surprise behavior
that several decades ago would have seemed unbelievably inhuman or ridiculous.

Paranoia sneaks in. It can happen to anyone. Coming out
from New York, I visited a friend in San Francisco. He has a
view of the Bay from the top of Russian Hill. Waiting for him
as darkness fell, the Easterner drew the blinds. My friend arrived
and asked: "What's the matter?" I found myself explaining that
in the exposed living room I made too easy a target. "For Christ's
sake!" he shouted, yanking open the blinds. "How can you live
that way!"

Yet, with existential sharpshooters abounding, was I entirely wrong?

At the asylum, Danvers State Hospital, near Boston, the
director, Dr. Tomislav Zargaj, smiles across his desk. He asks in
a sympathetic but also ironical tone: "*Are you perhaps looking
for a scapegoat for everything evil?*"

The psychopath as scapegoat—strange role, since the outlaw
makes it his business to cast others in it. The investigator pauses.
He no longer feels sure of his direction. Psychopaths of all persuasions have emerged, and they fit no simple category. Only one
development appears sure. A variety of revolutions, like many
whirlwinds, have been tearing apart the formerly secure middle-
class scene he once depended on, even while criticizing it. He
knows that bourgeois complacency, deceit, the war, pollution
have all invited savagely destructive change. Certain revolutionary evils do appall him. The hatred, intolerance, debased
language, guns and dynamite . . . Yet at the same time he feels
his own moral restraints, the ones he grew up with and thought
would always guide him, now giving way.

The world of the psychopath and the world of the bourgeoisie
meet like two colliding galaxies. A sense of craziness fills the air.
What to do in these circumstances, how to navigate? Resist the
psychopath, hunt him down, imitate him? Yield to insanity accepted as normal? Cultivate one's own latent psychopathy, per-

haps trying to adapt it to good ends? Could it be that in a violent and godless time psychopathy has become operative and welcome?

Before deciding, first explore what is mostly evil, negative. The following section details memories of some mad scenes passing for ordinary, together with close-in, usually grievous experiences of psychopaths in action. These accounts have to do with the war between psychopaths and conventional middle-class people. They also describe the mad and pitiless background from which the more destructive types of psychopathy spring.

Most of the scenes involve one soul doing violence to others, but obviously not every psychopath may be judged the same. A mass killer can hardly be paired with the poet who steals a parking space. The head of a business conglomerate and a master of orgies express themselves in quite different ways. But see in all these people [all names are fictional] a curious, cold passion, an attacking restlessness, and a need to dominate that will not leave them or anyone in their way alone, ever.

II

Psychopathic
Tales

1. TWO LOVE STORIES

Arthur remembers the delicate red-haired girl whose family, when she was growing up, had almost never touched her. She was neither cuddled, rocked, or spanked. Discipline consisted of ignoring the child. Her father was a biologist; her mother, hard to believe, a Ph.D. in psychology. Cynthia never was praised. If she did well, scored first in her class, this was what ought to be and her success deserved no comment. Whenever she failed to measure up, silent disapproval was the rule.

The family maintained a remorseless belief in excellence and the power of self-reliance. When, at twenty-one, Cynthia decided to move from Boston and try for luck in New York she was given fifty dollars and warned that the future was up to her: she would receive no more.

Arthur found her after she had been three years in the arms of the Nobel Prize-winning psychopath. She stood by herself at a party, cold, distant, dazed, and in anguish. Longing to escape the man, she had finally made the decision to come. In three years, "my first night out alone!" Cynthia's story was incredible. The Nobel Prize winner had beaten her again. She couldn't take it anymore. Saul would never leave his wife. He had broken his promise too many times. At thirty-five the head of a great new research laboratory, her genius with the glittering black eyes remained a family man with position and young children, and wouldn't change. Therefore, he no longer had the right to keep her in bondage.

Yes, almost a prisoner. By day she worked in a Manhattan advertising agency. After six he dictated her life completely. She was forbidden to go anywhere or see anyone, or have a friend

51

come in. Immediately after shopping for groceries she returned
to the apartment that Saul had found for her. There she waited,
and he came nearly every evening about six and stayed until
eight or nine.

The apartment was a bleak little place in the Eighties near
York Avenue, living room, bedroom, bathroom, and wall kitchen.
Saul had bought her an enormous bed and a hi-fi set. He liked
loud Stravinsky, particularly *The Firebird,* while they were
making love. There was no other furniture except a rickety breakfast table and two small wooden chairs. No rug. Bare floors and
walls. Bare overhead lighting. Only in the bedroom did she have
a reading lamp. After three years the apartment looked as though
she had just moved in. Her books lay in piles along the wall. She
always had dishes in the sink. The windows never had been
washed.

Twice a week she visited her psychiatrist. But far from
rescuing her, she confessed ruefully, he had been emotionally
drawn into the affair. Dr. Jones railed against the Nobel Prize
winner. Forgetting himself on one occasion, he seized her wrists,
begging her to leave the monster.

It hadn't been easy. The severe Protestant girl from Boston
and the ebullient jeering Jewish genius could not break free of
each other. Once, when Saul's family was on Martha's Vineyard,
Cynthia's lover took her for a ride on the Staten Island ferry
and to City Island for a moonlight dinner. Otherwise, for three
years, they went nowhere. Whenever they were hungry, Saul
ordered in Chinese food. Why go to a film or play? What need
for entertainment? For three hours every evening, one of the
century's huge minds was at her disposal. And she adored his
arrogance. Not only was Saul an acknowledged world master in
biochemistry. He dashed off beautiful love poems, which to her
despair he refused to have published.

Arms folded, leaping from his powerful thighs, he could
dance the *gopak* for a quarter of an hour without weakening or
gasping for breath. "Where else," he would cry out triumphantly, "could you find an authority on early Florentine madrigals
and twenty-first-century physics!" For he knew physics about

as well as his own field. And botany, and the history of the Toltecs.

When she complained of loneliness the Nobel Prize winner bought her a Siamese cat that, by itself all day long and unheeded at night, soon became crazed with solitude. Just as Cynthia hadn't been touched in childhood, she hardly touched the animal intended as her companion. Minou leaped about the apartment, bouncing off the walls, clawing the breakfast table and chairs. If she insisted on clawing the bedspread she would be shut in the bathroom. And Saul signaled his desire for lovemaking by depositing Minou behind the bathroom door.

Sometimes after Saul had gone home to his wife—he always did, as if to madden Cynthia, on the stroke of eight or nine, never a second before or after; and if he didn't make a move at eight, there was exactly, no more, no less, one hour to go—she would take a bottle of Smirnoff from the refrigerator and drink as much of it as she could, and presently two neglected creatures would be lying on the bed side by side, with the cat, unnoticed, rhythmically stretching and clawing the spread, and Cynthia drowsily half-asleep.

Saul ruled her with a bewildering alternation of tenderness and abuse. He defined all meaning for her; he constantly defined and redefined life itself for her. She wasn't allowed to think, except to ask. He would tell her. Nothing, no tiny secret of hers, evaded his intelligence. And when, shivering, knowing what was to come, she played the game of disagreeing with him, taunting his omniscience, he would pin her to the bed and begin the rhythmic slapping, far more humiliating than a blow from his fist would have been, until she burst into tears, and he took her roughly and they made love. The endless game was at once ecstatic and oppressive. He was a lover beyond belief, and when not boasting and teaching he wanted her all the time.

For two or three hours nearly every weekday evening she was utterly possessed by this man. The outside world turned into a dream. She began to feel that the advertising agency existed only in her imagination and that the people in her office were only dream figures. Her three-hour God filled up all reality. One night after he had gone, she lay on the great bed he had bought, the sheets still in a tangle, half-drunk on straight shots of vodka, stupefied from his lovemaking. Her cat miaowed, in heat again, orange eyes glowing madly, and she thought: I'm dying. Saul was slowly killing her. He didn't love her, and she had allowed herself to be turned into a doll-victim. Yes, their fantasies mingled in this barren little living space, and she inhabited a dream he had carefully built up within the shabby containing walls. But then God went home to his wife, little boys, television, and snug kiss good night, while she remained for one more lonely night pinioned in his fantasy.

Cynthia had begun to nurse a growing rage: hatred for the Nobel Prize winner's wife. The complacent bitch! She would call her to account one day. Threatening this to Saul, she had received a terrible five-minute slapping that made her decide to break away. She summoned up what courage she had left to tell him so. He sneered and laughed, and struck her lightly with a chop he had learned in an Oriental combat class. He was tired of her anyhow, because she was stupid. Without him she amounted to nothing, as she would find out, and after him every other man would be a bore. "So long, buster!" he called back over his shoulder and walked out.

Next day he telephoned her at the office.

"Let's stop all the foolishness, buster. Come on. Where else are you going to find anyone who can do it for you the way I can? I'll come around tonight, and you be home."

She told him that she wouldn't answer the door. He arrived exactly at six. The downstairs buzzer sounded for twenty minutes before he went away. Then the phone rang over and over again. Smiling, she watched it vibrate the fragile table. With each ring, she imagined Saul's power over her ebbing.

So she said, and Arthur believed this. The following night he walked her home from the party. She shivered and clung to his arm. No, it would be better if he didn't come up this time. Dinner tomorrow? Oh, yes. How wonderful for a change not to eat shrimp chow mein delivered from the Chinese restaurant.

Liberating Cynthia, Arthur threw open all the doors and windows to let the fresh air in, opening up life again, introduced his new girl to friends who welcomed her. He kept his

Madison Avenue walk-up, but they lived mostly at her apartment. She refused to abandon the place, expecting family phone
calls that never came. It didn't matter. Arthur started bringing
in furniture, a big stuffed chair, a rug. He confessed to everyone
that he'd never felt happier.

He reckoned without the Nobel Prize winner. All this time
Cynthia and her master had been in touch with one another.

The revelation came gradually. One night Arthur arrived
late at her apartment to find Cynthia crying. Saul was going to
commit suicide. What made her think so? She just had a feeling.
Arthur questioned her affectionately. Holding his hand, she
admitted that Saul had called up to tell her this. Then she insisted that Arthur telephone Saul's home to inquire. He refused,
saying it was a hoax. The call was a typical grandstand play.
She stayed awake most of the night, and they had their first bad
quarrel. In the morning she phoned the research institute. The
Nobel Prize winner was in conference.

The love Arthur thought he had soon went to pieces. The
phone in her apartment kept ringing. She had extracted a promise
from him not to answer it on the grounds that if Saul heard a
man's voice he would become violent and suddenly attack her
on the street. Smiling, placing her finger on her lips, she would
signal that they must let the phone ring. But it went on for
a half hour. Arthur felt himself being drawn into a psychotic
game. How did her former lover know they were in?

"Watching from across the street! Seeing the light on!" She
sighed. Arthur would look out and never see anyone.

One day he bought her a half-dozen roses, all the florist had
left. They turned out to be old, and soon wilted. The next night
he arrived to find a dozen powerful, fresh roses in a glass vase
standing on top of the hi-fi set.

"Oh, I thought they came from you . . ."

The phone rang again.

She would sigh, and look away. They had flash fights for
no reason. She was late for a cocktail party. Saul had waited for
her on the sidewalk after work and leaped into her taxicab. It
had taken twenty minutes to get rid of him.

"All right, Cynthia. It's time I talked to him."

"No, don't you see? It's not you he cares about. He'd only hurt me!"

The phone rang. This time, to Arthur's surprise, she went into the bedroom and picked it up. After a few moments he heard her say: "No, no, Saul. I love him. I really do!"

Then she was silent for a long time.

"Come on," Arthur said. "That's enough!"

She motioned for him to join her. Covering the receiver, she whispered: "He's drunk!" With a cryptic little smile, she once again laid a finger on her lips and beckoned Arthur to draw close.

He heard a curiously singsong voice at the other end: "I know I've hurt you sometimes, buster. But it's okay now. My claws are sheathed. Believe in me, buster. I'm going up to Cambridge tomorrow, but I'll be back. *Where else* are you going to find a green belt in Kung Fu lecturing on cryobiology at Harvard?"

Arthur slammed the phone down, and they quarreled again. The next night she reported Saul jumping out of the shadows and seizing her by the arm.

Early one evening the door buzzer in the downstairs lobby sounded. It kept on and on. Someone was jamming the button. Arthur rushed to the elevator and descended to find the buzzer stabbed by a pencil. But the mysterious enemy couldn't be seen. Only a note stuffed into the slot by the button. It read: "Shut up your goddamned cat!" and he remembered that Minou had been locked in the bathroom. Her wailing in the vertical echo chamber must have caused a neighbor to lose his mind.

By this time it was all crazily downhill. At Fire Island she lost his wrist watch in the sand. Later in the day they quarreled terribly and took a mid-weekend train back to New York. One of his most painful memories was watching her choose a seat by the only smashed window in the empty car and sit gazing all the way to Penn Station at the cracks radiating from the interior of the glass.

Secretly, it appeared, Saul had followed them there. Yes, he called the following day to tell her so. It was astounding how accurately he had described Arthur and their companions on the beach.

The madness spread and life sickened. There were shameful episodes. He was somehow persuaded to put through a call to Saul's apartment, pretending to be a doctor. His wife answered in a gentle voice, refusing to put her husband on the phone. He was sleeping, she said, and needed his rest.

Arthur was taking Cynthia to the theater. Distractedly he searched for missing tickets that he had set down on the kitchen table, and never did find them. Later he realized that she had slipped them into her handbag and had watched him sardonically in his search.

"I've betrayed him!" She sighed.

Arthur went back to his place then.

That night her call was frantic. She had taken sleeping pills. Knowing the phone number of her psychiatrist, Arthur waked him at one in the morning.

"Don't worry," Dr. Jones said angrily. "It's part of her act. She's made the same call before."

But this unrelenting game they've included me in . . .

"Oh, she won't die. She's probably taken one pill, or none at all. But can't you hang on for a bit? You don't realize how much you've done for this girl. Don't you know you've helped save her from that bastard?"

Arthur found himself crying from exhaustion. The psychiatrist and he were dolts when it came to dealing with these people.

"Save her!" Dr. Jones said. "Not from death. From herself. Go over there! Try just one more time!"

Cynthia lay in bed reading. She seemed to have expected his coming and calmly apologized for alarming him. With his clothes on, he went to sleep by her side.

Save her? The idea was ludicrous. Rather Dr. Jones and he had to think of saving their own sanity. Games beyond their ken were going on. Evidently sane, untroubled love could be a bore, and for some the cruel play was essential. Only this kind of mutual torture suspended life's meaninglessness. I gave nothing but good will, Arthur thought. Saul framed her life with vicious authority and gave it meaning, and that's why they tortured each other in this drab little apartment with the huge bed and hi-fi as life's only furniture.

Going through motions he didn't understand, Arthur took her to a dinner party. She charmed everyone, graciously playing to him and reaching often for his hand. During coffee, she left the table for a long time. He looked in the bedroom. Back to him, sitting on the bed, she gripped the telephone. "Bitch! You bitch! I know he's there. Let me speak to him!"

Arthur quit then. A few days later she called to denounce him as despicable and disloyal. Once she phoned, teasing, and Arthur could tell that in his turn the Nobel Prize winner was listening in. By this time—a month away from the scene—he felt only relief, didn't care, and answered with offhand good nature.

Unfortunately, the next day by sheer chance Cynthia came upon Arthur walking with his former wife and passed them with a murderous expression. Thereafter Natalie began receiving obscene phone calls.

"You bitch . . ."

The calls went on for days, and Natalie had to change her phone number.

Joy drank too much, and knew it. Her drinking was a matter of carefully deliberated choice. "Rather than give up liquor," she said one night, "I would shorten my life by ten years and end up broke with no one to care for me." A musician standing nearby said: "Your wish is granted."

Classically she had come down in the world. Once pale, dark-haired and pretty, Joy had been married to a legendary film star. He had long since gone on through two other wives. Although he was famous for being cheap—a fifty-cent and dollar tipper, grabber of taxicabs from old ladies, and refuser of help to his several children—he came to Joy's rescue now and then. Within a few years she had dissipated the small settlement he had made on her. Now at fifty, spent, gray, she knocked about the fashionable world accepting what jobs turned up. Generally on the strength of her name and her husband's eminence she was able to serve as a social secretary or ladylike salesperson at boutiques. Much of the time Joy managed. She had played small parts on the stage and spoke clear theatrical English. Everyone knew that the actor, cheap though he was, remained available as a last resource for her.

"Darlings," she would say, "I can always count on him, so long as I don't ask for anything."

So she continued in her mildly catty and self-destructive way to go downhill, a little each year. Even though she drank too much and soon wobbled and slurred—she imagined charmingly —Joy wasn't unattractive. I don't quite know why. Perhaps in part because she paid close attention to whoever was with her. At once amusing and vulnerable, bitchy, likely to catch you in some kind of ridiculousness if you underestimated her, she hardly ever came across as boring. You didn't quickly turn away from her to younger girls. Aging, foolish, adrift, she conveyed a sort of promise. Also, Joy gave the impression of knowing tricks in bed.

Then one summer evening in Sag Harbor she met the waiter. Vincent had come illegitimately from a German mother and Irish father. After growing up in Youngstown, Ohio, he had hitchhiked East and waited on table briefly in New York and New Jersey. His career was soon interrupted by conviction for rape and extortion. He had hit upon the technique of raping nice girl customers, then threatening to tell the parents that their daughter had been violated. He demanded fairly small sums in return for silence. Two girls had acquiesced. The third had exposed him, and Vincent spent his next six years in prison.

Two weeks after being set free he was charged again with rape, but the complaint was eventually withdrawn. As Joy drifted vaguely down, Vincent climbed. With rude good looks and a cheerful, breezy manner he became a fine hotel waiter. He shuttled between Long Island in the summer and Florida in winter. In between the seasons he knocked around and had fun. Somewhere along the way he discovered that it was better to seduce the guests rather than rape them, and that there was a lot more money in this. He learned to spot the rich, lonely women who would go for him and arranged with the headwaiter to seat them in his area.

Vincent was still cocky and brutal and enjoyed giving them rough treatment. It was surprising how many of them liked that. The day came when he learned that the one who so often came alone at the cocktail hour was the movie star's first wife. He got her in bed the first night, and for a fifty-year-old woman she wasn't bad.

At first Vincent was a little in awe of Joy. She knew so many famous people. This wasn't crap, he discovered, because several times he saw actors whose faces he recognized from the movies stop and chat with her. She had been all over. One time she got some money, took him to a mod shop whose proprietor she knew, and outfitted him with a new suit and a couple of jackets that made him look great.

They drank a lot together, and in the beginning he cooled it. Drinking, he knew, made him mean, and rages would come over him, and on these occasions he had slapped women around and raped them. He didn't want to do that now. If he played her right, with all her connections, she could help him go places. So taking care not to lose her, for a few weeks he did cool it and treated Joy with more respect than he felt. She was, after all, an old bag, and sometimes it embarrassed him to be seen with her. People, other guests and customers, looked at them knowingly. More than once he caught young girls staring at him with contempt.

She was getting a lot more than she gave, he began to realize. Who else would service this old bag the way he did? She wasn't even rich. A good lay all right, but her body was loose and old. Besides, he accused her furiously one night: "I'm not good enough for your friends, I guess. You never introduce me!"

"But, darling . . ."

"Don't give me any of that 'darling' crap. All you want is a cheap lay. What did you ever do for me? An old woman like you!"

"Sweetheart . . ."

He hit her then, for the first time. Knocked her right out of bed. She got up sobbing from the floor, and he hit her again.

What followed was the greatest lay of his life. She was hot all over him. He took her savagely, and it was the greatest. Vincent lay back looking at her bruised, wild, begging face and knew for certain now that he had her where he wanted. She needed it that way. He could make her do anything.

Joy's friends grew worried about her affair with Vincent. She wore outsize dark glasses, but the marks of her beatings still showed. In the fall they came back to the city and began living together in a dingy West Side sublet. When winter came she would follow him to Florida. No one could account for the relationship lasting as long as it had. Vincent was judged not only ignorant, but stupid and boring. Having demanded that she introduce him to her friends, he was surly and uncomfortable with them. He had developed the habit of treating her meanly in their presence. She seemed only to love him all the more for this, catering to him and waiting on him while he stood haughtily by.

One day I ran into her coming out of a doctor's office. This time her head was bandaged. He had split her crown with a candlestick.

"Joy, that's terrible . . ."

I bought her a drink, and asked how long she was going to keep on with it. Might he not some day drunkenly kill her?

"Yes, darling, he could," Joy agreed in the little-girl voice she had affected lately. "I suppose I'd better stop fairly soon. If I value my life!" She laughed. "But do I value my life?"

Speaking dreamily, she described for me the pleasures of degradation, the thrill of being at the mercy of a dangerous child. She had never before known such excitement. Cheat, liar, rapist, brute, the man who dominated her days and nights was completely unpredictable. Upon a given provocation, he might kiss or beat her.

It came down to this. Most of her life had been tedious. Even the days with the film star were empty. With no children, she had nothing to do except drink and have sex. And it was all so much the same. Nothing new ever happened. But with Vincent all that had changed. Now she knew the sweet sickness of being at the beck and call of a low-grade intelligence. She lived in a dangerous nursery with a violent, corrupt young man who might attack her at any moment. His coarseness and stupidity excited her. She was held in thrall by the game of survival played against the brutish child who held her prisoner. Every day and night turned into an enchanting risk-filled exercise in slightly teasing his evil temper, sometimes getting away with it, more often not.

Was Vincent a fabulous lover? No, most of the time he simply took her and plowed into her, but it was just this mindlessness of her young lord that excited Joy more than all the sensitive and expert loving she had experienced before. But lately, she went on, a new and more dangerous element had entered into their relationship. The rapist-waiter had gradually come to love her and need her, and hated himself for it. He had come to need an old woman. He was trapped by an old woman, and the young people all laughed at him, but just the same the bitch had got him where *she* wanted, and he couldn't do without her. Once he hadn't cared what she did in her free time. Now his love took the form of ferocious jealousy. Walking down West 56th Street, he happened to look in on Joy having cocktails in a French restaurant with a film producer—an old friend of her husband's. When she came home, he had split her eyelid with his ring hand.

From now on, he insisted, she wasn't going to see any of those movie bastards, or any of her old friends for that matter. To make sure of this, he had taken to following her at a distance. Apart from shopping, he expected her to stay home and watch dreary daytime television on a seven-inch screen. In this situation she began to drink harder, and he objected to that too.

"You old drunk! Give me that bottle! . . ."

Her universe had contracted to a sleazy apartment, a secret bottle, a flickering screen, and—tramping in and out, lolling, smoking, swearing—the modern equivalent of the stableboy who had brought her so low.

Joy, the stupid question again. Why?

"Darling, I suppose you think I'm paying for imaginary sins. But that's not true. I don't feel guilty about anything I've ever done. And you probably won't believe me, but I'm no masochist either. I hate pain. Have you ever been punched in the eye and had your lip split? Apart from being a horrible insult, it hurts terribly—not so much at the time but afterward. No, if I stay, and

I don't know whether I dare much longer"—she glanced fearfully out the picture window at the passersby—"it's because with Vincent, strange as it may appear to you, I'm alive every moment. He never once has bored me."

A month later he broke several of her ribs. She lay in the hospital hardly able to breathe and plotted at last to escape him. From her hospital bed Joy put through a telephone call to the actor, who was making a film in France. For once he responded more than generously and without reproaches, cabling $3,000 to her bank.

Slipping out of the hospital, she taxied to Bankers Trust, converted her money into American Express checks, and from the safe-deposit box she maintained, picked up her passport and some jewelry. Then with only the clothes she had on, purse, and flight bag, she drove in a limousine to Kennedy Airport and flew to Paris that night. The next afternoon she was enjoying cocktails on the Champs-Elysées with members of her husband's film company. An unusually warm autumn sun made her drowsy. The conversation of the film people flashed around her, and she was peacefully home again with her sort. But during dinner she began to yawn and stir and look around, and to find everyone tiresome. How vapidly fashionable, self-seeking yet directionless all their talk was . . .

Vincent knew nothing except that she had sneaked away from the hospital behind his back. He had no idea where she had gone. He did find that Joy had checked out all paid up. Where would she get that kind of money? From only one person, the actor, who, he had seen in a *Daily News* column, was now making a movie outside of Paris. No problem. Vincent got on the phone and called France, giving only the actor's name. Amazingly, within a few minutes he was put straight through to the set. The actor, in between takes, answered the long-distance call.

To his dismay, he met with a harangue. Some crazy person in New York was claiming that he had stolen Joy away. The man was going to the police. He would tell all the papers and gossip columnists. Further, if the actor didn't see to it that Joy boarded the next plane and returned to the States, the furious caller was going to raise such a stink as he, the actor, had never imagined, and further come on over to France himself and expose him and beat him up.

In terror, the actor first allowed himself to be bluffed into admitting that Joy was in France, and, second, that he had provided the money for her trip. He stammered and protested. He cried out "See here!" and tried in a civilized way to reason with the enraged caller. All his efforts were useless. Not only the day was ruined; his entire psyche was thrown off. He forgot his lines. He didn't know what he was doing, where Joy was, what she thought she was doing. As usual, she had been absolutely irresponsible. Always had been. Now she had fallen into a ridiculous and frightening predicament that he wanted nothing to do with.

On the boulevard, at her little table, Joy smiled dreamily.

"Don't you see that you can't stay!" the underling said. "You're making it hell for him. We've had to shoot around his scenes. That idiot from New York keeps calling. Look, we're willing to finance it, but you've got to leave. Can't you go back to New York so that this friend of yours, whoever he is, will leave us alone?"

He was lying in bed, naked, smoking, watching a football game on TV, when she came in.

"What the fuck do you think you're doing?" he asked her. "Do you know all the aggravation you've put on me?"

He kept on watching the game, and she went into the bathroom. It occurred to her for the first time that aside from a blouse and skirt she had bought in Paris, she had come back with nothing from her trip. Nothing for him. Timidly she went back into the bedroom and handed him both books of American Express checks, the first she had converted at Bankers Trust, the second the film-company underling had pressed on her just before she had boarded the Pan Am flight at Orly.

She was seized by the hair and tumbled on their sweaty bed. The sheets hadn't been changed since she left. Nothing was changed, she realized. It would be this way. Her legs embraced him. He tore her clothes off and plunged into her.

"Bitch! Bitch! Don't you ever do that to me again!"

2. WIZARD OF THE CONGLOMERATES

Lewis Hoagland, president of the conglomerate Garfield-Jones Industries, works on the top floor of the Manhattan skyscraper that bears his company's name. He has his desk peculiarly arranged—with a window at his back—so that outdoor light all but blinds the visitor. In addition, the light strikes two polished glass paperweights on his desk, giving an impression that you have come under the scrutiny of two translucent orbs; that your thoughts are being read and your capabilities assayed in a second or two.

So the president bedazzles all witnesses, begins dispelling resistance before a word has been spoken. Such tactics seem to make even sophisticated men uneasy. Face to face, no one has stood up to Hoagland or denied him for very long, at least not in recent years. His spirit roams free, dominating an industrial complex that spreads across the United States and through sizable areas of Europe and Latin America.

In less than four years he took Garfield-Jones to the moon. A space engineer who thinks of him with both awe and hatred has said ("Only that bastard could have done it") that the astronauts might not have reached the lunar surface in 1969 if Hoagland, whipping and driving his research and development teams, hadn't brought in a number of indispensable rocket components exactly on schedule.

Some day he will have to fail or at least occasionally fall short like anyone else. At present it seems that nothing can go wrong for him. His competitors and particularly Garfield-Jones's own higher-level executives admit that his whims wrench their lives around. They remain in perpetual anxiety over what he will do next. Yet many keep insisting on his ordinariness. Just a quick-tempered accountant, they say, a vulgar man with a genius for juggling figures and divining the flow of hidden money. Also an expert dealer in pain and shock. His system, if that is the word, has been to envelop the company in an atmosphere of continuing tension and disorder. Strangely enough, the technique seems to bring out the best in many until they drop. Now I hope to do the same for him.

This doesn't mean going into the president's background. How the child Hoagland was imprinted makes no difference now. Illumination of the past won't help us resist outlaws. The problem is rather to uncover the secret of their magnetism—then find the wolfbane we need to protect ourselves.

I served Hoagland as an occasional speech writer, luckily not from inside the company. My job was with Paul Keogh Associates, Garfield-Jones's public-relations counsel. Several times I helped rework the talk he gave before company shareholders at the May annual meeting. In preparation he dictated a three-hour jumble. The writer had somehow to fit this message into twenty minutes, but "Don't leave anything out, and don't change anything!"

That was the way he came on, the specialist immediately being placed under the thumb of impossibility and forced to squirm out as best he could. Still, I was safe enough. The outsider wouldn't be abused—or only one time, as Hoagland knew. Keogh Associates could easily afford to lose the account: major corporations were waiting in line for our services.

Having an ideal vantage point, we had watched the take-over by Lewis Hoagland and his friends of a dignified old family enterprise. Until he came, the company had confined itself to manufacturing relatively simple electronic equipment and power tools. Within months Hoagland changed this. Ferociously, he sent the old managers rolling. They tried to duck under his sword, but it was no good. Small, skinny, hatchet-faced, a forty-five-year-old vengeful child driven by apparently limitless energy had taken charge. The corporation's old guard had never heard of anyone like this newcomer with the shining black eyes who despite an adult lifetime of peering at figures never wore glasses, now seemingly bent on destroying them for no reason they could understand.

And no one could begin to keep up with the way he managed the company. He opened with a number of mystifying acquisitions, including enterprises whose products had nothing to do with electronics or machinery. Gradually, then, he filled in the spaces between them until three years later his competitors discovered that he had fashioned a nearly world-wide domain whose sections, reinforcing one another, fitted together perfectly.

His manipulations had nothing to do with honesty and dishonesty; he operated far beyond such concerns. Switching assets from one subsidiary to another, arranging transfinite transactions among European, Latin American, and North American affiliates, he moved so quickly that no government revenue service on earth could follow what he was doing. During this period he seemed off somewhere, dealing cards only to himself.

To rule over Garfield-Jones's acquired companies, Hoagland dispatched a horde of breathtakingly rude, jostling men. There was no way to resist them. These loud, unattractive, and oddly boring (even though menacing) individuals would descend on the captured affiliate and commence driving out all the old-line executives.

The most pathetic victims were those who stayed on at headquarters. We began to receive despairing phone calls; then the confidences of frightened men poured out at secret, drunken lunches. Monsters were rampant on the top floor. Working under them, particularly in the financial area, was all but unbearable. The president's door would be flung open, and a small, wild-eyed figure shaped like a hatchet would come flying out and split their heads with impossible questions. You might be summoned to come up with information at any time of day, often at night, even at home, with the phone starting to ring as your head hit the pillow. "He never stops probing!" a financial man moaned in the bar of the Commodore Hotel. "We're three steps behind him. Sometimes two steps but always behind. It's terrible to be behind someone!"

These people had a common problem. Even before Hoagland's arrival, Garfield-Jones's pensions were based on a noncontributory plan. An executive wouldn't be eligible for his due until he had been with the company for twenty years. Such an arrangement may have made sense during the benign era of founder ownership, but under Hoagland the hope of long service being honored was laughable. Still, incredibly, the veteran managers did hope. The prayer of somehow being able to outlast the terror, stupid faith that the new breed of men tormenting them would eventually go away, caused many of the old-timers to abandon all dignity. They ran around timidly, looking out of sunken eyes, rattled papers at their desks pretending to be busy, hung on eating every humiliation.

What brought the scene at Garfield-Jones home to us was a report given to the weekly staff meeting by Ted Vreeland, Paul Keogh's deputy. Ted was a small, sensible man about forty-five with crew-cut white hair. Usually he walked around smoking his pipe, nodding at everyone. But at this meeting he waved his pipe at us. It was time, he said, that we dropped the account.

True, a client's personal behavior in his own shop was theoretically none of our business. "Just the same, I feel that we're providing aid and counsel for the lord of a huge car, like a juggernaut. And the masses—"

"*Masses?*"

"White collar, Paul. Country club. Twenty to thirty-five thousand a year. The business and professional masses . . . dragging the tyrant's car through the sand, some being crushed under it, while he . . ."

Ted told how a former colleague of ours had come under assault. "For instance, what they're doing to Leo Niles. Hoagland wants a new PR director, an errand boy all his own, so they're trying to get rid of him. Well and good, you know, the civilized way: 'Sorry, Leo, better start looking. We'll give you a couple of months . . .'

"Hoagland and his gang have no conception that such common decency exists. I want to nail something down!" The ashes from Ted's pipe had scattered across the conference table. "A kind of lunacy. Meanness without practical reason. Humiliation for its own sake. These people not only want to fire a man but destroy his self-esteem in the process. Why? What kind of men have we got here? Rather than quietly unload the victim, they put him through a ceremony. Now listen to this—they bring the company psychiatrist in. What in the world for? A mousy little guy, he sits off in the corner. Leo has seen it. The show begins with a dressing down from Hoagland in front of the cronies he brought in with him, and sometimes one of the man's own subordinates. Then Hoagland goes into a tantrum. Leo still can't figure out whether it's fake or real, or starts out as a deliberate tactic and then becomes real. World-famed industrialist! Why does he bother! Hoagland shouts and curses and heaps ridicule on the poor fellow. Then he and all of them pursue the disgraced man to the outer offices and berate him in front of the stenographers. He goes stumbling away. Amazingly enough, not one humiliated man has ever talked back to Hoagland, or hit him. That's what I mean by *masses*.

"Leo, as you know, was appointed PR director about a year before the new crowd came in," Ted Vreeland reminded us. "For a while they let him alone. Why not? I'd say he's not only able but almost *too* conscientious. You see, he has a heart condition which he tried to keep hidden. But the company doctors know about it, or they've guessed it. Now Hoagland's crowd is trying to— The point is that there have been so many indiscriminate firings lately that they have got to get something on Leo, demonstrate to the satisfaction of the outside board members that he's incompetent.

"So they're alternately hounding and ignoring him. Why should he take it? Well, he is looking for another job, but with his heart he'll never get by any company's physical. Now he sits in his office smoking one Gauloise after another. Of all cigarettes. Perhaps they remind him that he was once a student at the Sorbonne, and might have taught philosophy instead of playing straight man to a sadist without style.

"I mean, Paul, Hoagland, when he contradicts a man, may as likely as not shout 'Hawss piss!' at him. What kind of a *lumpen sadist* is that! He despises elementary good manners. At dinner in the very best restaurant—San Francisco, Paris, Rio, he doesn't care—he pours ketchup on the Chateaubriand. Of course, this is done deliberately, to affront those he would refer to jeeringly as the 'gentlemen' of the old management.

"He insults good living. Laughs at wine and cheese, and ridicules French menus by mispronouncing the names of the dishes in front of the waiter. What he loves to do— In Brazil, you can imagine it, he forced the nice old Portuguese manager, Mr. Delgado, who has a delicate stomach, to join him at the dinner hour *at his desk* for hamburgers well-done on a bun washed down with milk, and made him go right on with his sales report while eating even this. In Jamaica he kept the plant managers after sundown, after eight, after nine o'clock without food or drink, until when one brave man protested, he grinned: 'Hungry? Why didn't you guys tell me?' And so they were sent on their way revealed as cowards subject to his whim.

"Also he lies, Paul. Claims to have attended a prep school that doesn't exist. Claims to be— Never mind, I won't descend to vituperation. All right, as of now they're refusing to acknowledge Leo's phone calls. For instance, he phoned Hoagland's deputy —what's his name? Govno—fourteen times about some policy matter. Then, happening to meet the president himself in the lobby, he mentioned that he had to have an answer. 'Sure, Niles,' Hoagland said. A few days later Leo got a call from the president's office. 'Why didn't you tell me about this?' 'But, sir,' Leo answered, 'I mentioned it in the lobby.' 'You didn't say anything in the lobby.'

"They say the coward does it with a kiss, Paul. Well, he also does the job with psychologists. They forced poor Leo to take a four-hour examination and found that he was 'tending toward emotional instability.' My God, why wouldn't he be unstable?

"But finally when I think of Hoagland I keep seeing his fingers. Those talons wrapped around the hamburger bun. And then I see Leo's fingers tapping on the Gauloise package, and—"

"Yes, Ted." Gently as always Paul Keogh got us back on the track. Our chief also had white hair. He had been sitting up straight and listening with his head slightly averted. Now he propped his finger tips together, and said: "A passing notion occurred to me, that all decay creates. Including possibly spiritual decay. Fecal matter nourishes all soils. For instance, the Chinese use human wastes."

Ted Vreeland smiled grimly around at us. "And in our way so do we, so does Hoagland. Is that it?"

"Also," said the head of our firm, "that was an interesting analogy you drew earlier. But aren't those who drag the god's

cart through the sand, some falling under it, aren't they wor-
shipers?"

"I had forgotten that," Ted Vreeland admitted.

"Just a notion."

"You mean there are people who are such masochists, or who
have so little to live for or believe in, that they'll even worship a
monster like Hoagland?"

A silence fell on our meeting.

We had been working elbow to elbow on one of his tortured
speeches. At the far end of his office the see-through wall clock
with golden hands and numbers chimed once, signaling eleven in
the morning. A door opened softly. Dr. Dunwoodie, the company
psychiatrist, slipped in and took a chair in the corner. There was
something medieval in his appearance, like a court dwarf.

A buzzer sounded, and without raising his head Hoagland
instructed the intercom: "Let him in."

A terrified man stood before us, blinking and clearing his
throat. It was the amiable old booze fighter with elephant ears,
Dill Hoover, the company secretary, who had been with Garfield-
Jones Industries since the 1940's. Hoagland let him stand and
went on correcting the draft of our speech. Minutes went by,
and there we sat, three of us, the president, Dr. Dunwoodie, and
I, and stood, one, the secretary of the corporation, ignored.

Finally the president looked up and said: "Didn't you tell me
you had some kind of financial background?"

"Yes, Mr. Hoagland."

"This man . . ." Hoagland abruptly turned to me, the obscure
speech writer, to witness the outrage. "He claims that he has a
degree from the Wharton School of Business! You didn't join this
company on false pretenses, did you?"

"No, sir." Dill Hoover tried to laugh.

Another silence was filled by a meek cough from the psychiatrist's corner.

"I told you to go to the treasurer and get from him a report
on *cash flow*. How the hell can you turn in a memo like this? What
information does it give me? Shit! That's what. I don't care what

kind of a degree you've got, Hoover. You don't know shit. *What's that you've got there?"*

Dill Hoover simply gaped at us, sweating and horror-stricken. The president himself seemed about to faint with rage. One story was that he couldn't endure anyone who turned out to be stupid, lazy, or disloyal, and if the person were not quickly removed from his sight he would actually rush into the presidential washroom and get sick.

"Is that a copy you've got with you?"

"Yes, I . . ."

"Tear it up!"

"I only . . ."

"Tear it up!"

In a sorrowful, dreamy ceremony Dill Hoover did as he was told.

"Throw it in the wastebasket. Right there! Throw it in! Now, listen. You come back to me in two hours. Not at five. Not at four. One o'clock! And you bring the report I asked for!"

Lurching, almost falling down, the secretary made for the door. As he did so Dr. Dunwoodie leaped up nimbly in his corner and followed.

Meanwhile a benign leader of men had taken his place in the president's chair. Turning about, Hoagland favored me with a pale, radiant little smile. It was both a knowing and a mocking look. Its effect, which I still have no way of explaining, was one of making me feel complimented by being included in his crime. Conspiratorially he tapped his brow, as if to say: "You and I know . . ."

I found myself smiling back at him.

"We're doing fine," he said. "Friday we'll work on it some more."

Beyond my understanding even now, the wafer of praise filled me with gratitude. I felt utterly privileged, chosen.

"Yes, sir. Thank you."

In the reception room I saw Dill Hoover slumped in a stuffed chair with Dr. Dunwoodie's arm around his shoulders, and thought: What kind of a zoo is this? Not with superiority—I was in the cage too.

Not surprisingly there has been a good deal of speculation about Hoagland's home and sex life. Married, he has no children. His wife is said to be a gracious and serene woman. She has appeared at Garfield-Jones headquarters once or twice, but otherwise, since as far as we know the president never entertains, no one ever sees her. No one, except a few cronies, presumably, has been invited to his Park Avenue town house (the blinds are always drawn) or the country place at Cos Cob.

The wonder centers on when Hoagland can possibly find time for love. He almost invariably goes home late, between eight and nine in the evening, sometimes later, carrying several briefcases filled with work to be done. And it's never a surprise when the computer that walks like a man labors madly on alone—or attended by a group of despairing subordinates—with all lights blazing on the top floor of his skyscraper well past midnight.

However he may be as a husband, in every other way Hoagland denies life and substitutes business in its place. He can be strangely naïve. To a vice-president getting married, asking for a three-week vacation (his first except for long weekends in three years), he asked in amazement: "How could anyone want to be away from this job for more than two weeks?"

Does he actually enjoy wrecking the simple family pleasures of the men who work for him, not know any better, or simply not care? The grief of the interrupted weekend. Hoagland, Destroyer of Sundays. How many times on holiday mornings a groaning associate has heard his wife whisper angrily: "It's for you." And the president's voice over the phone: "Come on in, will you. There's something I want to talk about." And the midweek exhaustion brought on by interminable late-evening conferences. A timetable of missed trains passing through the commuter's mind interrupted by the whipcrack of a question: "What's last quarter's figure from Düsseldorf?" Finally, the endless commute back home in the dark, a moist film on his face, children unmet and unkissed, his wife loathing all of it and somehow holding him responsible.

Once at a staff meeting the president suggested a new rule. Weekends each member of the staff would phone in to headquarters every three hours, wherever he happened to be, at home, out for a drive, on the beach, to make sure the company knew where he could be found. After this suggestion there was a silence. Then an anguished cry came from a young marketing man: "Oh, my God, sir, please, no!" Perhaps it was a joke. At any rate Hoagland chuckled and let the subject drop.

Travel with Hoagland. Flown to some of the most beautiful and exciting cities in the world, where Garfield-Jones affiliates have been established, he sees nothing.

From the start, he moves in a convoy. Garfield-Jones's black limousines speed to the airport. A miniature office has been fitted into the back of the lead car, and the president works en route. Aides hand him papers; he disposes of them. Into the terminal, immediately conveyed to the VIP Lounge. Hoagland works until boarding time, then rushes into a private compartment. Another office desk awaits him. Aides find seats all around. Pull down the window shades. Fastening his seat belt, he labors on. Take-off. He shuts his eyes for a few moments until the liner is airborne, then raps out a question, another, makes a note, and studies the next memorandum.

Apprehensively the men around him wait for his next question. The stewardess's offer of drinks is declined, or surreptitiously taken up later. Eventually, on a long trip, the cabin goes dark. Hoagland's head falls back on the pillow and he's immediately asleep.

At sunrise—after orange juice, cornflakes and milk—he resumes. The party hits Paris, Rome, Mexico City, running. He would run through the Vatican or the Taj Mahal without looking to one side or another on his way to a business appointment. His aides are already staggering. Into limousines waiting. Work. To the Hilton! There, in enormous suites, work on. Papers are strewn all over the beds and the rug. Bellboys look at them astounded. They can't conceive that this may go on for two or three days, that the party will invade the conference rooms of one quaking branch manager after another and hammer at him for hours. The president rubs his hands: "Let's go. It's only midnight!"

Uncounted hours later the mission has been completed. A nightcap? No chance. Everyone is stunned with fatigue. Besides, in all likelihood, they will be taking the night plane back to New York, arriving just in time to go to the office the following morning. Process to be repeated next month.

Even as Garfield-Jones grew, moving upward in *Fortune*'s list of the top five hundred corporations, we could watch employee morale deteriorate. On every floor you could sense a feverish and corrupt atmosphere. People encountered in the corridors seemed wary. On the phone, many talked behind their hands. Some stalked about, as if hunting small animals. Others scuttled from office to office, trying not to be noticed. And all of them in this bin of sadists and victims gave the impression of scuffling for advantage.

Since nobody could be sure of his job, the answer was to hustle. The employees turned into a collection of greedy, bad children. You would see behavior at once crude, clownish, and pathetic. One day I noticed a clerk actually bent over listening at the door of Hoagland's executive vice-president, Art Govno. Abruptly he broke and ran past me down the hallway. I could guess what was going on. He had heard Govno telephoning a buy or sell order to a Wall Street connection. Whoever he was, the eavesdropper would now be babbling the same order to *his* broker.

Nearly everybody went into the market that year. Stock prices were spiraling up, few more spectacularly than the price of Garfield-Jones Industries. At the most fragmentary hint of a news development affecting the company, every man and woman in the know ran to phone a broker. The idea, as old as the exchange itself, was to have brokers, friends, family, cousins, and maiden aunts (acting for you, if a disguise was needed) buy now, and then as the stock jumped, sell before it came back down again.

More sophisticated speculation within the company began shortly after Hoagland's arrival. It started with Garfield-Jones's engineers. For decades "the boys in the lab" had been developing new products and processes for a pittance. The most brilliantly conceived device (and this was true throughout American industry) brought them fifty dollars upon acceptance by the company, another fifty if the U.S. Patent Office accepted it, and that was all. Sooner or later it had to occur to one of these taken-for-granted creative people: "Before the story about a new lab development gets out, why don't I call *my* broker?"

"Why not?" Ted Vreeland had asked at another staff meeting. "Why shouldn't they leak confidential news? Everybody else does. The scientist has to protect himself, too. But isn't there a fathomless corruption here? Don't we accept such things too easily? Yes, I know that's old hat and naïve. Forgive me."

Ted also identified the adroitly managed news release as the main reason for the persecution of Leo Niles. If Hoagland's own man could be installed as head of the PR department, stock-boosting stories could be manipulated more freely and advance knowledge of them confined to a few chosen scientists and engineers and selected members of management close to the top. What they did with this information, and when they did it, would be their own affair.

And so, only a month after Ted Vreeland made his report to us, the day arrived when Leo Niles was summoned before Hoagland. At noon I stopped by Leo's office and through the half-open door looked in on an emergency. He was sprawled white-faced in his swivel chair. Grace, his secretary, had one hand cupped behind his head and was offering him a glass of water.

I wanted to call the company doctor, but he shook his head. *Can't let them know.* And accepting the way we lived, in Hoagland's universe, he was right. Soon he had some color back. I said not to talk, but he insisted that Grace close the door and leave us, and told me about the meeting.

Slipping the nitroglycerin under his tongue, he felt better, but still not very good. Hoagland's outer office had a sinister atmosphere. The girls are looking at me strangely, he thought. He tried to strike up a conversation with the president's secretary, but she murmured in embarrassment and looked away.

He heard voices rising and falling behind the heavy door that opened into the conference room. There must be quite a few of them in there, he imagined. Feeling terribly cold, he began shivering. Damn! He couldn't let them see him in this condition.

He went out to the corridor and walked up and down. He flexed his hands to get some circulation going. It was an ordeal to be commanded to appear before a meeting, having not the slightest idea why, and then to be kept waiting in the reception room for half an hour. To be on the safe side, he had brought along the annual report and layout, including his suggested revisions of the President's Letter to the stockholders. This was a subject that would practically have to come up—the deadline being so desperately near.

"Mr. Niles!"

"Coming!" He ran inside.

The faces were somber. He knew he was in for it. His only friend in the room was Dill Hoover. Apart from the company secretary, all the rest at the long table were Hoagland's appointees. The president didn't look up as Leo entered. The public-relations director wasn't asked to sit down. Nor could he have, since there was no empty chair. Leo placed his briefcase against a leg of the conference table and nodded to the eight men. Only Dill Hoover responded, with a grimace so fleeting that it was more like a tic than a smile.

Dill was obviously miserable. A month before, after four Scotches in his own living room, he had wept to Leo: "I've got to get out, and you'd better too!" His bloated face had been a piteous sight that evening. Hearing the voices of his wife and teen-age sons down the hall, he had laid his finger on his lips.

The silence that followed Leo's appearance had lengthened into a form of harassment. The public-relations director could feel his heart pumping and skipping. He could feel it stop with a thump, and pause, and go into patterned flight. His breath was short; his hands and feet were cold. Now Hoagland looked up. Leo Niles saw that he had been studying the proposed revisions of the President's Letter.

"What's this?" Hoagland tapped the draft Leo had submitted.

"Sir?" Leo cleared his throat. "I . . . er, looked over your . . . the latest draft of your letter, Mr. Hoagland. There were parts that seemed a bit obscure, so I—"

"Crapped it up," said Hoagland, tossing the draft aside.

"I'm sorry," Leo Niles said. "I must have been mistaken. I just thought that a few of the paragraphs were muddy, but I guess I was wrong."

"Muddy . . ." Hoagland looked around him. Everyone seemed to find the word amusing. "Show me something 'muddy.'"

"Well," said Leo, "I've got a copy in my briefcase. Just a second . . ." From below the level of the table he heard the president say: "He came prepared."

Straightening up, Leo felt his heart roll like a ball bearing. His hands shook, and there was nothing he could do to control them. "The passage here—" Leo read aloud: "'That part of this sum allocated to research will continue to be with the exception of portions hitherto designated as being subject to related activities.' I thought that paragraph needed clarifying."

"You thought," the president said. His round face was pale, and his little eyes seemed entirely black with no white area around the pupils. "Why?"

"I guess so that the stockholders could get a clear picture . . ."

"Why?"

Now, too late, Leo understood.

"Who *needs* them to get a picture any clearer than that? You, maybe? Who are you? Benedict Arnold around here?"

"Mr. Hoagland, I wouldn't . . ."

"Give me *that*."

Leo handed his draft copy to the nearest executive, but the man indicated that he should walk around the table and hand it to the president himself. Leo did, and Hoagland dropped it in the wastebasket. Walking back to his station at the foot of the conference table, Leo heard Hoagland's voice behind him. "That's not what I wanted to talk to you about anyway!"

Leo turned to face them. Hoagland was shouting.

"You denied that we had a perpetual-motion machine!" (Here I am not naming the actual device.)

Slowly the public-relations director realized what they were doing to him.

"Who gave you the right to tell the papers anything?"

This attack was so unfair and preposterous that Leo Niles

wasn't even frightened by it. He felt that he had walked into a den of lunatics. He knew that Dill Hoover, at least, would be aware of how ridiculous this charge was. He looked for a sign from his old friend, but the secretary of the company had shut his eyes.

"What do you know about whether we have a perpetual-motion machine? Are you an engineer? Benedict Arnold? What?"

He was about to be made the goat of a situation that didn't require a goat. The management of rumor was one more technique perfected by the Hoagland team for running up the company's stock price. Used sparingly, once every year or two, it always worked. One of the president's friends would drop a hint to his favorite security analyst or brokerage house that some astonishing development was in the works at a Garfield-Jones plant, say, in the Pacific Northwest. The stock would go up as speculators moved in. The mutual funds would react. Small investors would hear about it; the price would rise some more. At this point Hoagland would call a press conference or grant an interview to an important business writer. "Certain rumors have been going the rounds,'" he might say. "I want to get the record straight. Yes, it's true that our scientists are working on————. But as yet we haven't reached the stage . . ." etc., etc.

In this instance the word was that Garfield-Jones engineers had achieved a "breakthrough" toward constructing a perpetual-motion device that "will need no energy of any kind except the power of the sun, even on cloudy days."

Leo Niles's statement that such a breakthrough hadn't yet occurred (this time the lab engineers knew they had nothing and begged that the correction be made), followed next day by Hoagland's "setting the record straight," had resulted in an *additional* rise in the company's stock price—since Garfield-Jones's involvement in perpetual motion was not denied—and management also received high marks for honesty. Yet Leo now found himself being shouted at and so dizzy that he could hardly keep his feet.

"Who are you to make statements to the press!"

"I was instructed to, sir," the public-relations director answered quietly.

"*Who* instructed you?"

"Mr. Govno," said Leo Niles. He looked for Hoagland's right-hand man to confirm his statement, but Govno wasn't there.

"He says he didn't."

"He must have . . . forgotten, Mr. Hoagland."

"Forgotten!" Hoagland grinned. "More likely it's you who forgot. You're not around very much. I tried to get hold of you twice yesterday afternoon. Where were you?"

Grace hadn't told him. It was unlikely that they had phoned, and yet they knew he was away from his desk. Leo's memory went blank. Where had he been? Oh, yes, at the doctor's. But he mustn't tell them that.

"I was out. Just . . ."

"Sneaking out in the afternoons, eh?" The president chuckled. "Getting a little nooky, eh? A little poontang. I know you public-relations guys."

A roar of laughter went up, and Leo Niles saw that his friend Dill Hoover was laughing with the rest—as wildly as he had wept and moaned over the four Scotches in his living room a month before. He saw Hoagland turning this way and that like a master of ceremonies, and Dill Hoover laughing. He couldn't look at them anymore, and felt himself turning, picking up his briefcase and walking out. He heard Hoagland say "I'm kidding . . ." as he closed the door behind him.

"Leo Niles! Dead!" Dill Hoover slapped the desk in front of him. His mouth trembled. "But . . . last week! I saw him!"

"He died over the weekend," Ted Vreeland said. "How come you didn't hear about it?"

"Oh, I was away! On the Cape. I had to— I've just got in this morning! Dead! Oh, my . . ." He covered his face with his hands.

"You knew him a long time, didn't you?"

"Years! Long before he came with us. I helped— I recommended—"

It was obvious that he desperately wanted a drink but didn't dare pull the flask out of his drawer in front of the outside public-relations man. Not at ten o'clock in the morning.

"Go ahead," Ted Vreeland advised him. "What difference does it make?"

"I will . . . I will . . ." He tilted the flask like a baby bottle and took several gulps of his secret vodka. "Gone!" A tear ran down each of Dill Hoover's bloated cheeks. "Lord, I saw him . . ."

"The last time they worked him over, wasn't it?"

Ted Vreeland said later that he couldn't resist this, but was immediately sorry.

The company secretary gasped. Clutching his flask, he walked to the window and gazed miserably out. "You must have heard— It was awful. I was there. I was— I didn't *speak up*."

The agency man sucked rhythmically on his pipe. "You aren't the only one."

"No, but he was my friend!" Dill Hoover tilted his flask again. "Did Leo die . . . peacefully?"

Ted Vreeland told him what he knew.

At the end Leo Niles had an obsession. In May he wanted Christmas decorations all around him. So his wife decorated his oxygen tent with Christmas trimmings the day before he died. "She'd saved the tinsel and angels' hair and silver light bulbs." The tent became a Christmas tree with Leo inside of it, looking out. He asked: "Where are the red bulbs?" and she went out and got them. He wanted color. Leo's heart's blood instead of flowing was spurting, so he had that perpetual flutter—

"I *know*!" Dill Hoover cried, then made his confession. If there was anything in his life he would crawl on his knees to take back it would be the laugh that came out of him when Hoagland was humiliating Leo Niles. He would never forget Leo turning to him uncertainly, then feebly joining in the laughter, as if to say: "If *you're* laughing, old friend, it must be true. I am Benedict Arnold, only out for poontang."

Dill Hoover sweated. "Ted! Please tell me. Why did I laugh at Leo? The thing is it wasn't just fear. Something in me enjoyed the scene, made me want to kowtow to Hoagland while he was publicly ridiculing my friend. I don't understand! Does their cruelty appeal to something base in my make-up? Could I be that much of a pervert? Believe me, Ted, I'm not cruel by nature! Or am I?"

The president is reported to have said that he had nothing personal against Leo Niles, and hoped there were no hard feelings. At Garfield-Jones Leo's death inspired little comment. Hoagland's PR-director-in-waiting was quickly installed, and life went on.

Indirectly Leo's passing brought on a month-long enforced vacation for Ted Vreeland. At the weekly staff meeting after his friend's death Ted had put all of us, especially Paul Keogh, in an insufferable moral position.

"What is this lousy dog and pony show we're supposed to believe in? How long are we going to serve this evil individual? Polluter of souls, litterer of other men's lives . . ."

"Yes, Ted . . ."

Disturbed that day, our chief closed the meeting early.

So Lewis Hoagland continued to work his will on everyone. All of us without exception in and outside of the company bowed down to him and did his bidding. For me, the mystery of his dominating power remained. Hatchet-faced demon, I thought, what gods do you worship? If I could once see you down on your knees . . .

The night before the annual meeting I saw him that way.

The final draft of his speech was being typed late in the afternoon. He had gone home, this time to Connecticut. Trusting no one, no messenger service, not even Garfield-Jones's own, he asked me to supervise the final typing and personally bring the speech to him in Cos Cob that evening.

The house was a small stucco fortress secreted behind poplars and clipped hedges. A half-moon was up. Reflecting disks at ground level guided me along the curling gravel driveway, and my car threw a monstrous moving shadow across a hedgerow.

He appeared in the lighted doorway, alone. There was no sign of anyone else in the house.

"Here it is, Mr. Hoagland."

He accepted the envelope, but his thoughts were somewhere else. He smiled oddly in an abstracted way, and to my surprise I saw that he was dressed in green coveralls like a mechanic. I turned to get back into my car when, still smiling, he beckoned for me to follow him. We walked around the side of the house. Presently we came to a gate and the high brick walls of his back yard. He threw a switch and behind the walls the yard lighted up.

The gate swung open and he triumphantly extended his arm. I passed beneath an archway and into the light. Covering most of the grassy half acre I was confronted by what seemed to be a gigantic pile of junk. After a few moments I saw that it was connected up, a unit of some kind, sprawling like a wild cell under the floodlights.

Now the president, a sharp-faced little man in coveralls, held up one finger and retreated to a small workshop near a grape arbor. He reached inside the workshop door.

The enormous heap of junk started to move, grind, and clatter. Pistons labored. Blades of light began flashing. Pulleys whirred. Wheels turned against other wheels. The machine groaned and wheezed. Taut wires even sang. Rythmically, small motors coughed, sputtered, and whined. Then the night was pierced by a scraping sound, as if the machine had gone into agony.

"No, no!"

The first words he had spoken since my arrival came out of him as he turned off the switch. The machine abruptly rested, smoking, breathing exhaust fumes in small jets. Now the president ran to it, carrying a small toolbox and an oilcan with spout attached. He knelt before a rod and a shining wheel, wrenching at the connection between them and delicately applying oil from the spout. He spent several minutes kneeling in front of this creation, and the figure in coveralls seemed itself to have joined the colossal metallic tangle. Then proudly he stood up, ran back across the yard, and restarted his giant contraption.

"What do you think?" he called out to me.

"Unbelievable, Mr. Hoagland. What does it do?"

"Nothing!" He grinned. "Nothing at all!"

"It doesn't do anything?"

"Not a thing. Look at her. Isn't she beautiful!"

Lewis Hoagland performed a little caper in front of his wild model.

"*Never. She'll never be finished.* That's the beauty. She'll just go on getting bigger. You know what I'm going to do next? Bust through the back wall, buy the property in back there, keep adding on . . ."

The president of Garfield-Jones Industries steps to the lectern, surveys the gathering of more than one thousand stockholders, introduces himself, and calls the annual meeting to order.

"It's flattering to your management that so many of you have taken the trouble to come here today. Of course, it could be that you've all come to *vote us out . . .*"

A laugh goes up, directors and shareholders joining together.

"Now, Mr. Secretary"—the president turns to Dill Hoover—"will you please read the notice of the meeting and give proof that you've mailed everyone entitled to receive it such notice."

Mournfully, his elephant ears seeming to weigh his head down, Dill Hoover drones out the official word. When he has finished, the president steps to the microphone and begins as always: "Last year domestic sales and revenues reached a new high . . ."

From then on, once again, it's magic, a recital of uninterrupted conquests. All over the world the company has made more money than ever before, more acquisitions, more advances into competitors' territory.

I observe again that once on a rostrum the president no longer seems a small man. His eyes dilate and a tremendous financial intelligence shines out of them. He speaks to row upon row of entranced faces. Once more, they learn, he will increase their dividends. Not a doubting or hostile presence can be seen. Certainly no sign of disaffection from defeated Dill Hoover, or Paul Keogh, whom I have just noticed shaking hands enthusiastically with Hoagland, or the red, stubborn countenance of Ted Vreeland, who has been sent away to ponder justice on the shore of a Canadian lake. The ghost of Leo Niles definitely does not hover over this meeting.

Genially during the question period the president disposes

of two recalcitrant stockholders as though they were bright but uninformed children.

One of the middle-aged women wearing flower hats rises to cry out admiringly: "Mr. Hoagland, how can you possibly remember all those details!"

The president grins, goes into his triumphant little dance, and taps his brow. "I've got it all—right here!"

I see a heap of mechanized trash in the moonlight, a grin, a dance, no mourning of crushed men, and a congregation of adoring dollar-worshipers.

For them, for me perhaps, a mad god is better than none.

3. THE EDUCATION OF AN ORGY MASTER

In the middle 1960's Lee Raymond* was an eighteen-year-old male prostitute. He had begun his career four years earlier and was now well known on the homosexual circuit as a master of orgies. He also served women and mixed groups, putting on shows with girls, boys, or both, might furnish you with his own girl, but his principal clientele was male, and he boasted a list of about seven hundred johns, his customers in the United States and Europe.

A homosexual businessman friend who admired him enormously put Lee in touch with us. My wife taped a few sessions with him, and I talked with him. After a few visits he drifted away.

Snub-nosed, beach-blond hair, wide-open candid blue eyes, small in stature but strong, moving quickly like a boxer, speaking in modulated tones with untouched assurance, a Norman Rockwell cover of a boy from a small town near Manchester, New Hampshire, he lay back at ease, addressing us and the tape recorder without hesitation, at some time during the visit pausing to roll a joint, inhaling deeply with his eyes closed, the mari-

* He never gave us the name he was born with. In fact, no one outside of his home town knows his legal name, and he never goes back there.

juana seeming to complete him and make the flow of his memories and reflections come faster.

My father was in the Army until I was about six. I remember one situation when he finally arrived home, coming up the stairs with a duffel bag without any previous notice and I believe my mother had a boy friend up there, a sailor, and there was a fight and my old lady got hit.

Until he came back my mother and I did everything together, went to the movies and things like that. There wasn't that much difference in age between us—only sixteen years. When he came home he worked for a while in a machine shop. My mother took in washing and worked in a textile mill. All through this time I remember money worries.

It started right off. He resented the fact that my mother was showing me all the attention. He expected constant attention from my mother. He wanted her to fawn all over him and hang on him—sit at his feet sort of thing. You know. I used to do a lot of things to burn him up. Like he'd tell me to eat. I wouldn't say anything. I'd be nice and polite and wouldn't eat, and he dumped a bowl of spaghetti on me and a quart of milk and he beat me up. I didn't swing back or do anything and I got up and smashed the windows out of the house. I had orange crates full of books and threw those and walked out. I was thirteen. That was the first time I left.

One time I picked a wild rose for my mother, and the people downstairs, they flipped their corker because I picked the rose off the vine and a big fight ensued, and my mother's dress got ripped off. She was fighting with the woman. And my father was coming out of the house too, and got into a fight with the husband, and then we moved . . .

It wasn't too long after he came back that my father brought over a family from Germany, including a daughter. She and I slept in the same room together because there was not very much room for six people in a three-room house. I had relations with the daughter. This was when I was about seven years old. She was eight. She taught me all I know—well, not all, but she gave me my first experience in sex. She learned it from a concentration camp.

One night she asked me—she couldn't speak English very well—if I wanted—I don't remember the word . . . I forget it all the time. Something to do with fig bars. I said okay. So then she showed me what I had to go through to get, you know, to the goal which I thought was these cookies. She took down her pajamas and told me to put it between her legs, and this went on maybe for two or three weeks. But then we got caught. Her mother caught us and she hit me twice and she only hit her once. I remember that. Then a slap on the ass each and it seemed as if everything was going to be all right. There was nobody else home but the old lady, so she must have heard bad noises. The next thing you know I was waked up from a sound sleep, and it was just terrible. All of them yelling. Both of us cried, and for hours it was "Who did it?" "Your son showed her." "No, your daughter . . ." This went on for hours. They hit me and she got hit, and my family told them she would have to get out. I don't know why. It was just an ordinary kid thing.

I was about eight when I started teaching my cousins what I had learned. I fucked all my little cousins, lots of little cousins. And then next door there were four girls and I was making it with them. We used to make it in this turkey coop and I would make it with one and another would watch out through the window to see if anybody was coming through the back way. I wore suspenders, and they had an older brother. I guess he was about sixteen or eighteen, and the next thing I knew they said: "He's coming . . ." The brother was coming and I got my suspenders caught between my legs and I couldn't get them up, and he knew about it but he never said anything.

I started to school when I was about four and a half, and
I was baptized in the Catholic church. I started in the Catholic
parochial school. I was in this school about two years before
I was removed because of not enough money in the family.

I always read. I like to read. I read all the child stories, you
know, *Three Musketeers, Kidnapped, Little Men.* All the stories
that children read . . .

I used to do different sports and things. I never talked to
my father at all so he never knew I was boxing. He didn't know
about it till he read in the newspaper that I had been in a fight
and won, and he started telling his buddies about his kid—you
know, good at boxing. In a small town they eat up this kind of
shit anyway, and I quit. Even in sports, like whenever he started
bragging about sports I was in, I used to tell him not to because
I never did like to have people brag about me. I'd just stop
playing when he started bragging. At school I just stopped going
because I used to be an honor student and got my name in the
newspapers. Big deal in a small town too. Every time you get a
report card the honor students go in the newspapers. I didn't
bother to fail in my marks. I just didn't bother to go to school
anymore. I would just go for exams, that's all. But I still did pass,
for some unknown reason.

As a kid . . . there was this hen house on our property. I
shoveled out all the chicken shit, nailed some burlap bags over
the windows, and made it into a workshop. Then I manufactured
Christmas decorations, and like baskets and wreaths. I got these
things out of the cemetery dump. I'd go to the dump all summer
long with bags and get baskets, hoops, sticks, and ribbons. I
would iron the ribbons on the hot stovepipe and save them. Three
or four months before Christmas I would start getting greens
and putting them on the wreaths. I would take flowerpots out of
the cemetery dump and dig up plants out of the woods and sell
them. I picked up blueberries and blackberries and sold those.

And then sometimes I went out in the woods and hunted and fished, trapped animals and sent their skins to New York.

With the money I would buy clothes, hatchets, knives. I gave a lot of it to my mother. I used some to buy Christmas presents for my family.

Later on I got into trouble, many times. I broke five hundred windows, little plate-glass windows in a big barn. The kids squealed on me, and before the police got a chance to come or anything, my mother was coming up the hill from work and I was crying. I told her what had happened right away and my father made me go down there—he had to put the windows back in—and they made me get down on my knees and apologize. We had a big hassle over that. He humiliated me. It was wintertime, but I ran out with just my pants and T-shirt on.

The police came to the house one day and picked me up. I had broken into eleven houses and they had caught the others who had been with me. I had stolen things—whiskey, cigarettes and canteen sets, straw hats. You know, silly things, swords and guns and things like that. I would take them into town. There was a little restaurant where the kids congregated and I had auctions. We sold them.

Eventually they made me give back a whole duffel bag full of loot I had stolen. We went to court, and I was put on probation. I had to write the golden rule two hundred times.

I was in a car accident with some of the boys. We were drinking. On the highway going home we started racing this other kid. We were in a convertible and somehow or other we didn't maneuver the corner, and we hit one of those stations you wait in for a bus when it's raining in the country, knocking that into a river. We hit a tree and I went through the top of the convertible. I was unconscious for three days and was out of school for a couple of months.

The police were always following me. Because of my father mostly. He kept trying to get me locked up. They got me for breaking probation, not checking in as I was supposed to do. My father was always complaining and wanted the probation officer to take me away. I would go to court or jail. They would hold me for eight hours and let me out. Then it was continuous assault and all that. My father and I would have a fight, and I would leave home. Then they would catch me and bring me back. He would report me and go looking for me, and when the cops saw me they would always pick me up and question me about anything that went wrong.

I got sick of the whole scene. I couldn't stand it, and didn't care about the parole or anything. It was just after my fourteenth birthday. I decided to go to New York, and a friend of mine picked me up on a motorcycle. He was about four or five years older than me. We had worked in a junk yard together and got laid off.

He told me I wouldn't have any trouble making out in New York, but I didn't know what he was talking about. We went to a bar and got drunk, and I didn't see him again for three days. It was my first time in the city, and I was scared. I hadn't eaten. After I had been on the street for about three days someone picked me up on Times Square. He came up and said, you know: "What are you doing?" and I said: "Just looking in the window." He asked: "Would you like something to eat?" and I said: "Of course." He gave me a meal, which made me sleepy. I hadn't been able to sleep in Bryant Park. The police kept waking me and kicking me out. Anyway he wanted to screw me in the ass, but I went right to sleep.

I had no objections. I had just never heard of it before. I didn't have feelings one way or the other toward him. I just wanted to go to sleep. When I got up he said he had to go to work and I went out and never saw him again.

Then this other person picked me up in front of Playland on

42nd Street. He was gay too, and sort of . . . criminal. He took me home and asked would I like to take a tour of the South. I said sure and we had relations. He sucked my cock, and gave me a suit to wear. It was much too big for me, but I never had a suit before and I thought it was pretty good.

He knew an awful lot about pharmacology because he was a salesman for a big drug company. That's where I learned most of what I know about drugs. Speed, heroin . . . I tried them all, but never was addicted. We were only in New York a few days, and then went south, everywhere, Virginia, North Carolina, South Carolina, Georgia. I stayed with this man Jerry for eight months.

We stopped at all the big cities so that he could set up sample rooms, but the ultimate goal of our trip was Georgia. He planned when he got there to get this buddy of his off a road gang. His friend Dave was in for armed robbery. Dave had gotten himself out of the penitentiary and onto the road gang. They had signals arranged. We were driving along the highway when the truck came to bring the men to the road to work. Dave recognized Jerry. Then Jerry told me: "I'm going to drive by pretty soon— Look, this is serious. You don't have to go. You can wait here." But I wanted to go along. I thought it would be kicks, but it was just like picking up somebody at a drugstore because Jerry just drove down the highway and the man came dashing out of the field—he had a revolver he'd gotten from one of the guards—and from there we went to Atlanta.

Jerry had been overspending his expense account. I mean, he was just in too much. I'd pick out a thousand dollars' worth of clothes. He told me to pick out what I wanted, so I did. He gave the store one hundred dollars on account, and they haven't seen the rest of it since. I pawned the clothes, most of them in Washington, D.C., on the way back, and what I didn't somebody took from me.

In Washington we went to a party and there were some faggots there. Dave wasn't a faggot. I was in the bedroom. I was going to take a shower and go to sleep, being tired from all the driving we did. There was a crash and someone grabbed my pants and ran out, and they had hit Dave with a flowerpot and smashed his face all open. He couldn't go to the doctor, having just escaped from the road gang, so Jerry sewed his face up. Then Dave went off to stay with a girl friend, and that was the last I saw of him.

When we got back to New York Jerry's mother and father talked him into committing himself before he went to jail. He was hanging bad checks, and the company he was working for wanted the money he had spent, having overdrawn his expense account, and lied on it, so he decided to commit himself to Rockland. They locked Jerry up, and that left me on the street again.

Before he went to Rockland, he introduced me to a friend who was also gay and I stayed with him for a while and hustled Times Square. I was almost fifteen then. Soon I got myself together enough money and got my own apartment. I hustled in various ways. I've been a call boy. I've been a bar hooker and a street hooker.

Like most boys I hustled on Times Square, like the little boys who come in from Jersey and want the money so they can go to a rock 'n' roll show. They'll stand on Times Square until some faggot picks them up and then they go to bed and get five dollars. Or, to supplement that and have a place to stay—I've talked to boys who are working there now, and they say the classic thing is a buck and breakfast—they call it B and B. They sleep overnight, then get a buck and breakfast.

These boys from New Jersey—they're not hustling boys, actually. They're just clean-cut schoolboys, and if there's a rock 'n' roll show in town, say, for instance, and they don't have the money to go—the tickets might be four dollars—so they'll go to bed with some faggot to get the money, for the four dollars.

You talk about *Lolita*. I didn't even bother to finish it because it didn't shock me at all. It wasn't even interesting. You can get twelve-year-old girls and boys anywhere around. Like the ones on Times Square. The word gets around. Younger kids, much younger than I was, find out about this. There are many men on Times Square, faggots who like very young kids, and they even have a name. They're called kidnappers. And these young boys come in from Jersey, just for purely sexual purposes. They're twelve years old. You know, anything, give me five dollars and suck my cock, please.

I can call right up now and get you a twelve-year-old. Or a five-year-old. Twelve, five, two, a baby if you want. What happens usually—like with Puerto Ricans—you pay the family. This is true. The families don't have any money and they figure the child isn't being harmed, so they say: "All right, give us a couple of dollars and you can use our kid." So you can have a kid of any age then.

I got this pretty little queen to live with me. I had picked this queen up, or he had picked me up—I don't remember now—and we went home for Christmas and got drunk together at my apartment.

This queen looked like a girl. She stayed with me for—I don't know—four, five, or six months, and I hustled for both of us. I don't know why. When Jerry left, I was lonely. It wasn't really a love affair because there was no sex or anything. Well, only three times. It was just loneliness and the need for companionship. But we just couldn't get along, and then Jerry came back out of Rockland.

Jerry and I were going to a party. When I came back, before the party, in the afternoon, the door was locked. The queen had stolen my television, my hi-fi, and stowed them in the landlady's apartment. And stolen my cashmere shirts and pawned them, and there was nothing left for me. At the party I got drunk, and I was so depressed about the situation I decided there was no sense living anymore. I went to Jerry's from there. He had Tuinals, thirty-three-grain Tuinals, and I took them all and went to sleep.

The next thing I knew I woke up in Bellevue and later Jerry told me he had carried me down and put me in the car and taken me there. The attendants wouldn't help him lift me out of the car. They said no. So they took me and pumped out my stomach and, well, when I woke up I had a johnny on and I was in sort of a dream world. I didn't open my eyes. I just lay there, my arm

paining me so much because the intravenous they had been giving me was put in by half-ass attendants and instead of going
intravenous it was going subcutaneous in my arm. For about a
month it was bloated like this. And after I laid there for about
a half hour, someone came by and grabbed my penis. I never
looked to see who it was.

Not that I was groggy. I just didn't feel like moving. Then I
thought about it, and realized that here I was, and I had no
comb, no toothbrush, cigarettes, no anything, so I waited and
someone came by and grabbed my penis again. When he walked
away I noticed that it was one of the interns. So I asked him if
he could give me some pajamas or something to put on because
I felt funny lying there, and he said he could. I said I didn't
know how to put them on, and he said: "Come to the men's
room." I mean I had ulterior motives all the way along. When
he was showing me how to put them on he started playing with
me, and I explained to him my plight—that I needed a comb,
cigarettes, and toothbrush and tooth paste—and he said he would
get them for me if I would let him suck my cock. So he went
ahead and did it and I got my comb and toothbrush. Then they
shipped me upstairs. This was in Bellevue. They put me in the
psycho ward, and I was there for five days until Jerry's family
got me out. They said I was their son.

I got disgusted with the whole situation and decided to go
home to Massachusetts. So I put all the things I had in boxes and
gave it all to my family. There were various ashtrays and towels
and sheets I had picked up from the hotels along the way down
South and here in New York, from different hotels I slept in.

I went home and walked in the door just like I was home
from school and had been home that morning. That was all right,
but that night I got in a car accident with some of my friends
who were drinking and went to the hospital. My father came
in to visit me, and said that everything about the past, I mean
about leaving when I was on parole, was straightened out. But he
was two-faced as always. After all this time of my being away

down South and in New York, they still had kept the book on me. Eleven home breaks, truancy, incorrigibility, fighting . . .

The day I was ready to leave the hospital I got dressed and stepped out of the door of the hospital room and these two big men put handcuffs on me. They took me to the courthouse and I had a special court session. My father said he had evidence that I had stolen these things from hotels and that he didn't want me at home. The judge and my father decided to put me into C——— Hospital. I was there for a couple of weeks and the psychiatrists decided I was nuts—they never told me why—and had me sent to the institution at R———.

Everywhere I went, I had always kept my address book with me. But when you go into an institution they take away your things. They even take your clothes. I had become good friends with the man who takes patients from the hospital to the institution, and I got him to bring my address book back. He sneaked it to me, so I wasn't too lost. I could leave there and go to New York anytime I wanted.

It was easy. At this place nobody knew what was happening. The authorities didn't know anything. I would play cribbage with the attendants and then steal parole cards and walk out on the grounds. I could have left anytime. But at first I didn't want to. There were a lot of nuts, and I had a good time there. I stole my own charts and used to write funny quotations alongside. There were other parolees, girl nuts, and we would make it together like under the stairways and in the cornfields and apple orchards.

At first that wasn't possible. In the beginning I didn't even have cigarettes. I told the attendant that if there were any faggots in here I would get some. He advised me—he wasn't homosexual, he and I were just buddies, we played cards together—he said not to fool around with them because they were unreliable, and there had been times when they reported it.

But pretty soon I had this little Portygee boy. He was about ten at the time. A dark Portygee, a very pretty boy. Now being locked up in an institution, of course, sex is very limited, so that what is usually done is that some young boy is taken over and you have oral and anal intercourse with him, simply because there is no other means available.

He told me about other men who had given him candy or money to go to bed with him, but because the boy sort of admired me, that wasn't necessary. This boy was just the product of a large family. There was no need for him to be there. The family just decided he was the most troublesome and there were too many mouths to feed, so they put him away. Actually the boy was well behaved. Sometimes a little belligerent, but I could make him do anything I wanted to. With kindness. We had many relations.

Eventually I suppose this boy is going to turn out to be like some of the other boys in the institution that have been there for years. At first they aren't really homosexual—it's just lack of female companionship and no sex. At ten or eleven they haven't become homosexual yet, but as they get older they will.

When I was on the ward I took over a seclusion room. Being a young man myself—all boys sort of attach themselves to an older boy as playing the hero part in their lives—we fixed up the seclusion room together. I had him. He slept in one bed and I slept in the other.

I stole things out of the dayroom, and then I made it into a nice hotel room. I had curtains in the window. I had a bed-spread, rugs on the floor, the ones the nuts used to make in occupational therapy. I had flower plants I stole out of the hall-way downstairs. And the little Portygee boy would do just about anything I said. He'd clean the room and at night after visiting days he used to crawl under the beds and steal all the money and candy and give it to me. I figured it would be easier for him to do it, because then I wouldn't get in trouble if he got caught. Not only that, he was dark and they can't see anybody in the dormitory at night. Yes, I had him working for me. So of course I was never at a shortage for money, cigarettes, or candy. Every now and then I would throw a little party. I would buy them all Coca-Cola, give them each a cigarette, you know, I figured, you know, it would be nice.

Finally I just got completely bored with the whole thing. I did have lots of good times in there because it was interesting, but after a while it got quite boring. I had been waiting to see if my father would sign me out, and I saw no hope for that at all—so what I did was to steal a day pass and a parole card, and went out the gate, and took a bus to Providence. I had contacted Jerry from the nut house. I could have done it on my own but he met me there and brought me clothes. I didn't take anything with me. He brought me one of his suits, kind of baggy but okay.

I was fifteen then, and I went to New York. This was in August. In December the police and the court at home finally decided there was no sense in bringing me back. Not only because they couldn't find me but because there was nothing they could do for me there—there was no sense wasting the taxpayers' money, so they gave me a legal discharge.

I arranged it really. I had been out of the institution for a couple of months when it occurred to me that my family always had money problems. I decided that the one way to keep on the outside and to get a permanent discharge from probation would be to get them relying on me for financing. So I started sending them money by Western Union without letting them know where I was. Finally I contacted them. My mother kept me warned whenever my father went into a rage. She'd tell me to stay hidden because he would have me put away again. But when they got relying on my money, that was different. He changed. Then I went home and saw the probation officer, and sat down with him and my mother, and they gave me a legal discharge. I told them I was in the modeling game and they believed it.

Meanwhile I had renewed my old connections and gone back to hustling. I really set out to learn the business and I did.

The way the johns and hustlers operate, they all sort of work together. If a john wants to see a boy he might ask another john. Or he might ask a hustler he knows. It's a brotherhood, an organization—like the Masons.

One nice thing about the faggots is there's a grapevine. Once there's a nice boy in town and he stays around for a little while, if he's smart, he can pick up a fortune by going from one faggot to his friend and so on.

For instance, I would get a call because my friend Arthur told a john about me, and the john wants to import me into some town at such and such a fee. Or a john might ask if I know some boy and I say: "What type do you like?" and he'll say: "I want a six-footer with blond hair who's a body-builder." And you get him a six-footer with blond hair who's a body-builder, and he gives you a little kickback. You know . . .

During my time hustling on Times Square—I hadn't been hustling too long and being a cute boy and having a commodity to sell—one of the johns gave me the number of a boy he said would give me quite a few numbers and help me out. Now I had no idea what "quite a few" meant. I thought maybe five or six. This boy had at least five hundred connections! I was surprised at that time, but now I myself have a book listing probably six or seven hundred faggots. And the boy hustlers—it's overwhelming how many there are. By myself I know at least four hundred. The money the good ones make most people wouldn't believe. It's all tax-free, of course. Also they get inside tips on the stock market, things like that. A friend I saw today—he's been hustling only about two years, since he was seventeen, and he's worth now, I would say at a minimum, at least sixty thousand dollars.

The johns . . . you have to get used to the demands they can make. When I first got involved in the gay life, the first person I met who wanted to be urinated on, I felt it was kind of strange. Today I no longer think of it as a perversion because it's so common everywhere. There are so many johns who ask you to piss on them I would no longer classify it as a perversion.

Others like to get shat on. Then there are lots of sadists, and you have to look out for them. There are the masochists. Some just want you to talk mean to them. Some want you to hurt them, and some just want you to go halfway, and just wear boots and a motorcycle jacket and dungarees and hit them with a thick belt. There are hustlers who mostly specialize in this.

You take Vince. He works in a New York City bureau, and you can reach him there. He usually answers the phone himself. I'd say he was about thirty-two, even though he claims to be twenty-eight, because some people have known him for sixteen or seventeen years. He's so cheap. He'll go for a trick with a very rich person; just ride his bicycle over and chain it to a No Parking sign and run upstairs, have his little session, collect his money, run downstairs, hop on his bicycle, and off he goes. All this time he has been studying for a master's in psychology. Now he teaches—just where, I don't know. This boy is so money-conscious that he lives in a cold-water flat on Tenth Avenue, and he doesn't even take his leak before going to bed without calling up a john that might like to be pissed on.

He just wants money for money's sake. He's been in Europe several times. Of course, now he's getting older and it costs him a little more, but he goes over as cheap as he can. He gets a bicycle and he pedals from one country to the next—seeing johns, you know, all over Europe.

Sometimes I would go on a retainer, get paid by the week. The johns give you spending money every day and usually you can save some of that. Then you get a certain fee at the end of the week. Lots of times you get tips that bring in more money. If you are nice, you get a fat tip, you know, and you get your round-trip ticket. They might buy you clothes. It's good.

For instance, there is this one rich john. He has all the money he wants, and I think his objective is . . . he's a young man and he wants to see boys turn out sort of—you know—good, be married and have children. And he wants to feel he's playing a big part in it, you see. He likes to have them come down and stay in the town he lives in. He'll rent them an apartment, get them a car. Good Samaritan sort of thing. Yeah. They go to school and play the small-town game, and that's what he wants. But it's just not for me. But he digs me just the same, and asks me to come down there sometimes and I make out good.

There are also clearinghouses. Boys in certain big cities like L.A. and New York; one boy might know a thousand johns and maybe himself know five or six hundred boys. All over the world he's known and he gets calls, say, from Paris. "I want to see a boy. You know some boys here in Paris?" they ask. And he knows so many johns and so many boys that he can give you a number any place you go.

It's international because any faggot that's got any kind of money will travel all over the world, and he might meet you in Los Angeles, or you might meet him in New York, Paris, London . . . anywhere.

Then there are a lot of heterosexual people who would like to see me and a girl make it together. Also, quite a few heterosexual people like to see a boy every six months or so. And of course a lot of out-and-out homosexuals are married men with families and children. I would get many calls from women. I know this one who looks like a sweet grandmother. You go in, and she doesn't want to do anything but get fucked and fucked and fucked. She has boys come in. She likes to see boys make it together, and she pays very well. Once she wanted me to get her a lesbian. A real bull dyke, she said. She wanted a real good girl, too. Then there are other women who have five, six, or seven boys at once. Then some married couples like to have a boy come in. I know many guys who like to see their wives get fucked. And they pay. I've been with gay cops and vice-squad men. And, too, if you want to get into the religious line, there are many gay priests. As a matter of fact, the priest who gave me instruction for my confirmation was homosexual.

When my own name started traveling with my phone number there was no need for hustling anymore. My phone was ringing constantly. If I felt pretty good, I would see as many johns as I could every day. Sometimes as many as twelve. But that depends on who you're with. If you can fake your orgasm without letting them know it, then you can save yourself.

The little grandmother, the little teacup, that sweet old lady I mentioned, you would never suspect her at all. She has a kind of house. I never worked in a house where there were women. But I introduced my girl Julia to this woman, and she has tricked for her. Julia is very good with homosexuals. A few of them have never had a girl, so they want to try it. So they come down and buy her. She doesn't have any difficulty with them. They have no trouble getting an erection, and as a matter of fact their orgasm is quite rapid.

Unpleasant experiences? Yes. One of the most unpleasant I can think of is not getting your money. But you can run into difficulties where somebody might want to tie you up, you know, and you get out of there right away, because there are a lot of sadists and you can get yourself hurt if you're not smart. You can't always tell who's going to be a sadist. As soon as you get any inkling you just get out. That's all. I mean you have to be able to feel them out. You have to know how to hustle, that's all. You've got to be a good hustler.

There are a lot of tricks, you know. A girl, for instance, has to learn how to get in and get out and not make the john feel he's being rushed. When she gets into bed with him she should be able to make the john think he's just the best thing that ever hit the earth. Learn how to whisper and talk to him so he gets off his rocks quicker. Things like that.

All that goes for boys too. I've found that a prostitute has to have a real good memory because then you make the john feel very personal. Like when he calls on the phone, never let him say who he is. Say: "Oh, how have you been?" Get him talking if you don't recognize the voice right away. Then you say his name. When he calls and says hello I can usually recognize the voice right away, and I say: "Oh, howdy, Bob, how are you?" and it makes them feel personal, instead of them thinking of you as a prostitute.

Try not to say to a john: "How much do you pay?" I mean if you know you're traveling in the better class of people. Don't let them think they are paying you. It's better if they're just

making you a little gift. Have your stories ready, whichever one
is best for the john you're with. I need help putting myself
through school. Or I need clothes. Or I'm helping my mother
and father. I always have some little story. Sometimes I get very
elaborate and end up blowing my own story because it gets so
good I come to a punch line that's just so right that I have to use
it, and then everybody—myself included—cracks up, and they
know I'm just putting them on.

The better class of john, they like to talk. So after you have
performed your duties, then . . . or you might talk beforehand
too. I usually don't talk much until I'm out of bed and paid. For
some reason—psychological thing—I usually can't talk to a john
until I'm out of bed. I never know what to say, you know . . .
But once I'm out of bed I can talk freely. I feel better, once it's
over and done with.

Do I ever have any feeling of repugnance? No, I looked at it
this way a long time ago. Say you have this repugnance, and you
won't do this and you won't do that when you're in bed. Then
don't do it. Go to work. If you're going to do it, it's just like any
other job—any other profession. Do it and do it well and get out.
Make the money and get out. It's like when you get up in the
morning and brush your teeth. If you feel too lazy you don't do
it. You start letting yourself go, and your teeth are going to fall
apart, and so it is in your business. It's the same way.

Oh, I got to it gradually. It took me a long time to realize
these different weaknesses and strong points in myself and in the
johns. I started off as what's known as strictly trade—don't do
anything in bed. Then I graduated to other things, because I had
to reach it with myself before I could do it, you see. And so of
course when I first started doing other things there was a repugnance. But soon I realized if you're going to do it, do it and make
your money—I mean, why fool around? So that's what I did.

I would add too that each prostitute has his own angle to
push. One guy will be a big weight lifter, muscle boy, you know.
I push the angle of a sweet young boy. I sort of shy away from
the vulgarities when people talk and I play my innocent little-boy

role because that's the role I am pushing. It's what I can sell best because I look that way.

Like, you see, girls that are very voluptuous and big, they can't play the little-girl angle. But that's the role my girl Julia pushes. I showed her how to push the little-girl angle. That's what she is, and people will buy that, just like they buy any other angle.

You're selling a commodity. There's a definite market for this commodity, and if you sell it well you make money. If you don't, you don't. It's as simple as that. It's cut and dried. As far as occupational hazards go, like a sadist, if you run into him and get hurt, it's just part of the game. A bricklayer can have a brick fall on his head. A steeplejack can fall off the steeple or wherever he is. So in this game there are a few occupational hazards, like a sadist, or like syphilis and clap. It's all in the game. But it depends on the clients you're dealing with. There are people that are always clapped up because they're dealing with people of the lower classes. Dealing with a good class, I've never had anything. I had one crab once, just one. Nobody ever has just one crab, but that's all I had. One crab. And that was the extent of my hazards.

My girl, she prostitutes herself. I don't arrange her things. I've been going with her for about two years, and she decided— we decided together—that it would be more profitable for both of us if she went out and hustled. And so she meets people and she hustles. She makes money, and if I need money she gives it to me and lets me handle the money anyway.

She doesn't mind when I have relations with other people. She knows it's part of the game. I have no jealousy about her either. None at all. We have talked about that a lot and I think jealousy is an emotion that's built into you by society. Because she goes out to see . . . goes to bed with other people, that's all right. I'm sure she doesn't ball with them the way she balls with me. They're just fucking her, that's all. She doesn't give herself, in other words. That's the way she puts it.

Having sex with someone is simply getting your rocks off.

Making love is a process that takes time, and over a period you develop a definite relationship and understanding. It's a mutual compatibility, and the relationship is gratifying to both people— even further than the climax. What about prostitution and homosexuality? They're fine. Homosexuality is fine by me, except that I find it more gratifying to have relations with a woman. As for prostitution, if someone has a need, it should be legal for him to have the services of a prostitute. There's nothing wrong with what we do. Of course, I may break a few church laws here and there.

I've already put it before. There's a difference between having sex with someone and making love with someone. All the men Julia sees, they don't make love. They don't do anything. They don't have sex. They don't do anything except come. So there's no danger of her going to anyone else. She'll stay with me as long as this goes on.

Julia is happy with the life she's leading now. She's very happy. For one thing, she has gotten away from her family. They're terrible. They just sit and drink beer and watch television and then go to bed. It's immoral. Nowhere. Nothing ever happens . . .

She's secure because she's with me. Now she's got someone . . . All her habits were bad. Her eating habits, even brushing her teeth and washing her face. She had nothing before. She gets her own johns, through madams and like that. For the time being I want to continue the way we are. I want to groom her and make her into the person she ought to be right now, and would be except for the bad family training she had when she was young.

She had never heard anything about taking care of her fingernails. Never heard of . . . you don't eat a baloney sandwich and drink a Pepsi and that's all you eat for a day. She never brushed her teeth before she went to bed, or when she got up. I had to teach her about using douche bags. About the pill. I had to teach her all this. She was a virgin when I met her. I was the first one.

I just want her to be a beautiful little girl, that's all. And take care of me. She gets up and cooks my breakfast. I enjoy that security. I want her to be highly presentable. If she could be a high-class call girl, she would make more money that way. It's advantageous to both of us. If we're still together in five or six years, and if things have been going along all right, I'll marry her. I'll have children, I think. I don't believe in rushing into marriage. If we do get married I wouldn't mind if she kept on hustling. I know other married women who hustle. I know a man who's a schoolteacher and his wife hustles and he knows it. And she's got a two-year-old kid.

I'm not particularly generous. I am conservative. I have investments, stocks and securities, and a bank account. I have a mutual fund. Oh, if I'm in the mood I'll spend. I spend freely, too. I mean, we go out and go to a movie. We go to a bar, and we take taxis. Then I spend a hell of a lot more than I save. Because . . . I just enjoy it. When I want something I buy it. I went through this stage where I had seventeen suits all at one time. Now I don't want so many clothes. You have so much trouble deciding what you're going to wear. I've had fifty shirts. I give them to my father.

Julia and I are both going to school. I have to be in at one o'clock. I have typing for an hour and a half every day, accounting for two hours, and I have special courses in English, business math, public speaking, and salesmanship. Julia takes shorthand, typing, and spelling.

There's no sense in being limited. If you don't make a success in one field, you need something else to fall back on. At least I have my fingers in the pie and I'm playing many different games.

I think it would be fun to buy an island in the Bahamas and make it into a health club sort of thing, and have all my friends that are heads pay so much to belong to this club. There would be boys for gay people and girls for the straight ones. The whole thing is just fun. You know . . .

It would be a gas to run a charm school for hookers and hustlers. Like Lee's Charm School to finish girls and boys alike, teach them how to be good hustlers, give them a little class, and charge them so much for a lesson, I suppose. Prepare the boys and finish the girls. I'm taking accounting so I'll know how to manage the books.

Something bad just happened. Since last time . . . it's very bad. This sadist. I've tried to tell her: if you're not sure, look directly into his eyes. A sadist looks at you in a particular way. You just have to sense it. Julia didn't use her head. It was this friend of a friend, in from Akron. At first he seemed all right, but then he began beating and cutting her. I was home and the first I knew she was crying and sobbing on the phone. I could hear him sort of laughing in the background. I knew where she had taken him, of course, so I said: "Keep talking! I'll be right there . . ." and went over with Leonard, this friend of mine.

Why did he let her call? I don't know. I guess he gets his pleasure that way, with the phone call. When Leonard and I got to the hotel, I saw this man sneaking off the elevator and knew right away it was him. I could just tell. I thought I might go after him, but what was the good? That would only get us into more trouble.

We went upstairs, and she was beaten-up and bleeding. She said he had worn a necklace of razor blades. He had carved up her breasts a little, but not so bad. There was a slash across her belly, but not very deep. She's going to be all right, but that's the end. I can't let her keep on, as she has been, because she's just not intelligent enough. She'll never learn to sense and feel dangerous situations before they happen. I'll have to get her with the right johns from now on, only the ones I can vouch for personally.

Soon after we talked with him, Lee Raymond, still eighteen years old, met a Dutch banker and began making regular flights to Amsterdam and London. This was a cultivated man, and proud of the sweet-natured young American boy he had acquired. Just as Lee had played Pygmalion for Julia, so now he became the banker's protégé. The homosexual businessman who had introduced us to Lee reported with awe that he was (he used the expression) "traveling in the highest circles." Lee's backer was unusual in a number of respects. First, he gladly acquiesced when his loved one asked if he could bring his girl over to live with him in a cottage on the banker's estate. Second, he was so pleased with Lee that he didn't mind sharing him with a number of his friends. Hence, in the next two years a succession of Johns, Johanns, Jans, Juans, and Jeans contributed to Lee's education. He could now be seen at the opening of art shows, the theater, and film festivals. He was beautifully tailored and at ease with everyone. "He speaks fluent French and a little German!" the businessman said. "And he's got a Swiss bank account . . ."

Our friend pointed out to us that Lee has no official identity. Nobody knows his real name. He has never worked anywhere that would require listing a social security number. A false passport has been arranged for him. For taxes and other purposes he doesn't exist on any government record.

His patron remains passionately in love with him. Recently he set up Lee and Julia in Germany. Hand in hand they stroll the battlements of the Dutch banker's castle. The Rhine flows swiftly by.

4. THE PSYCHOPATH AND THE GOOD SAMARITAN

. . . he, willing to justify himself, said unto Jesus, And who is my neighbor?

And Jesus answering said, A certain man went down from Jerusalem to Jericho, and fell among thieves, which stripped him of his raiment, and wounded him, and departed, leaving him half dead.

And by chance there came down a certain priest that way: and when he saw him, he passed by on the other side.

And likewise a Levite, when he was at the place, came and looked on him, and passed by on the other side.

But a certain Samaritan, as he journeyed, came where he was: and when he saw him, he had compassion on him,

And went to him, and bound up his wounds, pouring in oil and wine, and set him on his own beast, and brought him to an inn, and took care of him.

And on the morrow when he departed, he took out two
pence, and gave them to the host, and said unto him, Take
care of him; and whatsoever thou spendest more, when I
come again, I will repay thee.

Which now of these three, thinkest thou, was neighbor
unto him that fell among the thieves?

And he said, He that shewed mercy on him. Then said
Jesus unto him, Go, and do thou likewise.°

GIRL, 18, FOILS AN ABDUCTION
THEN IS KIDNAPPED AND SLAIN

UPI, Dec. 26, 1960 [names and locale changed]—
Dorothy Gaines, 18 years old, intervened when a man tried
to kidnap another girl from a lounge early today.

Instead of taking the other girl, the man kidnapped
Miss Gaines, drove her 20 miles, stabbed her to death and
left her body by a road, the police said.

Hours after the discovery of Miss Gaines' body, the
authorities charged Edwin Smith, 20, of Chicago, with the
girl's murder.

He was arrested on the strength of a description of the
kidnapper and his automobile by witnesses at the Melody
Lounge, where Miss Gaines had worked.

In Boston, the rapist cornered Faith in an alley. At knife
point he drove her against a pile of boards. She remembers
the smell of decaying leaves and the slipperiness of rotten lum-
ber. A powerful, practiced man had dragged her in here with
one hand over her mouth, the other forcing her arm behind
her back in a cruel hammer lock. Then she was released. The
silver blade waited an inch from her throat. She couldn't see his
face in the shadows, only the knife. Now he was fumbling at
her thighs. The terrible unreality of the moment paralyzed her.
She was thrown back, and above dark, wet branches she saw
a tranquil sky and fleecy clouds. Twisting from him, she realized
to her amazement that people were passing by along the sunlit
sidewalk only thirty feet away, that a busy morning in the city

° Luke 10:19–37.

was going on as usual in full view. She felt a shock and went to her knees. The man had hit her in the face. More than a rapist, he might well kill her whether she resisted or not. Screaming away from the knife, Faith broke free and ran, almost reaching the sunlight when he caught her again. She screamed but no one on the safe street so much as looked her way. Clutching at the corner of the building, she reached out and all but touched a passerby. "Help!" she called to him. "He's trying to kill me!" This man in a gray business suit stopped to look at her with distaste and said, "That's your problem" before walking on.

The attacker gave up then and ran. Faith's experience has marked her in an unexpected way. The disagreeable mien of the passerby has turned out to be more painful in memory than the rape attempt. She frequently dreams of one but not the other. In her dream the disdainful countenance appears, and the same man always tells her: "That's your problem." She thinks she hates this expression more than any other in the language.

Is the storybook Good Samaritan outmoded? I remember, very young, near Boston, being caught in a snowstorm after midnight. My car had a flat tire on the highway. No other cars could be seen. A freezing wind blew curtains of snow across the road. My fingers were numb. I had trouble managing the jack. Then out of the black cold a taxi rolled alongside. The driver stopped and helped me change the tire, almost angrily refusing pay. For years afterward, and now still, I've been mystified by his decency.

This sort of rescue has become less frequent, with reason, since a growing number of predatory psychopaths make such good deeds unfeasible, even stupid. The Samaritan has to watch himself. He can no longer easily afford the spiritual luxury of helping people out of pits. Nearly as often as not, an accomplice close by may push him into the pit. You pick up a hitchhiker and, not liking the way you drive, he kills you. Or you are murdered by a boy you take into your home on Thanksgiving, because he thinks (perhaps rightly): Why only on Thanksgiving?

Unhappily, the psychopath, whenever he can, turns decency

into foolishness, and today one of the violent sort lies in wait for
the classic Good Samaritan. Sometimes it even appears that the
two have been drawn to each other, and made for each other.

Lore taught high-school English literature in a New England
resort town. A small, dark girl of twenty-seven with close-cropped
black hair, she lived by herself near the sand dunes. A north wind
would bring faint highway traffic sounds to her cottage. When
the wind blew from any other direction, or on calm days, the fall
of waves on the beach could be heard. Also neighing and nicker-
ing from the riding academy across the water.

A miniature cove separated the dune area from the main part
of town. Lore's cottage, not far from the lighthouse on the point,
had been built decades before a tacky cluster of small homes
was fabricated in the mid-1960's on filled-in marshland at the end
of the causeway. By accident now, as the developers happened
to draw their map, she lived at the edge of this community, with
neighbors near, but secluded behind a partition of reeds and
scrub oak.

Like most such towns in the area, H——— was gloomy in
winter. Spring changed the scene entirely. Tourists explored the
historic wharfs and cobblestoned side streets. Fishing parties went
out. Seasonal art galleries opened, as did the prosperous summer
theater. On warm nights Lore could hear dance music from a
new marina, which she would try to block out with Mozart or
rock 'n' roll from her own record player.

Next to teaching, perhaps even more—except that this was
pleasure and she preferred duty—Lore loved to ride. At the academy she boarded her horse named Brother. Several times a week
she would go on long rides through the woods, returning home
close to the shore along the dunes. For company she kept Mike,
a big tail-wagging black-and-tan mongrel, who, even though
usually good-natured, growled and bristled if you moved too
quickly toward Lore. Most of her devoted acquaintances were
girls. Not that she was unfriendly to men. At the time, vacation-
ing and alone, I found Lore sweet and responsive, even physically
a tender girl, but remote. She was gently ironic, played guitar

softly, and refused to show her poems: "They're not good enough yet."

What separated us most often was her obsession with duty. She seemed always to be correcting papers, tutoring, or teaching at night. During summer, duty involved conducting remedial classes for hopeless students. She volunteered as a visiting nurse. You couldn't put two nights together with her as you might with anyone else because she was so often busy helping other people. I said: "Lore, for you the Christian spirit has become an illness. Try not to be quite such a good person."

But the need to rescue others wouldn't leave her in peace. Even when persuaded for an evening not to go visit a sick old woman or retarded boy, Lore would grow restless and unhappy, looking over her shoulder. I saw finally that in order to enjoy a night out she had to exact from herself a week or two of penance, or service, and that nothing could be done about this.

Of all Lore's lame ducks, Paul Adamson concerned her more than any other. He was a thin, undersized sixteen-year-old who came to her in last-ditch need of tutoring. Though quick and alert, he consistently failed in his classwork, having twice stayed back a grade. He was also reported as being noisy and disruptive in class. Lore found this hard to believe. For one thing, by her side evening after evening, reviewing the courses he couldn't master during regular school hours, Paul showed aptitudes he had never demonstrated before. At first he could only concentrate for two or three minutes at a time, but soon he could stay with a lesson for at least an hour.

She was helping Paul find himself as a person too. The boy had a wretched background. His mother had been a violent alcoholic. All through his early boyhood she had made a practice of locking him in closets when he was bad. Then at times she would play with him flirtatiously, as though they were the same age. Paul's father had divorced his mother and married again. Paul stayed with them, tolerated his stepmother, never talked to his father if he could help it. The older people lived a grunting life together. He despised them but didn't let out his contempt. Except for his occasional bad behavior in class (disorderly enough for school administrators to recommend psychiatric treatment),

Lore said, Paul had almost unbelievably good manners. "He's so polite!" she marveled. "I'm trying to get him out of the habit of saying 'Yes, Miss Barker,' 'No, Miss Barker,' all the time."

Apart from the improvement in his studies, he was also gaining physical self-respect. He dressed neatly now. Tired of being pushed around and laughed at by stronger boys, he began a mail-order study of karate and weight lifting.

Toward the end of summer I caught a glimpse of Lore's protégé. He lived across the street, several houses down. The Adamsons had the only two-story house on the block. From a small second-floor balcony, an imitation captain's walk, Paul could look down between two scrub oaks on Lore's front doorstep. One evening under the door light we were saying good-bye. She drew away, murmuring: "There's Paul . . ." and I saw him on the balcony watching us.

Less than a month later, back in New York, a phone call came from Frieda, also a teacher at the high school, telling of Paul Adamson's midnight assault on Lore, how he set her house on fire, and the murder and horror that followed.

> This young defendant, just two months past his six-teenth birthday and under the care of what is assumed to be the most competent health clinic in our area, effected an atrocity that staggers the imagination and grips one's spirit. The offense was obviously planned and the execution was done with dispatch.*

A week before, Lore's dog Mike had disappeared. She searched everywhere on foot and on horseback, near the causeway where a car might have hit him on the beach, along the dunes. She felt sick, and only Paul Adamson seemed to care. He had taken to helping her around the house. A fair carpenter, he volunteered to adjust the lock on her front door. Every day he would inquire: "Have you found him yet, Miss Barker?" and shake his head, looking downcast.

* Probation Officer, State Supreme Court.

The night was exceptionally warm and humid for September. Lore was working late as usual, correcting papers, with soft Mozart on the record player. She heard a sound outside. Then he burst in, breaking the screen-door lock he had pretended to fix.

"What are you doing here?"

The one who had killed her dog had no answer.

"Go home, Paul!"

He came at her.

"Go home!"

He caught her by the throat, and they fell on the bed. Lore fought and talked at the same time. In the beginning the boy was no stronger. For many minutes she fended him off, and pleaded and reasoned, and promised that if he would go away "I won't say anything!" But she was appealing to a mask. He began clubbing her with karate blows. Again and again he hit her on the neck with the side of his hand, and he came on with increasing energy. Paul reached across the table at which they had studied together for so many months, yanked the gooseneck lamp from its socket and wound it around her neck. In another minute she would have to give up. She made a despairing effort and pushed up from the bed, forcing him back. Locked together, they struggled toward the door and crashed outside into the yard. There they fought in the oblong of light outside her front door, crushing the flowers in her garden, Lore gasping and crying, the pain and night slowly fading. He stuffed garden earth into her mouth and Lore lost consciousness.

She awoke on fire. Two neighbors, Mr. and Mrs. Fred Gregory, were beating the flames out of her clothes. They had found her lying on the bed with fire all around and had pulled Lore out just in time. Had they arrived several minutes later, she would probably have been dead. As it was, her back and arms were badly seared.

What no one knew as yet was that Paul had sought to destroy all evidence of what he had done by dragging his teacher back into the house, using his school papers and Lore's sheet music to set fire to the bed and curtains, and turning on the gas burners. He then ran to the dunes in back of the house, and from that high ground saw the Gregorys intervene.

Lore's rescuers, people in their early fifties, had only the vaguest idea of what had taken place. Lying dazed in the front yard, Lore, in the words of the police report, "feared to reveal the assailant's identity."

With her house now obscured in flames and smoke, Lore's trial gradually became the Gregorys'. According to the official report:

> They immediately took her out to the yard and she regained consciousness. Apparently it was at this time that Paul Adamson was observed on the scene and Mr. Gregory told him to go and call his father for assistance. The two ladies then proceeded from Miss Barker's residence northward to the Gregory residence. Fred Gregory said that while he was well aware that an attack had occurred and that Paul was on the scene, he did not associate the two ideas and felt that Paul was awakened in somewhat the same manner that he and his wife had been. He said that he had unwound the hose and was proceeding to turn on the faucet when he looked up to an object that Paul was bringing down on him. He said the object hit him on the forehead and instantly blinded him with blood and shock. He stated that he momentarily saw Paul and was partially able to grab him and could feel the blows about his face and head . . . he passed out . . . and did not regain consciousness until he was in the Intensive Care Ward of the Medical Center. . . . He suffered a punctured lung and a broken jaw that was wired together for 45 days. According to Mr. Gregory, recovery, psychologically and physically, lasted [required] about a year and there are still areas in his face on which he does not have feeling.

The night continued as if in slow motion. The two women fled down a dark lane to the Gregory house. Lore gasped out to Henrietta Gregory what she had dared not say before, that Paul was her attacker, that he had gone mad, and that they were still in danger. Quickly they locked all the doors and windows and put in a frantic call to the police. The worst possible mistake was then made: Lore and Mrs. Gregory armed themselves with kitchen knives.

Paul had followed them. With a heavy stone he smashed the plate-glass back door and entered the house. The women ran out the front door into the lane. Lore, much younger and quicker, made for the dunes. Paul overtook Mrs. Gregory. Police later found her dead on the road with sixteen stab wounds. As she had died, her husband lay unconscious near Lore's blazing house. Lore crouched in the reeds, her arms and back throbbing unbearably. She remembers the fog bell clanging while Paul searched for her. She heard him thrashing in the reeds and saw him once standing on a dune. The police didn't arrive for twenty minutes.

After a while Paul tired of hunting for her and decided that he would go home to bed. The police reported that "the defendant was found in his home. He had taken off the clothes he had worn during the assaults and had thrown them at the base of his closet and had attempted to wash the blood off his body."

In a statement Paul later explained:

> The first thing I did was to wash my hands and change into my pajamas and then go back to bed. The thing about everything that happened that night was that there was an absence of emotions. I was just numb. I had no feeling at all, or sense of right and wrong. It's hard to explain—it's like being paralyzed. You are aware of what's going on but you have no control over yourself. It's really frightening when you think about it . . .
>
> A few minutes after I went to bed, Doris, my sister, came into my bedroom and looked out the window. She said there had been a homicide committed. After she said that, I asked her what a homicide was. Your Honor, normally I knew what a homicide was but my mind was a total blank that night. Nothing registered . . .

Why had he gone after Mrs. Gregory?

"I just wanted to talk to her . . . I never even intended to harm her. I just wanted her to see things as I saw them . . . I didn't want any of this information to get around. I just wanted it to be among the three of us . . ."

Had he earlier killed Miss Barker's dog?

"Oh, yes."

Why had he tried to kill Miss Barker, battered Mr. Gregory and stabbed Mrs. Gregory to death?

Paul Adamson thought for a while, and then answered: "Roughly out of madness."

Madness previously suspected, yet at critical moments during his sessions in therapy—when the decision might have been made to commit him—a condition artfully covered.

Two years before, at the Child Guidance Clinic, a consulting psychiatrist had written: "I predict that Paul will become a serious problem if he is not given psychiatric or psychological help within the near future."

In drawings made during psychiatric tests, he depicted his father and mother hung up dead by the heels like Mussolini and Clara Petacci, with both bodies carefully labeled.

He thought about buying an entirely black outfit so that he could "go into a synagogue and scare the Jews."

A therapist reports him "writing his father's and mother's names on two bullets he has, as, he believes, American soldiers wrote Nazis' names on bullets before firing them." The consulting physician questions whether Paul may be "testing therapist to see if she will panic at possibility of his acting out his hostility." She concludes: ". . . at present therapist feels he is testing her more than actually planning murder . . . much of the threats are to shock the therapist and test [her], and the therapist should neither panic (which in turn would scare the boy) or ignore them (which is almost a dare)."

Paul's behavior during the sessions seems to have improved for a time: "While the boy is potentially dangerous, he is apparently responding to the relationship with the therapist and therefore is much less dangerous than many people with similar problems . . ."

Dr. L—— might have recalled an earlier entry in her casebook: "Paul described how he feels he was at present standing in the middle manipulating his parents but at the same time somewhat of a bystander who feels he must suppress all feelings. He would like to laugh out loud at them but cannot. Tentatively stated that he would like to learn to laugh again."

Another entry passes without comment: "When questioned about direct retaliation or fights with his peers [he] denied he had ever done so and stated he would rather wait and get back at them when they weren't expecting it."

Two days before Paul broke into Lore's cottage, the doctor makes this note: "He came to our session in much better spirits today, looked at me several times instead of always looking away, and even smiled once or twice. He then asked me how sex was performed."

But there was no sexual assault on Lore—not in the sense of rape, penetration, orgasm. The attack had simply been murderous. Might it have been prevented? Doctors at the clinic could produce a record of their warnings: "dangerous . . . in a paranoid state . . . incipient paranoid schizophrenia . . . in need of institutional care." But none of these general diagnoses account for this curiously emotionless bolt of vengeance falling on Lore.

Now the probation officer comes into the case. His role is to determine whether convicted persons—and society—will benefit at some point if they are allowed to go free on probation, reporting to the court at stated periods. For someone like Paul this review becomes academic, since the perpetrator of such a killing can hardly be freed for many years, if ever. Even so, the probation officer files his report and recommends sentence.

Unlike the therapists at the clinic, Fred Brice found Paul to be a psychopath, or, in the term he preferred, a sociopath, and told the court that his attack on Lore could best be understood within the framework of psychopathy. He wrote that "sociopathy or psychopathy is not always recognized as mental illness but it is more the form of an infantile pattern of relating to people."

Why had this infantilism exploded into violence? Very possibly because (the officer learned) at the end of June, some two months before the assault, Paul had scored poorly in his final English examination—in spite of Lore's tutoring. Throughout the summer, while continuing to study with her—the courteous bystander with his "Yes, Miss Barker" and "No, thank you, Miss Barker"—he waited and planned.

Brice pointed out:

> The Court should note that when the idea of measured performance is presented to a sociopath, it seems to strike him with terror . . . these [are] people who must avoid critical evaluation of their performance as it occurs in school. *The factor of self-esteem* which is related to homicide and insanity must not be forgotten. In our opinion he attempted to kill Miss Barker for two reasons: First, because he felt her responsible for his poor grades in English and, second, he needs to do something about the world of objects around him in a concrete way to make his mark on them.
>
> When one continues to perform as poorly as Paul Adamson has, we are faced with the critical loss of self-esteem. So his motive, then, is a drive for achievement and the removing of a barrier that was blocking public approval or at least public notice.

Yet for Brice, as well as for the psychiatrists examining Paul after the murder, the psychopathic mystery persists. They find themselves trying to fathom the thought processes of a smiling, affable young man, eager to please, flashing for his questioners "pseudo sophistication and polish."

The Court Record is filled with observations such as these:

> Throughout the interviews, the defendant always seemed to be trying to determine his behavior on what he could perceive about the probation officer. To pervert and paraphrase what Saint Paul wrote, "he is all things to all people" with the hope that he might put the make on a few.
>
> . . . A candid observation of life might prove that were a socialized person to commit this crime, he would indeed be insane, but if there were one who *had never been socialized* and do this, it would simply be a biological man trying to rid himself of a problem. The probation officer can detect no conscience in this person, and what appears to him to be emotion is, no doubt, tension when he is frustrated in the expression of his instinctual drives . . .

From a court-appointed psychiatrist:

> He still tries, in his own crafty way, to determine what is expected of him in the way of responses and then offer that particular response. He attempts to be charming, ingratiating, and at times to communicate on an almost peer level . . . Paul seems to have some difficulty in abstract thinking. When he was asked to define his crime, he did it in terms of punishment [and went on] defining not only second-degree murder, but first-degree murder, and manslaughter in the same way.

And again:

> Paul put forth a great deal of effort being charming and seductive . . . He finds it very difficult to believe he is guilty of the crimes with which he is charged and is very careful, that is, very vague, evasive and guarded in talking about things . . .
>
> After detention, awaiting trial, Paul told the examining physician that he was planning a camping trip with his brother. When asked if he really intended to be away on a camping trip this fall, he became quite red, flustered, and stated that No, he was just thinking about it.
>
> At times I thought he might be depressed, but he always denied any depression . . . There are no disturbances of orientation or memory . . . At each interview there was a great attempt on his part by coaxing or persuasion to learn from me what I thought about him and his possible chances at the forthcoming trial. He showed an almost precocious legalistic knowledge of the possible charges that might be made against him.

Paul was sentenced to the state penitentiary for life. Mr. Gregory has recovered and married again, but he complains of both pain and numbness in his face and suffers recurring headaches. When he grows tired, he totters a little.

Girl friends stayed with Lore for a while, but she lives alone again on the other side of town. She rides Brother as always and has another big mongrel on the watch. The burns on her back and arms healed well after several grafts. Lore helps fewer people now, and only those whom she feels she knows quite well.

"I went over to my house the other day," she wrote, after being discharged from the hospital, "to see what the fire has destroyed." Her experience remained incomprehensible and unreal.

> Everything seemed so lovely, so tranquil and rich with autumn foliage—certainly as though violence were impossible even to begin to conceive there. But there was my charred house.
>
> It made me try again to grasp hate and brutality. The real tragedy is the mind of that 16-year-old boy. Who's responsible for that? Hate takes as long to build as love, I suppose. His life over at 16—why why why? I can't for the life of me figure out all the connections in his mind. There is overwhelming evidence that he planned this sometime in advance. It's hideous to contemplate. But I need to know why—his why. How could he plot and plan to murder one of the few people who cared for him? Well, these things I hope to learn some day.

The same week Paul Adamson composed this statement to the presiding Superior Court Judge:

> . . . How sad when I look back and see what I have done. I only hope and pray that somewhere in Mr. Gregory's and Miss Barker's hearts that they can forgive me for the terrible thing I have done!
>
> Now that I look back on that tragic night, I feel a lot of remorse and sorrow. And I am only sorry that I wasn't committed to a proper hospital where I could have gotten some help before this happened!
>
> Yes, I do want probation because probation means a second chance—a chance to prove myself. If I am granted probation, my future plans will be to work my way through college (in this day and age it is imperative to have a college degree, if you want to get ahead and be a success in this wide and wonderful world we live in) and after graduation I hope to settle down and have a wife and family to come home to every night! . . .

How do I feel about going to the State Prison? Personally, I don't like the idea!

One of the things that society seems to support and I disagree with is "Capital Punishment." I don't think anybody has the right to take another man's life. Life is so precious. It is the only thing that man can't put a premium on because it's priceless! . . .

Well, Judge, I only hope that you give me probation. I am very sorry for what has happened and I think if you give me probation you will never regret your decision!

Your friend,
Paul Adamson

P.S. Thank you for giving me this opportunity to express myself.

After being sentenced Paul sent Lore a bottle of perfume. In an accompanying letter, he apologized for having killed her dog. He continues to write her. Paul inquires anxiously whether she has a permanent boy friend. He sees no reason for having to spend all this time in prison and expects to be released soon. As soon as that happens, he intends to marry her.

5. LESSONS FROM A MALIGNANT GURU

"Looking over your notes," the novelist said, "you say here: 'Today, in many parts of the world, psychopaths are calling the bourgeoisie to account. Damaged children of violence and neglect, they aim to shatter the comfortable uses of hypocrisy, especially middle-class niceness. The role they are playing is that of brutal instructors.' I know what you're getting at. Two summers ago I ran into one of your 'brutal instructors.' We clashed. I wasn't ready for him and got the worst of it."

A violent scene?

"No, not physically, but it was still crazy and shocking. Two years later I can see it as a trivial debacle—an unbelievably petty episode. Just the same, it was the kind that shakes you, and the memory remains sharp and unpleasant. We found ourselves in a textbook situation: it illustrates your theme perfectly. Two 'nice people' up against what you call the outlaw intelligence.

"Denise and I had a bad time with this man. We only hope it was educational. Actually, thinking about it, given that we're living, or about to live, through wild and revolutionary years, the quick survival course we went through might serve a purpose. Not that he intended it that way. I'm just saying that, without meaning to, my malignant guru may have helped us to build up the paranoid defenses everybody is going to need from now on."

You may (*he began*) have heard of Baxter Crowe. He's a reporter—he might prefer "journalist"—specializing in exposés, all the inside details of corruption among the rich, powerful, and talented. I would say he writes in a baleful style, the way he moves. Walking about, Baxter bears himself as if impaled on a poker. See him once, and you won't forget that slow, furious strut. I think he can best be understood as a self-taught person, a desperate autodidact. Crowe never finished high school, which is fine, but not with him. So you'll notice that many of his attacks on the Establishment have to do with the fraud of higher education, proving many times over that he never needed one.

Crowe works for the most part as a TV reporter strictly behind the scenes—the calculation of every program director being that his baleful countenance, if projected on screen, would cause a massive switching of channels.

A key to Baxter is that he can't bear the success of others. For instance, Ralph Nader's prominence infuriates him. And he makes a second career out of baiting successful writers. A correspondent who had just won a Pulitzer Prize, out celebrating with friends, was faced by Crowe in a rage: "You're not a reporter! You can't write! You're not original! You don't even do your own legwork! You're just a fucking thief!" "Hey!" the prize winner complained, dazedly looking around. "What's wrong with this guy?"

He couldn't have known that the individual glaring at him had long ago purposefully adopted the boorish style. Years before, Crowe arrived at a life-changing perception: that civilized middle-class types—as opposed, say, to hard hats—nearly always shrink from head-on rudeness. As a rule they back down, back off, look away, stammer hastily, trying to find some area of agreement, and retire as quickly as possible. Observing the identical bourgeois backdown many times, Crowe set about making himself a master of confrontation. In New York he took up boxing, hanging with tough black prize fighters. Soon, among nonviolent intellectuals, he came to be known as a man more than ready to punch out a difference of opinion.

Crowe believes that he lives by the ideal of fierce, stripped-down honesty. But this really isn't so: a strange malice works in him, corrupting his truthfulness. He invokes morality enough, but given a situation that involves simple ordinary humanity . . . it's odd. I've watched Baxter. When the most elementary kindness is called for, his face goes completely blank. For instance, he apparently has no idea of what it means to betray a confidence. There was talk about this minor producer. He was supposed to have enjoyed a beautiful affair with a young actress. "Affair!" scoffed Crowe to a roomful of listeners. "They never once made it all the time they were together!" How could he know that? "He's my best friend. He told me himself!"

I didn't see much of him over the years, but heard stories. A streak of cruelty ran through most of them, though some of the episodes had a certain humorous style. Supposedly, during a brief stint as a television executive, in his skyscraper office, he snarled at a young writer: "I'll show you what I think of your story!" and threw the script out the window. Other confrontations were meaner. At the studio, his secretary gave him a box of cookies. Baxter kept them on top of his desk, never unwrapping the package, and there it stayed for the poor girl to look at, day after day. One story editor, everyone feared, was slowly going out of his mind. He fought against his deterioration, trying to keep his head right, but slowly lost ground. Every morning Crowe would lean into this man's office and inquire: "Well, are you winning or losing?"

Baxter has been married once and divorced. His teen-age daughter loves him very much, and he's appreciated by his wife as a scrupulous provider of alimony. Since his divorce, he has humped many women, as he puts it. Most of these have been hit-and-run affairs. Again cruelty comes in, stories of petty mistreatment and humiliation . . .

All at once Baxter's life fell apart. Fury came up into his throat, and he had to undergo surgery at the base of his tongue. He recovered well enough, but the operation exhausted him for a long while; his voice was now more rasping and hostile than ever, his neck withered, taking on a stalklike appearance, and a tracheotomy left a small scar below his Adam's apple.

Later a friend reported seeing him in the Village. Surprisingly, he was mild-mannered. Crowe said he had found *satori,* peace, enlightenment. I met him over a country weekend, and he seemed tired. His hair was sparse and graying. He actually asked my opinion about something, and listened politely. His old domination and aggression asserted themselves in only mild form: he took over the kitchen and, appointing several girls as assistant cooks, created a thick peasant soup that everybody admired. At last he seemed to have changed into a person who might—in a sour, amusing way—be relatively congenial.

At this time Baxter was a fiercely partisan advocate of Big Jim Garrison, the New Orleans D.A.—their faces look much alike— during the pursuit and hounding of Clay Shaw, before Garrison's case collapsed in court. Baxter had been completely taken in. An independent television group had named him special correspondent, but he badgered them so contemptuously, articulating in detail what cowards they were for declining to dramatize on screen Garrison's truth as Crowe reported it, that they called him one morning and said don't bother to come in anymore. Dropped from his New Orleans assignment, never having imagined that he could be dispensed with, he came to us that evening, tired and dejected, with a touch of ruefulness, and we offered him all sympathy, dinner, and so on.

After that we saw him every once in a while. He landed a job, teaching film journalism, and, we presumed, had finally found some kind of ease. When he telephoned to ask if we wanted to mind his cottage in Old Lyme, Connecticut, while he spent three weeks in England, even offering the use of his car, I hesitated. But Denise wanted the sunshine, and relief from New

York's dirty air would be good for the baby, so we accepted.

The day of his flight Baxter came by to drop off a set of keys and deliver the car. He also handed us a set of instructions covering care of the house, as well as the lawn and garden, plant by plant. The specifications detailed times of day for watering each lawn area, which nozzle to use, the precise amounts of spray to shower on this plant and that one. My older son—the karate expert I wish I were—studied the various messages later and said: "If I'd seen these in advance, I would never have gone down there." To tell the truth, I haven't looked at them yet. I made the mistake of remarking to Baxter offhand: "I'll be working all day. Denise will be handling the lawn detail most of the time," and I should have been warned by the angry glance he shot my way. After this, saying good-bye, I noticed him watch intently as I locked the car, to see whether I was doing it right.

Baxter flew to England, and next morning we headed into what must have been one of the most dismal Julys in the history of the Connecticut shore. It rained practically every day; I think we went to the beach three times. His cottage was a damp little two-story trap. Overhanging elms held the moisture in. The floors creaked. Although everything was arranged just so, we could hardly turn around without bumping into fragile patio tables or a rickety beach chair.

During brief moments of sunshine the back lawn turned into a bright postage stamp. But Crowe had diminished the already cramped yard by building a small cabin a few feet from the main cottage. In the end he had created a lower-middle-class paradise, the kind you see from train windows close to the tracks. It lacked only a plastic dunking pool.

A few minutes before leaving, Baxter had informed us that two college teen-agers would be spending weekends in the smaller cabin. One was a wormy boy with pale soft arms and legs who ran about casting resentful glances over his shoulder, once or twice referring to the absent Baxter as "Old Crowe." His girl appeared—a beautiful, utterly detached witness who stared into space much of the time. They too had found out about the arrangement at the last moment, and obviously didn't like our being there. We made a few attempts to be friendly but, meeting only with grunts, soon gave up.

The wet, dark weeks seemed endless. Having to stay indoors, the baby cried a lot, and toward the end of our stay we could hardly wait for Crowe to come home. It didn't occur to us to be worried about his returning mood. Denise watered the grass and plants now and then, but since the rains seldom let up there had hardly been any need to do even that. Crowe's garden was blooming. Every week the mowers came in and cut his lawn, and the grass dripped green. The only damage we had done was to take a fairly well shredded bamboo umbrella to the beach—he had suggested this—where it had been ripped by a sudden gust. I collected Baxter's mail at the post office and maintained a record of the few phone calls he received, keeping them—a mistake, we will see—in my jacket pocket.

Knowing our host to be fussy and precise, we worked hard to put things in order. The cottage was cleaned up and down. The car was fine. In fact, when he had turned it over to us, the interior had been filthy, with an accumulation of soiled, presumably discarded, manuscript pages, sand, and crud. I swept that out, clipping the pages together and leaving them on the car floor where they had been, weighted with a stone. I had worked at his desk, placing his papers off to one side, along with his mail. Now I carefully put the papers back. His shoes remained as he had left them in the bedroom, with powder in them, aligned along the wall like cruisers mothballed up the river. One accident marred our last day: the baby kicked a salad plate off the kitchen table, breaking it in pieces.

I drove to meet Baxter at the airport. This is bound to build up blood pressure. Kennedy frazzles the nerves. Its road signs are unclear. Parking spaces spread over an immense area, and planes taking off and landing depress you with their endless, uneven roaring.

Casually he had asked us to stay the weekend after his return. I remember, in the parking lot, wishing that this arrangement hadn't been made. The baby might be bothersome with all of us

crowded in the small cottage, and, besides, Denise and I wanted
to get back to the city.

His plane landed early, and he had already phoned to ask
where I was. He arrived exhausted, in a foul temper. The trip
seemed not to have gone well.

"Where's the car?" he wanted to know in the parking lot.

"Two sections from here," I told him, joking a little. "You see
that black boy with the transistor radio leaning against the fence?
I took my bearings from him."

"Suppose he moved!" said Baxter in his grating voice.

He got behind the wheel, and we drove out. A sign confused
him, he took a wrong turn, and we missed our exit. Savagely
under his breath, he began cursing the designers of Kennedy's
road system. I looked sideways at him and realized that missing
the exit meant immeasurably more than a few minutes' incon-
venience. His very manhood had been affronted by the incompetent planners.

When I drive I grip the wheel with both hands, peering out.
Baxter, I saw, guided the wheel with one finger tip, demonstrat-
ing his prowess for the imaginary camera he always has looking
over his shoulder. My God, I thought, his ego is on the line even
when he's steering his car. This man poses for his own home
movie every waking moment.

"Where's the registration?" he said. "And the insurance card?"

I looked in my wallet. Where could they be? "I guess Denise
must have them."

This caused him to turn pale and silent. A few minutes later
he said: "What about my phone calls?"

Here was something that could be scored as my fault, not
grievous but a fault. The main fault was not to anticipate the sort
of accounting he would expect. For him anything less than a
neat list of callers, with messages and phone numbers, laid out,
like his shoes, next to the phone would be a profound insult. I
had the few callers' names—about six, I think—and their phone
numbers all right. Now I read them to him from the slip in my
pocket.

He interrupted. "Did she say to call her, or that she would

call me?" And "Did he say to call him, or that he would call me?"

All I knew was: there's the name, there's the number. Call it.

"I want that list typed up!"

Fine . . .

"The police came around," I said, "about that boy. They said for you to call them." For nearly two years he had been trying to have a neighborhood boy put in an institution for repeatedly throwing stones at his daughter.

"What was the cop's name?"

I hadn't taken the name, and probably should have, but in this small town with only a few police at the station nearby, Baxter must have talked regularly to the man on the case and known who he was.

Still off guard, I didn't sense his mounting rage. On the ride back we bickered over a number of questions. Lately he had become an enthusiast of the Palestine Arab revolutionaries. I held out for Israel, and we argued. Then who should he bring up but Claude Lévi-Strauss and structuralism! Like many self-educated people, when Baxter comes upon a new—for him—idea, he imagines that no one else can be in on it. You would think that Lévi-Strauss had been cringing in some dark corner of the Bibliothèque Nationale until Baxter discovered him. Now the French anthropologist had joined Big Jim Garrison in Crowe's pantheon. Baxter went on about structuralism. I should mention a peculiar effect that always descends on me when he talks for very long. I grow sleepy, but more than that, I hear the faint sounds of a violin. While Baxter expounds, a little old man is playing a violin somewhere. I can't explain this. Now, as I lay back saturated with Lévi-Strauss, this shabby little man, good-naturedly sawing away, appeared behind my eyelids.

We arrived in Old Lyme at six in the evening. Our homecoming was grim from the moment he stepped out of the car. "The plants!" he had said to Denise on the phone from the airport. "Did you water the plants?" Without even taking his bags into the house, he marched to the back yard. It was lush and green, and in flower as though a greenhouse had been dropped over it in his absence. At first we didn't comprehend this strange, ritualistic march, which I realize now, after reading

Ardrey, must have been a weird working out of the Territorial Imperative. Compulsive tramping. Baxter fancies himself a wolf, but in anger he's much more canine, stiff-legged, growling, with his hairs up. Before our eyes a curious ceremony began.

In his mind's eye, before going away, he had obviously photographed his miniature estate in detail. We watched grim-faced paranoia marching. It marched about the grounds checking every single plant and flower, practically every clump of grass to determine whether it had been watered. We woke slowly to what was going on. It was a silent inspection, oppressive, insolent, incredibly hostile, unbelievable to us. And, of course, there was nothing wrong. Nothing. But his manner remained thunderous, and he was gray with rage.

We put the baby to bed. Denise had prepared an elabo-rate welcome-home dinner, which Crowe ate practically none of. He left the table before dessert and commenced an inspection of the house. He looked into the refrigerator to see that it had been properly defrosted. Then we heard him tramping upstairs. But not in the baby's room. I wish he had gone in there. I would have interfered, and the whole business would have exploded more to our advantage. We decided to ignore him, and went out on the back porch for coffee.

I said to Denise: "This is a bad scene. Even if he did invite us for the weekend, we'd better leave."

"How can we?" she said. "You mean wake up the baby now? It's too late."

"Tomorrow morning then."

How innocent to honor an invitation that was nothing but a trap to keep us on the premises until his inspection was over! True, we had nothing definite to act on, except his horribly op-pressive manner, and a good night's sleep might take care of that. Besides, had he not given over his place free? Did we not owe him? Thus the overcivilized intelligence rationalizes and decides not to act, hoping for the best.

By the way, it occurs to me—you don't make this quite clear—that the psychopathic style needn't at all times by its nature be antibourgeois. Similar craziness, though perhaps not medically speaking psychopathic, can also arise from the deranged middle-

class soul. I mean as Baxter Crowe moved through his inspection
routine, we were seeing a small animal of property on the prowl—
a mini-bourgeois with the violins in his head strung too tight,
but middle class all the way, enraged in advance over possible
defacement of his holdings by vandals disguised as nice people.

Baxter went out and inspected the gas tanks. Coming back,
he said: "We're low on gas. Have you called the company to
bring in a new tank?"

"Yes, I did."

"When are they coming?"

"They said tomorrow morning, Baxter."

We mentioned the broken salad plate and torn umbrella. He
made a disgusted face. "All right," he said, "you'll replace those."

"Of course."

I had given him a check to cover such incidentals, but what
did it matter?

"What have you done to my desk?"

"Nothing, Baxter, all your stuff is there. And your mail too."

"I didn't ask you to collect my mail!"

"Sorry."

He sat down to look through the letters that had come in.
Again we watched a curious ritual. You wouldn't think a man
could open his mail insolently. Crowe managed even that. Just
as he drove his car—with the home movie going. He cut open
each envelope with a small penknife, and then shook, or, better
say, fastidiously sifted, the letter out. This was done very slowly.
Who knows, he may have been imitating a Japanese tea ceremony. Maybe Lévi-Strauss opens his mail that way. I have no
idea. The implication of the prolonged, finicky sifting out of the
letter was that news of enormous import would momentarily
drop from the envelope, and that in the meantime, pending the
drop, all conversation would be frivolous and unwelcome.

We went out on the porch again, and we heard Baxter abruptly go to bed. That night the baby was up three times. Tight-
lipped in the morning, Crowe answered "Yes" when asked whether
he had been kept awake. We were in the cramped kitchen. When
I moved past him, he bridled, pulling his chair closer to the
table. A few minutes later I saw him, frozen-faced and on the

march, carrying two copies of *The Village Voice* we had left on the porch, thinking he might want to see the back issues, and depositing them in the garbage.

Now we were ready to leave. If only I had told him sooner, but we waited too long. He was at the small table in the kitchen. "All right," he said. "I need that list of names and messages. All the people who called me."

From here on I began to pay for what I think of now as the Sin of Being Unprepared. Or perhaps—"Let's have no trouble, if we can help it"—the Sin of Middle-class Restraint. At some point earlier I should have said to hell with the free use of his house and car, the three free weeks in the country he made possible, and all the rest of it. I ought to have recognized that—for whatever reason, it didn't matter—we had been the target of a salami aggression, slicing little by little, against our dignity as civilized guests, and said, striking first: "Knock it off, Baxter. We appreciate what you've done, but we don't have to stand for this." But I didn't act soon enough.

What happened to us was ridiculously small and petty. Yet in a way we made the same disastrous error as the Clutters did in Kansas, according to Capote's account, and the family in Santa Cruz, California, last year, five killed by one man and dumped to die in their own swimming pool. This is the error, more than that, the sin, when confronted by an aggressor, even in the pettiest circumstances, of thinking that *this can't be happening to me,* and if I act reasonably, if possible good-naturedly, act with restraint, or don't act, the aggression will pass.

A train schedule had materialized on the kitchen table. Consulting it, he said: "By the way, you can make arrangements to take the four twenty-two."

So entrapment was complete. And insult. As though the discredited guests, friendless, carless, had no other option and like refugees would have to struggle as best they could, with their baby, suitcases, traveling crib, and so on, to the Old Saybrook station, and stumble aboard the train back to New York.

L'esprit de l'escalier, staircase wit. The retort that comes into your head, leaving, on the stairs, that you wish you had summoned up during the crisis in the salon. The cool you wish you'd had, and, worse, so easily could have had. If I had used my head just a little, I could have answered tolerantly, making him seem the small, ill-mannered person he was: "Sure, Baxter, we understand. You're tired. You want to be alone. You couldn't sleep last night. Fine, we'll go over to the Manns. They've asked us for the weekend anyway." Which was true. Instead I took umbrage. Turned out of somebody's house! *This can't be happening to me.* Even having already planned to leave, I said: "Hey, this is short notice. What's the matter?"

Crowe blew up. "You've let me down! You didn't leave a list of my phone calls! You've messed up my desk! You've been absolutely irresponsible. If you'd let me have your place free for three weeks, you'd expect things to be taken care of better than this!" Remember that his house and grounds were spotless and blooming.

"We have different standards, Baxter," I tried to say calmly.

"Bullshit!" He sneered. "And I want that salad plate replaced. I want a new beach umbrella. It's too tight here. Too tight. I want to be alone. So you can get on the train. And don't get uptight. It spreads bad emanations."

I had two passing visions, of an anguished dog snarling on his turf, and an avenging angel out to drive us from his crumby Eden.

"I am uptight!" I said. "I think this is lousy. You have all the information you need. It just isn't in the form you want. And who wouldn't feel oppressed? With all this marching around and inspecting!"

"That's just your weirdly convoluted paranoia!"

"Look, Baxter, if you feel this way, I'm sorry. I'll give you your list, and we'll be glad to leave. Not by train, of course."

He walked away. Denise had come in and watched the scene in amazement. At no time had he said anything against her. In fact, a week later she told me that, on the porch, he had shaken his head and wondered how she could put up with my disorganized ways. I've since learned that this is a technique of his, to take aside another man's wife or girl and commiserate with her for having to put up with something or other. Unfortunately, she didn't alert me to the porch conversation "for fear of starting trouble"—another of our endless succession of mistakes that night and morning.

Now she went upstairs to pack. The baby was still asleep, and we all moved about the house separately. I phoned Hertz to arrange for a car at noon. We heard the door bang and Baxter's car started up and he was gone. I telephoned various people to call off appointments and say good-bye. They said: "He's crazy. Why go back to New York? Come on over and stay with us."

But it started to rain again, and the incident had been so depressing. Crowe's outburst and his pettiness hung like a bad smell over everything. Neither of us had ever come up against behavior of this sort. It was all so mean-spirited and crumby. Rather than stay around, we preferred to leave the unpleasant vibrations behind and get back to Manhattan for a while. After a drink with friends, we did, in a red Hertz Fairlane.

On the way back to New York I started blaming myself for letting it happen. Denise kept saying: "Come on, it wasn't that serious. You sounded quite cool." That may be, but I don't think so. The crazy scene had put me down. Crowe had rudely gotten rid of us. On the wrong turf, at the wrong time, not wanting to be there, uneasy on another man's territory—Ardrey is right—in a bad, exposed position generally, and confronted by icy rage, I did nothing much but play the good fellow. And after all this, trying to be cool after the fact, I left him a polite note thanking him for the three weeks.

And one more bringdown had to be gone through. During the ride to pick him up at the airport, I had—for who knows what reason—thought I had better take along my checkbook. Home in our apartment I discovered that I'd left *that* in his car. This meant phoning Baxter to ask, in a tone somehow neither hostile nor in the least ingratiating, to mail it back to me. In reply the rasping voice allowed: "It would be possible."

Friends out of the line of fire can always come up with suggestions as to what would have been the best way to counter Baxter's rudeness.

"Punch him in the nose!"

"Just smile and leave."

"Laugh at him . . ."

Any one of these, of course, might have worked. I've been to the Old Lyme area quite often since the episode without running across him. If we meet again and trouble starts, I hope to do better. Meanwhile the memory . . .

I've spoken with two psychiatrists who know Baxter. Both consider him disturbed, one believes "very sick." But what remains mysterious, and more to the point, is the unbalanced person's ability to unsettle and even change the heads of sane people. It almost seems that, under pressure of a certain kind, sanity can be more precarious and vulnerable than a delusional system.

Chesterton, among others, has pointed out that arguments with the insane nearly always end badly for the person in his right mind. The paranoid individual, for instance, may make loony assumptions. But once he proceeds from them his logic won't have any holes. He's completely sure of himself. His destructively organized universe admits of no surprises. He has no doubt whatever about the plot against him and the evil intentions of others, and in identifying the plot he confronts you with coils of persuasive reasoning.

The strange thing is that psychotic conviction directed full force against you can possess such evil magic. With petty logical hammerings the disordered person can change perfectly ordinary circumstances into a vicious and distasteful scene, and may, if he's persistent enough, succeed in overwhelming and turning upside down the perceptions of innocent people.

When I think of our experience, the irony persists. The plain fact, as Denise said, is that we were good guests. Beyond this, we may fairly describe ourselves as a man and a woman of good will, moving through life, we hope, with most of the accepted virtues. I mean we clean up our trash. We're warm to our friends and pleasant to strangers, courteous most of the time, reasonably generous, willing to help out and give the other man a break. That kind of thing. But then, granting the pettiness of the episode, such ordinarily decent, trusting people turn out to be patsies: a disturbed individual easily entraps them and their civilized defenses don't work.

In these circumstances, you can mislay your ability to think straight. It didn't cross my mind for several days that Crowe's bad manners could be attributed also to the fact that he doesn't know any better, that for lack of proper bringing up or whatever reason, the idea of graciousness—even in the face of a few things gone wrong—was never made available to him, and that for a person of this background, nagging punctiliousness passes for gentility.

But here again, the trouble is—if, as you suggest, Crowe and others like him, even including *good* rude people, are on the verge of inheriting the earth—I may be citing bygone standards of behavior that don't mean anything anymore.

Several days after we came back home, a typewritten note arrived from Old Lyme. It read:

> Could you also add to that check an amount that would cover replacing the fifth of vodka and the half gallon of Almadén wine. I always thought that replacing consumed spirits was a taken-for-granted must with guests.
> I sent the last letter to the wrong address. In it I itemized some more costs: $10 for a service charge to fix the burner thermostat (fucked up by someone, not a Crowe, turning off the emergency switch); $2 for a ruined plastic washbasin; $10 to replace the broken umbrella and dish.

Reading the note again, I can see the dismal humor of it: the spectacle of this man running around his premises searching for damage, rummaging through drawers and closets seeking evidence of dirtiness, and noting—"Ah hah!"—the absence of nearly emptied bottles left behind as booby traps. But at the time I thought he still had my checkbook. If he didn't mail the book in a few days, I was ready to go to his house and demand it. Until then I wouldn't laugh off the new charges; also I had become temporarily demented by contagion, and felt the need to answer his claims item by item.

No, we hadn't touched his practically used-up half gallon of Almadén Chablis. It stood around for days on the kitchen sideboard and then disappeared. Presumably the kids drank it. There had been no fifth of vodka, but a miserable little pint, perhaps half or two-thirds full, which unfortunately we had finished and not replaced. I had thought this would be covered by the check for incidentals I had given him, but conceded—how degrading to bother—that we were in the wrong here.

We hadn't touched the thermostat either. Nor, good Lord, "ruined" the two-dollar plastic washbasin. If I remember, we sent him an additional check for $13.50 or something like that. We had already, before his note came, picked up the damned salad plate at Bloomingdale's. It was a cheap pattern, costing about $1.25. Then the umbrella, a replica of the sleazy bamboo job the wind had torn on the beach. We bothered to go to the store, by the way—again afflicted with contagious madness—because I didn't want him to have the money for these items, which he would have taken, to spend on anything else, and also with the of course mistaken idea that receiving one cheap salad plate in the parcel post might make him feel a little foolish.

At Bloomingdale's, feeling a bit odd buying a single cheap dish, we mentioned to the boy waiting on us that our summer host had demanded the replacement. "Wow," he said, "it's an epidemic. You're the fourth customer to come in this week who had the same thing happen. All two-dollar items or less. I'll gift wrap it!" But I told him no, there was no point.

There's no way around it, the man put us through changes. What we hope is that the lessons we learned in Old Lyme will help us in future dealings with your psychopaths, and other madmen and outlaws. We can pass on this much:

First, it may seem a minor point, but beware of a person who walks stiffly about as if prodded by an oversized suppository.

Second, never underestimate the effectiveness of carefully staged petty cruelty, no matter how absurd it may appear in the beginning. I mean the crippling little maneuvers designed gradually to corner and degrade you in your own eyes. For instance, where we were concerned, immediately demanding payment, say, for a broken dish when we certainly would have offered it. Denying the other the grace of offering. Pursuit of small discrepancies.

Systematic deprivation of grace in tiny little ways can bring down even a relatively secure person if he or she hasn't been on the watch for it. If you find your confidence and self-esteem being whittled away by such tactics, remember that you're probably not crazy, faulty, or inhuman. The one doing it to you is.

Third, we learned that an almost universally disliked person will act in destructive fashion sooner or later.

Fourth, psychopaths, outlaws, and other ambulatory madmen *notice things* more keenly than most of us. Since for them all territory, including the territory of self-esteem, will be a potential battleground, they study the opponent's position—everybody is an opponent—in detail. Before any given clash, the time and circumstance of which they will choose, they'll be likely to have examined you for areas of weakness and vulnerability.

All this puts the sane, decent person in a bind. The sad truth is that the best way to deal with psychopaths and outlaws is to become more like them. When you detect such a person in your life, don't, above all, placate him by trying to be nice. Immediately start preparing your defenses—which means, become functionally paranoid—and put yourself on a war footing. You have to go into the same game, watch the psychopath just as he has been watching you, coolly and secretly search out *his* possible weaknesses. But what a way to live! That's the problem. Who wants to be a bastard, even for survival purposes? Still, in the kind of world growing up around us, it may be that we have no choice.

How to detect a psychopath or outlaw in advance before he can injure you? One rule: Watch out for somebody who, perhaps for indefinable reasons, makes you feel uneasy. Trust your unthought-out animal wariness. Also be careful of a person with whom arrangements—even if apparently nailed down—somehow always seem to go wrong through your mistakes, never theirs, and you're constantly made to feel responsible for this. The easiest way out, naturally, is to avoid such individuals. But if you can't, and have to live with their presence, then become yourself hard and calculating, aggressive and predatory. Understand that you're faced with evil, and stay on the watch until that evil passes. How to accomplish this while keeping hold of your essential decency remains, for me anyhow, a mystery still to be solved, but I know that from now on I'll try to manage it.

A fifth lesson we learned at Old Lyme, as I've stressed, is that mental disorder can be contagious. Once you allow yourself to be drawn into paranoid territory, you start thinking wild, hateful, suspicious thoughts. The disdain I feel for Crowe depresses me. It's not my style. There never can be any satisfaction in despising another person so. But I can't rise above it; the Christian spirit just won't come through.

Once you've caught the illness you can find yourself in the morally debilitating position of growing so angry that you *wrongly accuse* the outlaw who has tried to injure you. I began to be convinced that Crowe was holding back the return of my checkbook. But as it turned out, my newly acquired craziness worked that way. His didn't. I telephoned him. He had mailed it to the wrong address, had just put it in the mail again, and it arrived the next day.

Curiously, on the phone, he suddenly demanded: *"Why* did you tell me that Denise would do most of the watering? *Why* did you do that?"

"Baxter," I said, "that's none of your business."

"We have just ended our conversation," he grated, and hung up.

I'm not sure that the matter of who watered the plants really upset him that much. More likely, what brought on our clash took place in the car coming home from the airport. When he was going on about Lévi-Strauss I didn't take him seriously. Worse, this was unintentional. I couldn't help it; waves of sleep had come over me. In my reverie, behind my eyelids, the gallant little old man was playing his violin. I smiled, and of course Baxter saw me.

The other day Denise brought our little boy home from the playground. His face was covered with blood. Another boy, older, about two and a half, had brought a small metal truck down on his nose. This one, known as "the monster" among the mothers and nannies at the playground, regularly attacks all the others. He ranges among the seesaws, swings, and sand piles, a completely unrestrained little terror. His baby-sitter lolls around reading. The other children's mothers and maids are the ones who prevent him from biting and hitting and smashing the nice boys and girls bloody.

One day the little monster's mother came with him to the playground, instead of the baby-sitter. She was cool, aloof, and beautifully dressed. In her presence he changed into a different child. He sat by his mother's skirts all morning long, never once venturing forth, leaning against her elegant knees and sucking his thumb.

I thought of Baxter Crowe in our play area. His mother won't come, and we have no nursemaids. He's not about to go away. So, for the time being at any rate, if he doesn't fall sick again, he remains on the loose, threatening sorrow to anyone who becomes involved with him. In this playground, paranoia has long ago taken over from the golden rule, with innocence the worst of sins.

6. MADNESS RISING IN NEW YORK

These events all took place recently within a twelve-month period.

I am walking down Lexington Avenue with my wife and baby, six months old, in the polluted twilight. Sulfur dioxide chokes us and we cough. We've just come in from the country, weary and shabby, I hauling a suitcase, she with the baby in her arms.

Out of the dusk appears a taxi with dimmers on. The driver leans out of his window and shouts: "Hey, you want to sell that kid?"

We simply look at him. Who can it be? He's into a joke, of course, but do we know this man?

The degenerate hawk face peers at us. "C'mon!" He beckons.

"The baby! How much do you want for it? I pay good!"

We're not in the least unnerved but just dumbfounded. No calculations we might make could include this. Approaching our corner, we turn left off the avenue, and now have our backs to him.

The voice pursues us, aggrieved, complaining. "I'm serious!" We have hurt his feelings.

"C'mon . . ."

Traffic lights change on the avenue. With a last shout, he guns his motor. We turn and see him borne away in the rush of cars.

The mom-and-pop tobacco and newspaper store operated by a middle-aged couple has abruptly become the scene of a loud and angry dispute. I can hear voices from down the block, and enter cautiously.

A Puerto Rican laborer has gone out of his head. So have the owners gone out of theirs. The quality of their Madison Avenue shop in an expensive neighborhood entitles them, they believe, to charge a penny more than the base rate for a pack of cigarettes. The laborer from a construction job down the street has just found this out, but too late.

In a hurry for a smoke, he tore open the pack of Camels and lit one. Then counting his change, he yelled at Joe Berman: "You cheat me!" Before my arrival they argued for several minutes, growing angrier. The Bermans cared most of all that their honesty had been shouted at and their floor actually spat on. To be charged with unfair dealing was an outrage, especially by a foreigner as ignorant as this one. Their customer knew only how much a pack of cigarettes cost everywhere else in the city, and that these *ladrones* were trying to steal from him, and when he caught them at it, they still refused to give his money back.

"Police! Police! He's got a knife!"

"Pig! I ain't got no knife. Gimme my change!"

"You already opened it, I told you. I can't give you your money back. The pack is damaged. You ripped the cellophane off. Can't you see? You're smoking one of them right now!"

"Pig, you no cheat me!"

"Twenty-four years we've been here, and nobody, not one person, ever made such an accusation. If you don't like it . . ."

"Gimmee my wan cent!"

". . . go back wherever you came from!"

"I keel—"

"Oh, well!" shouts Joe Berman to the ceiling. "Why not! I might as well die here as anyplace else!"

"Go on, give it back to him," I murmur to Ada. "It's only a penny. What's the difference?"

Behind the cash register she folds her arms. "Not one cent! What right has he got to come in here accusing—"

"*Puerca!* I got rights like you!"

"Ada, can't you see—"

"I see nothing. We owe nothing."

"Here!" I remember again that absurdity removes pressure. Change the game somehow. Yesterday I broke up a fight between two truck drivers, black and Italian, by calling out: "Hey! Never fight in front of witnesses!" They stopped, looking at me as though I were crazy. So now in a respectful manner I smile at the Puerto Rican and hand him a penny from my own pocket.

"No, no!" He backs away. "Not you! These *thief* got to give me!"

"Get out!"

"Get out of here with your crazy accent!"

"Police—"

"*I* get police!" The laborer stands in the doorway. He throws the opened pack of Camels at the storekeepers' feet. "Then I come back."

"Oh, yes!" Joe Berman laughs miserably after the man has gone. "Do you think he won't? He'll be back, with some of his friends. You'll see. Ignorant bastard. They're all crazy. And what can we do, two defenseless people?"

"I'll tell you one thing," Ada promises from behind the cash register. "Let him come. Not a cent will he get from us. Ever!"

I feel a pressure in my head. Jackhammer. Garbage trucks.

Horns. Moving toward Fifth Avenue, planning to sit in Central Park for a while. One particular horn intrudes on my nervous system. It grows louder, a repeated honking. The horn putting an iron bar through my head has both a tormenting and tormented sound. Someone is obviously driving himself crazy. Herself, as it turns out. In her Lincoln Continental a woman seethes and spits behind the wheel. A small murderous thumb presses down on the horn, filling this usually quiet side street with a blare of hatred. Standing on the curb with his hands on his hips, a young man looks at her. His station wagon has been blocking her way. Therefore she is blowing her enormous horn to make him climb into his car and drive off. But in response, he simply stands there observing her.

My head filled with terrible vibrations, I search up and down the street. No police anywhere. A dozen passersby are holding their ears. I shout at her through cupped hands, and after a few seconds she lets up, her thumb still resting on the horn. I speak to gritted teeth.

"Please, could you—"

"I'm *not* going to stop *until he moves.*"

"Well then . . ."

He remains motionless, somehow managing to speak without opening his mouth: "I'm not moving until she *cuts that out!*"

But you both won't give in.

BLARE! BLARE! *BLARE!*

Kill, get away, or be deafened. I make for the park, like all the others holding my hands to my ears. I'm three blocks down Fifth Avenue, nearly to the zoo, before the sound of her horn fades away.

The other day, Jack R. tells me, he inflicted the revenge he always wanted on a hornblower. He lives on the seventh floor of a new apartment house near the Lexington Avenue subway. Around noon the traffic jammed up on his side street and a shirt-sleeved man resembling a mole stepped out of an open convertible, looked down the block, got back behind the wheel, and began honking.

Jack raced to the kitchen, took an egg from the refrigerator, opened his window, and let fly. A beautiful hit splattered over the convertible's inside windshield. The driver reeled dripping out of the car, with his arms outflung, and seven floors above in his library the public-relations man danced.

This is balanced by a dismal story. Several weeks ago Jack was forced by a red-faced sweating bull of a client to join him in each drinking *nineteen* martinis. They started at lunch and went on all afternoon and through the cocktail hour. At about seven in the evening the client slumped to the floor. Jack staggered to the phone and called his wife for help, then crumpled in the booth. A company limousine was called to take the client and his PR man home. They are both alive but haven't spoken since. So far as he knows Jack still has the account.

My wife and I are having dinner with friends at a Polynesian restaurant. It's an immense dark shadowy place. The management has turned the big room into a jungle on a tropical island, with palm trees, grass shacks, waterfalls and recurring rain, electric guitars and grunting songs. We have two planter's punches. All at once out of the darkness there is thrust in front of me a grinning black face with luminous teeth. This face says in a high-pitched voice: "Hello!"

"What?"

"Can I sit down with you?"

"All right . . ." I lean away from the dummy's grinning familiarity. My friends laugh, and not sure what to say, I ask, "How are things with you?"

"I'm in trouble."

"What's wrong?"

The black face grins. "My girl friend is mad at me. She says I don't take her out enough."

"That's too bad. Why won't you take her out?"

"I need some money. You've got money. She'd like *you*." I have no answer for that, and the piping voice inquires, "Would you like to meet my girl friend?"

"Sure I would." I feel stupidly nervous.

"She would really like you." A chuckle follows. The head bobs and the teeth gleam. "You'd swing together."

"Well," I think I will ask and finally do, "why don't *you* swing with her?"

"Man, I can't take her to the places she wants to go."

Again "Why?"

"They won't let me in!"

"Come on. These days?"

"The tables are all reserved!"

"I—"

"You never *saw* so many reserved tables." The bright black eyes concentrate on me. "That's hard, man. I mean, if it was just me, I wouldn't be caught dead in one of those honky places. You know, as a customer. But she's got this hang-up."

I tell the dummy angrily: "Well, I can't help it. I'm sorry." And the people around me are nervously smiling.

More softly, the ebony face murmurs: "I need help, man."

"What do you expect—"

"Give him some money," my wife tells me, and I quickly put out three dollars on the tablecloth.

"Thanks, man. My girl friend thanks you."

The black face recedes into the shadows, and no one at our table jokes about the apparition after it has gone. How would money help?

I never saw the ventriloquist's face. Whom have I been talking to?

I am to tape a radio interview. A newspaperman and popular author will talk with me about my new book. It's a warm, intimate sort of program. Through the force of his personality, the nationally syndicated writer is known to bring out the best in his guests.

A Chinese girl enters the studio. We shake hands and she smiles: "Call me Bob." Everybody in the business knows this, of course, but as a matter of routine my interviewer and I will never meet. The Chinese girl will ask the questions. Then her voice will be snipped out of the tape, and Bob, when he stops by network headquarters, or perhaps back in his apartment, will read off her lines in his voice. Having access to my replies, he then may insert particularly clever queries which, as his listeners know, "draw the guest out." How easy it becomes to accept this kind of thing . . .

A brown fog had settled in. LaGuardia was closed and there was nothing to do but take the train from Penn Station to Boston. I sat next to the old sergeant wearing a miniature billboard of battle decorations.

With the three fingers remaining on his left hand he clutched the Dixie cup. The train lurched but his crippled hand was steady and he lost only a drop or two of the Carstairs blended whiskey poured from the pint bottle.

"By that time the Japs were about finished," he said. "We had the last of them pinned down in Manila Stadium, and we took our time and hit them with mortars. After a while we went in. We came in through the outfield gates. Nobody stopped us. They were ripped up pretty good, lying all over the grass. We couldn't find any left alive, except there was this Jap officer coming out of the third-base dugout. He was swinging one of those big swords in both hands."

"A samurai sword?"

"He had one of those big swords, and when he saw us he ran to home plate. He waited with his arms bent out, holding the sword like it was a bat, as if he expected us to pitch to him. Then he swung. He started running the bases, still hanging on to his sword, and we all just stopped and watched him. He went around second and headed for third. He was yelling at us. It was crazy." The sergeant tossed back his whiskey. "Sonova bitch tried for home."

"Did he make it?"

"No, I shot him. When he started to slide. Do you think I was going to let that bastard score?"

A bad snowstorm hit New York. Drifts had built up, especially in the cross streets. A thaw followed, then a freeze, and another storm brought fresh layers.

I had an appointment at Rockefeller Center. Crossing Madison Avenue at 86th Street, I saw in front of me a tall, ungainly old woman dressed in black. She was foundering in the snow. As I approached, she gave up struggling and simply waited, appearing to slant out of the drifts around her, gazing at me in mute despair.

Someone had to rescue this tattered schooner of a woman. She must have been well into her seventies. Her face was webbed and her eyes were rheumy. She could hardly speak, and then whispered in thick German that made no sense to me. She had on a black quilt covered with veils. This costume had no hooks or buttons so that her old breast was open to the weather. Her cracked black shoes splayed out as she slipped on the ice, and I caught her.

"Help a little. Please! Take a step!" I urged. She couldn't understand anything, and fell heavily against me. We clung to one another, leaning against a drift.

I saw my wife coming out of the grocery store across the street and I shouted to her. She came over, and I said: "Take the other arm!" Together we helped the old woman to the curb.

"She's German. Ask her to make an effort."

Upon being spoken to in her own language she began to declaim, gesturing as she spoke, making it harder than ever to hold her up. She wouldn't stop.

"What's she saying?"

"The poor woman!"

"I know that. Tell her she can talk about it later."

She lunged about, waving her old silken arms, and my wife translated: " 'It's my husband's fault! Why did he bring me here and then die? I'm an old woman. I can't talk to anyone. I have no friends . . . I have nothing . . . I'm sick . . .' "

"We've got to get her indoors."

"Not here. She has to go to Jager House to meet a lawyer. She hopes there'll be a letter from Switzerland."

We inched along 86th Street. This meant lifting and carrying her two long cross-town blocks. It was exhausting because she let herself go practically inert except when, in her deep old woman's voice, she denounced her husband for dying and abandoning her among alien people.

"Tell her to keep moving!"

The snow came to our knees, and we slipped on hidden ribs of ice. We fell once, all in a heap. My wife was covered with snow. My clean shirt was wet and my pants were bagged and sopping. Finally we managed to carry her as far as the Methodist Episcopal Church between Park and Lexington.

A sexton helped take her into the church. We led our old woman to a bench and blew on her hands and rubbed circulation into her arms and legs. A cleaning woman provided a big diaper pin, and my wife secured the folds of silk so that they wouldn't fly open.

These measures had an unexpectedly powerful effect. We could hardly believe it. She got to her feet, speaking in a low and dignified tone, and nodded to us almost regally.

"What did she say?" I asked.

" 'Thank you very much. I'm all right. I can walk by myself now.' "

She moved slowly, like a great black vessel under sail. We watched her make it to the corner and disappear.

The next day, late for another midtown appointment, I looked for a taxi. Once again I crossed Madison Avenue. Although it was a bright morning, the weather had become more severe. A gusty wind blew the snow around. People on the street were hooded and muffled. The snow was dazzling, and I wished that I had brought my dark glasses.

I stopped. A figure wavered before me. A tall, exhausted old woman in black stood helplessly on a slant in front of an enormous snowdrift. Her arms were flung out to the icy sky.

Mother in flapping black silk! Forgive me, but it was somebody else's turn.

A taxi answered my signal. I climbed in quickly and asked the driver to take me to Lever House.

My dentist has just died. A sad, vindictive little homosexual, longing for love. Youthful protégés abounded, actors, golden boys on motorcycles. Each year, and especially as he passed fifty, the new ones seemed younger. In trousers too tight, he cruised miserably from one to the next.

Professionally a superior craftsman, adept at drilling, decisive, tender, and consoling to the person in the chair. Otherwise, away from his office, a hornet buzzing with greed and self-pity. In business, mean and sharp, overcompetitive, unfailingly engaged in quarrels with a succession of partners.

Until he died I thought I had heard about every kind of hatred, or rather that no new expression of it would surprise me. But I'm told that when the news came—that, near the end, he was about to stumble aboard a Detroit plane to fly out and die with his sister in their home town—the two partners, roommates, with whom he had started a restaurant, cackled and cheered. Already twice in court with him and about to go again (he refused to concede that his latest golden young barman was robbing the cash register), they could hardly wait for the final announcement.

It came within a week. Dr. Marvin Garr was dead. The partners danced and ordered champagne. Again, I'm told that they invited friends to the celebration. Would they believe it, the little bastard was gone. The gray-faced passenger huddled in the aisle seat would never return.

Next morning, even with their hangovers, they joked and chuckled.

"Say," one of them laughed over coffee, "do you suppose he really is dead? It couldn't be a false rumor, could it?"

"Oh, *no!*"

"Call his office!"

"You do it."

"All right!"

One of the partners dialed, and they waited expectantly in their dressing gowns.

"You don't imagine—"

"Shh! Answering service—"

"DR. GARR IS IN DETROIT."

"Are you sure, dear?"

"DR. GARR IS IN DETROIT."

"It's too much!" The partner on the phone doubled up with laughter. "Here, you try. Go ahead. No . . . for the full effect, hang up and dial again!"

"DR. GARR IS IN DETROIT."

It was too good a game to keep to themselves. They got in touch with all the people they knew who had been acquainted with my dentist, asking them to join in.

"Call his office."

Next day the answering service received the word, and all communication with Dr. Garr was cut off forever.

My friend Leonard Browne was walking his dachshund, Igor, a little before midnight. It had been cool and misty all evening, and now the heavy atmosphere diffused the glow of the street lamps. Leonard shivered, wishing he had put on a sweater under his raincoat. He guided Igor off the curb in front of the Greek restaurant near his own doorway. The dachshund stubbornly held back, took his time, and urinated against a parking meter.

He heard shouted oaths from within the restaurant. He turned to see what was going on, but the plate glass had steamed over, and he could make out only rapidly moving figures. Then the door burst open and two men came running into the street, shouting: "Taxi! Taxi!" and one of them bellowed: "God damn you, son of a bitch!" at a driver who went by without seeing them. The two men filled Madison Avenue with their raucous noise. Even the dog was astonished, and squinted at them. Two or three people hurried by, escaping their wild presence, and Leonard was suddenly enraged.

One was tall, pale, and rangy, wearing a black sweater, and he sawed his arms, signaling at the occupied taxis going by. The other was short, also in a black sweater, resembling the labor leader Jimmy Hoffa. He was in a vicious temper. He danced with rage, yelling in the street, waking decent people with his aimless hatred.

Leonard, with cold anger rising, thought: You should die. Staring at the bantam hoodlum he wished death on him as he had never before called down harm on another human being. A taxicab stopped and the two got in, the bantam still raging and swearing. As the cab pulled away, Leonard bent forward and glared through the dark at this man to let him know that he had been observed and cursed for his loutish performance on the street. The cab was rolling away when he saw a wild white face appear in the back window and then violent gestures directed at him from behind the glass. A block down Madison Avenue the taxi swerved to a halt. An angry face peered out at him. Igor was at the parking meter again, and Leonard, with his hands in his raincoat pockets, remained still.

From their point of view he was like a statue in a white raincoat standing next to the Greek restaurant. The bantam leaped out of the cab and stared at him. Leonard made no move. The man was poised on his toes, shouting, making a finger gesture. Igor trotted to another parking meter and Leonard followed him, breaking the lock of hatred in which both he and the bantam were caught. A hand came out of the cab, pulling at the man, who furiously shrugged it off but took a step slowly backward, preparing to get back in the taxi. Cooperating in a mutual withdrawal, Leonard guided the dachshund toward his front door. The hoodlum got back into the cab, but the taxi still didn't move, and the faces at the back window continued to watch him. Leonard then pushed open the door to his apartment house. Once inside he leaned against the lobby wall.

"Anything wrong, Mr. Browne?" inquired Mike, the doorman, stepping out from the telephone switchboard.

"No, no," he answered. "Nothing."

But he had seldom been as afraid, and—he knew—with good reason. It had been insane of him to let his hatred out like that. When you revealed such hatred, you had to be ready to risk fighting and perhaps dying. Leonard shivered. There was such terrible violence in New York. In the elevator he resolved that from now on at night, walking the dog, he would carry in his pocket a small hammer, or possibly an aerosol container of Mace, or one of those butane lighters, the kind that can dart out a quick long flame against enemies in the dark.

Ivan has just been out of the mental hospital for two weeks and already he believes that he is being followed. They are following him. Especially the poet who sends him blank letters every day. Nothing in them. And the sinister novelist who is trying to hex him.

On the mall at Rockefeller Center Ivan looks around anxiously.

"He's probably down those stairs."

"Who?"

"B———." He names the novelist.

I have always liked Ivan, and now look forward to having lunch with him. He finds me conservative and restful. We get along easily, often talking over professional football, about which he is an expert. Part of his recurring illness is total recall. He can't un-remember anything. When enough information accumulates in his head, he blows a circuit and does wild things. One kind of relief for him is to explore sports facts. Instantly he can recall any sort of statistical information you want about football since the professional game began—yards gained by Red Grange in his first year with the Chicago Bears, Cliff Battles' punting average the year before the Boston Redskins transferred to Washington, and so on.

The kind of input that sends Ivan to mental institutions from time to time swells the dossier he is always building in his head relating to the plots being hatched against him. He knows of one master plot and many little ones reinforcing it. Ivan won't bore you when he details the obsession of his pursuers. He even laughs about them: "Why do they have to pick on a crazy person? I'm in trouble enough already." He also tolerates my attempts to reassure him.

"You're all right, Ivan."

He nods several times, appreciating an outsider's good will and assuming a deferential air in the face of my obtuseness.

"Nobody's trying to upset you."

Twirling his spaghetti (thin as he is he eats enormously) he inquires, glancing warily about the restaurant: "What about those phone calls?"

"Which ones?"

"With nobody at the other end. Just silence."

"Oh, hell, that happens all the time in New York. It can just be a malfunction on the line or—it could be—someone with robbery in mind checking to see if anyone's at home. But that happens to everybody, not just you."

"I can hear them breathing."

"Look, believe, trust me, there's no plot. Haven't the doctors told you? It's all in your imagination. People are too *busy* to plot against you. They have other things to do."

He smiles. "Last night. The pebbles at my window. Handfuls of them."

"Nobody's following you, Ivan. You simply have to force yourself to believe that. Otherwise how will you ever get well?"

Now there's a glimmer of acceptance in his bright eyes.

"Are you sure?"

"Of course!" I answer him heartily. "Now then, have you been writing any poetry?"

I know that sympathy and warmth will only be partly helpful in easing the fears of people like Ivan. Beyond sympathy, it's good to chat in a comforting, even trivial, bourgeois manner. Bring them back to the familiar world in which their morbid anxieties appear silly. It works. Soon he is laughing and telling stories about his days on the radio as a child prodigy who couldn't be stumped on sports questions.

We have a good lunch; then, in Rockefeller Center, we stroll among the boxed lilies. An emaciated figure with gleaming eyes waits for us.

"Hello, Ivan . . ."

B———, the novelist, steps out from a doorway.

My friend Cadwallader has been described as a Virginia Gentleman with liberal leanings. His wife, Ann, is a beautiful girl active in antipollution causes. They have a big and bad-tempered dog, a Doberman. My friend may be thin and not strong, but his dog terrifies all visitors. The dog even bites at people who try to pat him.

Cadwallader enjoys listening to both jazz and rock records, and may be counted on to pick up the recording arm of his stereo-orthophonic machine in order to replay an especially good passage several times over, remarking quietly: "Notice the way Miles comes in here!"

One night they went to a coffeehouse in the Village and about three in the morning brought home an obscure guitarist with corn-silk hair. They were going to listen to some records and thought the taxi driver, some kind of rough-and-ready Italian, would be interested in hearing them too, and he said okay. Ann went in first to tie up the dog in a corner of the living room.

They played the records. Ann served delicious scrambled eggs and bacon to the cabdriver and the guitarist. In the middle of George Harrison's "All Things Must Pass" album the driver went out. The doorbell rang and he came back, saying: "That's twelve-fifty you owe me!"

"You left the meter running!"

"Whadja think?" the driver said. "You think I'm in this business because I like to stay up at night?"

"But," said Cadwallader, "we took you home. We gave you drinks and scrambled eggs, and a chance to listen to some good records."

The Doberman growled.

"So what? You still owe me twelve-fifty. Pay up."

"I most certainly do not intend to pay you twelve dollars and fifty cents."

The taxi driver knocked Cadwallader to the floor. The guitarist ran into the street and disappeared. The Doberman snarled and leaped against his rope. The driver had straddled Cadwallader and was pounding him. Cadwallader writhed to avoid the punches.

"Hurry!" he cried to his wife. "Get him out of here!"

"Oh, dear God!" she said. Ann is a big girl, and with all her strength managed to drag the dog away.

"Lock him up!" groaned Cadwallader. "All right," he said to the man on top of him, "if you feel this strongly about it." He shouted: "Pay the driver what he wants!"

"Oh, dear, how much *does* he want?"

"Twelve dollars and fifty cents! Please, if you don't mind, could you get off—"

"Not till I get my money, Buster," said the driver, remaining on top of him.

"I think I've got it!" Ann called from the bedroom. She came in with the money and handed it to the driver, saying: "I really don't see any reason to tip you."

"It figures," the man grunted. He got up from Cadwallader, counting the bills. "That'll teach you to be a wise guy," he said, and left.

"Poor thing." Ann sighed, touching her husband's swollen cheek and bleeding lips. "Let me get you a facecloth."

"I think he loosened a tooth," Cadwallader said.

On the way to the bathroom they let the dog out of the hall closet.

I found myself in the poet's car, uncomfortably wedged in the back seat between two of his friends, ratty-looking people, with the only girl in the car sitting beside the poet up front. In the East Sixties near Lexington Avenue, we were looking for a parking space. But the avenue and, it seemed, every side street were clogged, with many cars double-parked. After ten minutes, the poet exclaimed: "Got it!"

Ahead, a black limousine was pulling out from the curb and had begun to maneuver around a Volkswagen already waiting for the space and backing slowly into it. "Hey, somebody else is there," I said. Then our compact shot into the opening that, according to every traffic regulation in the world, didn't belong to us. The poet crouched at the wheel, fiercely peering out.

We could see the driver entitled to our space looking back at us from the Volkswagen with amazement and fury. At first he gesticulated and made signs that we should get out. The woman with him also turned around in disbelief. Our intrusion simply couldn't be, yet there we were. Finally the man emerged from his car and came toward us with measured, dignified steps, a tall, sun-tanned person of about fifty.

The poet is frail and diminutive, no more than five feet four, but he turns a ferocious, wild stare on all strangers. The one approaching could not, of course, tell how small he was. As he leaned in on our carful, the poet said in an absolutely dead voice: "I'm staying here . . . I'm insane!" and glared up at the law-abiding man. Our decent antagonist, I could see, was probably by no means timid under ordinary circumstances. But as he and the poet stared at each other, he suddenly grimaced, and a dazed, defeated look came over his face. We hung in silence. Then the man said wearily: "I know a nut when I see one," and walked away, got back in his car, and drove off.

"It works every time," the poet said.

Looking out on Park Avenue, I see a bearded man in a black top hat at the wheel of an old Plymouth. I notice that he's driving ever more slowly. His car is on fire. Stopping at the corner of 96th and Park, he tries to peer under the smoking, steaming hood, gives up, and begins running around the car in circles. The dignity of his black hat, heavy suit, and beard contrasts with his staccato little dance. He reaches out to people, but they pass by, pretending not to notice the smoke and steam and licks of flame. Presently he disappears into the corner luncheonette, can only be making a phone call.

Observers gather at the other three corners of the intersection to watch the burning car. He comes out of the luncheonette, followed by several patrons, who also stand at a distance. Shortly, with a blatting that fills the avenue, two huge fire engines arrive. A half-dozen firemen in helmets, carrying hoses and axes, rush toward the car. Its owner, suddenly understanding that there will be no half measures, shouts and thrusts out his hands, as if to hold them off.

The firemen hack open the hood and send torrents of water into the engine. The Dalmatian mascot on top of the truck barks endlessly. The owner cries out, begging them not to destroy the motor. The hacking and hosing continue. Steam rises over everybody. The owner of the car once again goes into his forlorn little dance. He almost rushes at the crazy men with the shining hats, axes, and hoses. He calls to a policeman to make them stop.

156 *Psychopaths . . .*

The officer, ignoring him, chats in friendly fashion with the driver of the second engine. Then it's all over. The blatting horns sound. Turning away from the smashed and still smoking car, the firemen leap back on their trucks. The Dalmatian barks. They roar away, and the corner is momentarily deserted and silent.

The man is left with his smoking, savaged automobile. Through the entire experience not one person has spoken to him. Now he wanders about the sidewalk, occasionally approaching passersby, taking one or two by the elbow, showing them the evidence. They shrug and walk on. He gives up. For several minutes he stands contemplating his dead car, and then he is gone.

Twilight comes. I look out and see that the car's license plates have been removed. Less than an hour later, in the early dark, I hear tapping. Under the streetlight I see a group of Puerto Ricans passing cushions out from the interior and taking off the wheels. Before long everything of value has been stripped from the hulk that has now settled at the corner. After three days, a tow truck carries it off.

"True, but don't forget," the fashionable young lawyer said to me, "triumphs are possible. We, the good people, can still win. What you have to do is strike back with style. Go with the tempo, meanness, and insanity. You know, psych out the mad city. I suppose what I'm trying to say—you've touched on it—is that there may be such a thing as good psychopathic behavior. And in certain situations it may be absolutely required for survival.

"For instance, a few summers ago we were flying to Europe. The city had passed through sinister days. It was a good time to leave New York for a while. The weather had been hot and sticky. Every day was dark and hot, with foul air. There seemed to be a perpetual cloud cover. Hatred was in the air, too. News of black riots came in from all around the country, and there had been a few violent incidents in Harlem.

"Do you know Francesca Baldwin? The heiress. Somehow that old-fashioned designation suits her. Then you know she has all the money in the world, and does exactly what she likes with it. Feels no guilt about having millions. She indulges all her impulses without question. Wanders into a store and buys twenty-five pairs of shoes. Flies suddenly to Brazil. Smokes the very best, all that. Lives for all groovy moments. Seems not to have the slightest idea of time or fear, never regrets or apologizes, has no morals that I've heard of, and also never blames anybody for anything. The worst condemnation I've ever heard her express was: 'What an uncool, detached thing to do!'

"When she heard about our plans, Francesca decided to send us off in luxury. This meant an air-conditioned limousine with uniformed chauffeur for the ride to Kennedy, and ice buckets filled with champagne for six in the car. You can imagine, it was great. Corks started popping and soon we were all high, with a little grass to help, as the limousine carried us a mile a minute toward Kennedy, with Rome only a few hours away.

"It was Sunday. Not so many cars on the road. I noticed the chauffeur glancing fearfully over his shoulder. Then we all became aware of a shadow, a big, beat-up old black Rambler, crowding closer and closer to us, and ragged shirts, bare torsos, and black faces staring in at our celebration. The driver of our limousine accelerated, but the other car—it must have had a souped-up engine—easily stayed with us. We'll never know what they had in mind: a little fun, a drag race, scaring whitey, or actually wrecking him in a ditch. But they were a tough and mean-looking crowd, and our people, myself included, shrank and we were afraid, and our chauffeur's puffy face had turned the color of oatmeal.

"All this time Francesca had been talking away about nothing that I can recall. Suddenly she caught sight of the carful of blacks alongside us. To my amazement, she began to wave, then beckon to the people in the other car. The black faces seemed to grow blacker, staring. An expression of childish delight came over her. She looked eight years old.

"'Open the window!' I did, and Francesca reached into one of the ice buckets. Then, holding on to several of us for support, she leaned halfway out of the limousine window and, at sixty miles an hour, held out an unopened bottle of champagne.

"In the other car, you never saw such stupefaction, disbelief, and then really wild excitement. A big dark hand came out and grasped Francesca's arm, and in a second the transfer was made. We pulled her back in. She was waving. All the blacks were waving, and the man beside the driver was flourishing the bottle and pretending to open it with his teeth. Then the car fell away, back out of our sight.

"'Francie!' shouted a young doctor in our limousine. 'My God, don't you know they'll be remembering this for the rest of their *lives*. They'll tell their *grandchildren* how one time on the Van Wyck Expressway . . .'

"So will we. I still wonder whether she saw our danger— if indeed there was any—or whether she was just having fun, and the blacks appreciated exactly that. Was there an element of calculation in what she did? I don't imagine she knows. She has probably forgotten. Francesca hates explanations anyhow. I'd say she's incapable of them. I also believe she's different from the rest of us, from you and me, and goes through life without reflecting, her brain taking one snapshot after another—in other words, she has a new head, possibly the head of the future that you're so concerned with.

"Of course, she can afford to live that way because she's so rich. Oh, yes. The reason all this occurred to me, I remember now. Do you know what several dear friends call her, meaning it affectionately? Lovable Little Psychopath. Does that fit in with your conception?"

7. LAUGHTER, HUMILIATION, AND PAIN

The art director came from one of Chicago's tough neighborhoods. He fought his way up through art school, won several scholarships, traveled and studied in Europe, and came back to score an almost immediate success in New York. At thirty-four he reached the top position in his field at a famous advertising agency and had an income of more than $75,000 a year.

Naturally he left old chums behind. Many of his boyhood pals were in jail. Others after struggling a little had fallen back to become parking-lot attendants, grocery clerks, the manager of a diner, proprietor of a shoeshine parlor. The best that his close friend Ben could do was acquire a street-corner newsstand. There Ben suffered: he had wanted to be an artist too. Now, instead, he worked twelve hours a day on his corner dispensing newspapers, magazines, and cigarettes. Life was pinched for him. His wife endlessly complained. They never went anywhere, and their two children, boy and girl, were sallow, pinched, and noisy.

With all his success, the art director remained a kindhearted man. One day after a doleful letter from Ben, he decided to give his friend some fun, invite him, all expenses paid, for a week in New York, and show him around. The inside world of advertising art and television would open up for the visitor from Chicago, and he would go to the theater and to great parties.

But Ben was afraid. "Those people will put me down," he said. "I'm nobody. Nothing. All I have is my dumb newsstand. I look funny. I'll stand out from everybody, and they'll laugh."

"Ben! Nobody's going to take that attitude. You're my old friend, and that's the way they'll treat you."

He was finally convinced. His wife bitched, but he was used to that.

"Why not me?"

"Because nobody asked you, that's why."

He persuaded his cousin to run the newsstand for a week, and as if in a dream Ben flew to New York.

In Manhattan, he was more terrified than he expected. His old buddy lived on Park Avenue. He was surrounded by people with big jobs and famous names. Ben was introduced everywhere. There were actors and models, and executives with mod suits and suntans, all of them nice to him. The art director, of course, had briefed them to be nice. Ben wasn't so dumb as to be unaware of that. Still, even if he couldn't talk, even if he hunched his shoulders fearfully and could hardly get up the courage to say "Pleased, I'm sure," it was some experience just the same. Beautiful girls did speak to him. One went so far as to casually put her hand on his knee, and made him feel as if he belonged in the same room with her, which of course he didn't.

The fourth evening, at some producer's penthouse, Ben found himself standing alone—as had happened a few times when the art director stopped to say hello to an important connection and talked for a moment or two. But this time Ben was on his own for quite a while. He was in the middle of the living room all alone, hunched over, holding his glass of whiskey in two hands, feeling that his suit was much too old and wrinkled and heavy as iron. He guessed nobody knew at this party whose old friend he was. Nobody came up to talk.

Feeling panicky, he moved over to the fireplace and tried to slouch against it, but the mantel was too high. He was slouching against nothing, leaning sideways, hardly daring to look over his shoulder, when all at once he felt a fearful chill. A thin, creepy guy with sideburns was watching him. At that moment one of those silences came down. It accidentally fell on the party, and out of the silence the guy with the sideburns leaped across the room with his arms wide open, embracing Ben, calling out in front of everybody: "Ah! A failure!"

At some point during his visit Ben might have expected to come up against a little rudeness. Perhaps even a drunken insult. Instead he had the luck to run into Fred Rackley, master of psychopathic humor, specialist in the put-on and entrapment of the innocent. The skinny guy with sideburns, who barely avoided a punch in the mouth from the art director, sent Ben to the American Airlines terminal at LaGuardia without even a flight bag, where (no late flights to Chicago) he slept all night in his clothes.

Called by some the Professor, Rackley is well known in a minor way, almost a celebrity. The cross he has to bear is that he hasn't become really famous. Only insiders react to his name. Chic and even talented people (stage, screen, television, literary) in New York, London, Paris, and Rome consider Rackley fabulous, but no one else recognizes him on the street. He still can't impress the more perceptive headwaiters.

This man accomplishes a little but in mysterious ways. A small family income enables Fred, his wife, and two small daughters to drift around pretty much where he likes, through Europe, back to New York, out to the Pacific Coast for a while. He has friends—a set collects around him—everywhere. Some day Fred will, should at any rate, be remembered as a source. Decades ago he invented a style copied everywhere now. It might be called sympathetic sadism. Inquisitive sympathy is what distinguishes him from imitators and other connoisseurs of cruelty, and makes them appear coarse and merely brutal in comparison.

Another Rackley story.

The free-lance editor was down. The world treated him badly. He had written an emotional book reviewing the story of his life, and no one had paid much attention to it. Two marriages were shot. He was forty-three years old, with no children, and his former wives didn't insist on alimony. He almost wished they did, so there would be a family to talk to, even quarrel with. But they seemed perfectly content to forget about him. Roger had difficulties with women, not sexual, at least not from his point of view. Physically he was dogged and strong. Perhaps it was the woodenness of his opinions or his gloomy dogmatic manner, but almost invariably he bored them. After shorter and shorter periods of time their eyes would glaze over. Neither his wives nor various girl friends seemed especially enthusiastic about going to bed with him. They didn't quite *not* want to. Rather, when he insisted, they acquiesced with no particular relish and their ecstasies struck him as perfunctory. This more than anything else made him gloomy.

There had been one glorious exception six years ago, and he had incomprehensibly thrown his luck away. She was an identical twin, dark, lively, romantic, and loving. Everything he prized. Yet it was her girlish romanticism that threw him off. Something idiotically destructive in his nature made him mock her sweet impulses all the time.

She had been the one who wanted to get married. But testing her, testing himself, who knows, he kept making light of the idea. Looking back, he could only shake his head. What had impelled him to put down this warm, giving chick? Hurt her, for example, pretending that she and her twin were half-people sharing a single soul. Roger made Vivian cry too often, not really meaning to. One evening in a bar, after she left for the ladies' room, someone asked him who the nice girl was, and he replied: "Oh, just some chick who's doing my laundry this week." He had always been thankful she didn't overhear that, and cursed himself for saying such a vulgar thing. Thereafter he was nicer to her, but one Christmas holiday she went home to her family in Seattle and decided to stay.

So now, down on his luck at forty-three, womanless, he decided what the hell, he would drive out from New York to San Francisco, where his old friend Fred Rackley was holding court for a few months, and rap with him, learn new things, meet new people. Fred always had ideas and knew how to turn life around.

Roger climbed into his old Buick and it was a heavy trip, with breakdowns here and there, daylong waits in strange Wyoming garages. He arrived in San Francisco exhausted yet with new hope, anxious to see Fred again and confess his unhappiness with no inhibition or reserve, letting it pour out. What made better sense? Fred had known both his wives, had seen his romance with Vivian flower and break up, and understood everything in his crazy way.

There he was, as Roger knew he would be, in a big apartment on top of Russian Hill, surrounded by new friends, all fabulous chic and aplomb, in a mod jacket and tight pants, an enormous splashy cravat made out of the American flag, and, naturally, sandals. There would always be the ridiculous touch, the put-down of himself as well as everyone else, that entitled Fred Rackley to call himself Prince of the Contemporary.

"My boy," said Rackley to the bedraggled editor, "who in the world is your tailor? We've got to do something about you." And while Roger unloaded his sorrows, the heaviness and flatness of life, memories of lost romance, Rackley fluttered around him in a series of charades, pretending to be a Brooks Brothers salesman, fitter, tailor, and cameraman. All the while he was outfitting Roger in a tan frontier costume with a red bandanna, Stetson, and, of course, space shoes, and there Roger was in front of a full-length mirror, laughing in spite of himself at his space cowboy image, feeling at the same time wild, foolish, and crazily attractive.

"Tonight, old boy," promised Fred Rackley, holding up one

finger to the wind. "Party at my place. In your honor. You will meet the girl of your dreams."

And it was she! Incredible! Glorious! At last for the wanderer, a break. Second chance! Vivian, more beautiful than she ever had been, gracious, womanly now, and no ring on her finger. She was on the sofa with a tall blond guy who looked like a surfer, but she immediately detached herself from him. Roger held her gently by the elbow. She laughed in appreciation of the space cowboy just in from New York, saying: "Wow, you're beautiful." They went hand in hand to the balcony and looked out together over the Golden Gate. She was living in Sausalito, across the Bay. "You'll have to come." He couldn't remember being so happy.

He was the envy of all the others, he could tell. They were all watching him. The big surfer made no move.

An ocean liner was coming in. Sundown, the Golden Gate, his girl again. "Do you remember," he asked, "the last time we crossed a bridge together?"

"Yes, in New York!"

"No, no! That afternoon in Connecticut, driving over the river from Old Lyme. Remember what happened?"

"Roger, we did so many things."

"The boat that ran into the drawbridge. They hadn't raised it fast enough! The mast fell into the water. The boat capsized. The people swam for their lives . . ."

Oh, that time, yes. How could she ever forget it.

They fell silent, and then he said hoarsely: "Vivian . . . I've got a lot to make up to you."

She answered with a catch in her voice: "It's all right . . . don't think that way."

"But I have to," he insisted. "I'm a different guy now. You'll see. You know what you promised the last time we talked on the phone?"

She frowned.

"That if we ever met again, and neither of us had gotten married, you would . . ." He bent to kiss the small mole on the back of her left hand. It wasn't there. There was no scar there either.

She was looking at him with as much pity as he had ever seen expressed on a woman's face.

"Oh, hell," she said, "Fred Rackley is such a wicked bastard. Forgive me, can you? I'm ashamed to have let him put me up to it."

Gradually he understood. "You're—"

"Poor Roger. I've never seen you before in my life. I'm Carol."

"Vivian?"

"She's married. Three years ago to an engineer. They live in Oregon."

Roger stared, then blurted foolishly, "Well, then! God, how about *you!*"

"Honey, I'm getting married next week. To the big guy. Here he comes now. Isn't Fred a perfect shit? Good-bye, dear."

Later, with remonstrances heaped on him, Fred Rackley looked politely astonished. "Come on!" He raised his eyebrows. "You wouldn't ask me to pass that one up, would you?"

Pleasure in shafting the innocent didn't begin with Fred Rackley. He has simply perfected the game. In the Rackley tradition, we have a painful lesson to the victim often coupled with a breathtaking insult to life itself. Lenny Bruce understood this. Remember the young comedian who made his reputation imitating the voices of the Kennedy family? A few hours after the assassination, Bruce strolled onto a night-club floor: "Well, one thing's sure. Vaughn Meader just got screwed!"

The laughter of cruelty projects the psychopath's pitiless view of creation. In the world of psychopaths, performance is all. The medicine for failure will be compounded of cruel quips, symbolic destruction, laughs from your fellow men. The psychopath refuses to put up with death, the lowest form of incompetence. Death, disease, and deformity will be fair game for his jokes. The essence of his game is to put down, put on, send up losers.

The put-on is evil surgery. Psychopathic humor despises the ones who don't make it, and also those who fall from grace. The destructive new man (that is, the cold-natured bystander, as opposed to the headlong, impulsive type of outlaw who will usually be too impatient for such pastimes) probes others with shocks for his amusement. Beyond this, he demands that the victim face up to his situation. Playing destructive games, the psychopathic joker intends a sort of cruel therapy.

Humor ruinous to dignity demands that the butt of the joke change his act and get with it or die. Under such shock treatment, the victim must rise up out of his innocence or crumble into hopelessness. Thus, psychopathic probing and exploitation of another's weakened condition has become for many a substitute for bourgeois kindness, which glosses over inadequacy. We have then one more technique developed to torment the bourgeoisie, a truth-telling assault on values—belief in decorum, avoidance of embarrassment, the decency of the white lie—that the middle classes hold dear.

But the laughter created by Fred Rackley is born out of more than random, lighthearted sadism. It arises from a despairing sense of the ridiculous: a knowledge gained early that everything sacred has gone out of life, excepting perhaps the sacredness of celebrity enjoyed by actors, politicians, athletes, some writers.

Modern psychopathic humor may have begun with Rackley. Long before the adoration of Lenny Bruce, in the late 1940's, Rackley was making fun of misfits, unsuccessful people, and victims of misfortune. Before sick jokes became popular, before spastics were gleefully mimicked on the street, Rackley was imitating the kind of people who imitate spastics. The great essays by Susan Sontag and Jacob Brackman on camp and the put-on could have paid tribute to him. Glorification of the trivial was his specialty two decades before these studies. Worship of celebrity too, as well as pretended worship (the two sometimes being almost indistinguishable), and seeking out the celebrity gone downhill and no longer famous.

A routine (early) Rackley send-up invaded the morose privacy of a once-famous boy actor, ten years older and forgotten, hunched gloomily over a bar. Television had passed him by, except that in the dead hours of late afternoon his adolescent countenance would now and then appear in an old movie. Now in

the bar, close to his middle thirties, all that was gone, and he
stared at his Scotch and water. Then suddenly, abashed, peering
at him, a crazy guy wearing sideburns drew close and spoke his
name with reverence. Would it be all right to shake hands? Just
talk for a minute? The former child star got his fist ready. But
the guy appeared honorable enough. His manner was guileless,
humbler by the moment. Could I have the privilege of buying
you a drink? He was courtly, all attention and respect. The actor
began to feel better. Okay, if you want to.

"Are you sure it's all right?"

Yes, sure.

"I don't want to impose . . ."

At this point Rackley's companions couldn't stand the game
any longer and left, collapsing with laughter on the sidewalk.

But it wasn't only a game, except insofar as life is. Rackley,
who had never been famous, felt sorry for the abandoned child
star. The phenomenon of Lost Celebrity moved him to the psychopathic humorist's equivalent of tears, which is to heap mockery not always or entirely on the man but on the situation itself.

In Fred Rackley's world, celebrity remains supreme. In a
bar, the story goes, he stopped with a half-dozen of his cronies
for a drink. One of them pushed into a brawl with Anthony Quinn.
The big superstar flattened him with several punches and dis-
dainfully went off to the men's room to wipe the blood from his
fists. Revenge had to be. The six cronies along the bar turned to
Rackley, who nodded purposefully, and they got ready. Presently
Quinn emerged, glowering, and slowly walked past them on his
way to the street. The six held back, waiting for Rackley, but
their leader was gazing after Quinn with adoration, and just
before he reached the door called out meekly: "Hi, Tony!"

Starting small, wiring the beds of newlyweds, entrapping
young marrieds in orgies, setting up true-confession games that
end in undignified exposure, shame, and quarreling for all except
the Rackleys, who manage to slip away before their turn—these

were young amusements soon abandoned. Years later more elaborate put-ons were preferred. Posing as Jerry Lewis (whom he resembles, but not too closely) in a poorly lit San Francisco restaurant, signing autographs, bringing it off perfectly. Employing the arts of humiliation to bring himself down, for instance, by means of a dreadful comedy act in a small Los Angeles floor show, during which not one joke drew a laugh, and customers struggled to get out, first in pairs and then by the tableful, as the sweating, desperately cheerful Rackley's gags fell dead one after another.

He still inspects your mail, of course, believing every letter in the world to be his property. He will confront you with your worst enemy at a party, just to see what happens. Eavesdrop on your most intimate conversation. Perhaps record it. Anyway, if the fancy strikes him, repeat it all. Yet who else will be so curious, care so much, and perhaps—when everyone else finds your plight boring—lend money, possibly a substantial amount, dress you up for more fun so that your absurd life can go on?

A legend in his lifetime, only not big enough. You often hear people—especially if they have known him only a short time—wondering about the "layers" of Rackley. Is he *at heart* without pity, or does he feel pity in such devastating fashion that he must play hilarious games in order to make it from one day to the next?

Psychopathic humor can save the joker's life. Several years ago a friend owned the Cafe Renaissance in New York. Late at night a famous comedian, not so well known then, came into the restaurant.

"Oh, Christ!" muttered the owner.

"Why?" I asked. "Don't you like to have celebrities here?"

"You'll see."

I did soon enough. The comedian, say Rod Munday, was, and he is now, rotund, beguiling, and insanely funny. But he's crazy and loud, and on all the time. This may prevent him from going mad, but it fills up your room, particularly a dignified place like the Renaissance.

He knew Rackley years ago, and could have been an early

disciple. But Rackley, whatever role he may be assuming, qualifies as a coherent person. Munday hardly ever does. In the area of the nervous system where most people experience a feeling of identity, he maintains a guesthouse filled with a thousand characters. No central individual feels permanently at home in Munday's head, because he's always being somebody else.

That night a number of his characters populated the Renaissance. Within a few minutes Munday had put on a dozen patrons, becoming in turn a cowboy, gangster, businessman from Duluth, dance instructress, old lady rocking on a porch, and a game warden challenging the size of a pompano one diner was about to eat. Each of these routines lasted from thirty to sixty seconds, all of them designed to change the heads of Stanley's customers.

Just as the owner was about to escort Munday from the main dining room, the comedian proceeded to the bar. Stanley relaxed. A half-partition separated the two areas. Munday now sat down next to a man staring into his beer. His manner became quiet and confidential, but nosy. He elbowed his neighbor gently in the ribs and began talking to him.

"Go up and listen," urged Stanley. "You'll see what I mean."

This victim again was obviously down, meager, narrow-shouldered, wearing rumpled gray slacks, a white shirt open at the neck, moldy green Dacron jacket, and brown shoes. Were sales slumping? Had the district manager bawled him out? For whatever reason, he was noticeably glum in this fancy rendezvous with red and black trimmings and gas lamps. He had obviously wandered in off the street, not realizing what kind of place it was.

I stood behind Munday. With confidential nudges, he was rumbling sympathetically: "Beer, hmm? Poor man's refreshment? Mmh, yas. You look peaked, mister. Life gettin' you by the short hairs? Scrimp and save, right, boy? Beans, corned-beef hash, codfish cakes, chicken livers, TV dinners. Dollar in the collection plate, that about it? The wife yellin' at you? Sure . . . say, how much do you make? Seven, eight, nine thousand. Kind of hard on the old self-respect, eh? Well, some have it better than others, that's all. Turn around and look at me. Seen my face before? Of course, you have. On TV. All over the tube. Know how much I make? Half a million a year. That's right. You're sitting next to a man right now who makes one half a million dollars a year. Makes you think, doesn't it? No nine-to-five stuff either. Work when I want to. Snap my fingers, new girl every night. Now then, hey. I've got a proposition for you. Here's an idea. Think it over. If I can arrange it, and I'm pretty sure I can, *how would you like to change places with me?*"

During the last part of this, the man had begun to tilt on his stool, leaning away from Munday, not drunkenly, but with a desperate twining of his toe to find the floor. Abruptly he shoved back from the bar, and his stool was spinning as he marched past me with his hands rammed in his pockets, shouldered out the door, and vanished.

I found myself with a strangely bereft little fat man. Munday spread his hands in real or pretended bewilderment.

"Sensitive little bugger," he said. Which character in his head was speaking? Did he appreciate the damage he had done to the miserable beer drinker? Idle question, because Munday had not *himself* been patronizing the poor man but rather, in the Rackley tradition, *imitating* the kind of oaf who mocks failure as well as deriding the culture that produces him.

An hour later this same type of Zen put-on placed Munday's life in danger—then saved it. For a number of weeks the Renaissance bar had been haunted after midnight by a somber Cuban with a gun. He sat on a corner stool drinking rum and smoking small cigars. Not exactly glaring, he still made people uncomfortable. At first Stanley supposed that the man might belong to a syndicate he knew nothing about. He dressed with twenty-years-past gangster cool, wearing a pearl gray hat, stickpin, even spats, and all the rest. Perhaps a refugee from Castro by way of Miami, he seemed to be emulating the hoodlums he had admired in old movies. Just the same, his presence was intimidating. Though he had no connections that Stanley could discover, there was the gun in the shoulder holster. The man made no threats, said nothing, tipped the barmen reasonably, and appeared to be waiting. The Renaissance management decided to hold back a little longer before bringing in the police. This dark individual had a razored uptight Latin moustache, seemed utterly humorless and a nut besides, the kind who might come back later and shoot up the place.

With the bar filling after the theater, Munday took it into his head to imitate the sinister Cuban. He glowered at his own image in the mirror, fingered an imaginary moustache, and went through an elaborate ceremony of lighting a cigar that wasn't there. At first the man didn't notice anything. But then the drinkers around him, even the bartenders, began to break up. Munday poured on his imitation, twisting his fat face until it somehow became thin, cruel, and ferocious. The moment came when the butt of the routine caught on.

He got up from his stool and approached Munday in a gun fighter's slouch.

"You very funny fellow!" He shoved the comedian against the wall. "Funny little fellow!"

And there was nothing to be done to save Munday, no time.

The gangster reached slowly for his gun. As he did so, a huge lavender handkerchief whipped from Munday's pocket was waved in his face. The comedian minced toward him. The Cuban jumped away, but found himself cornered.

"I'll sthwyke you! I'll *kiw* you!" lisped Munday, dancing in and flicking the man again and again with his gauzy weapon. Witnesses fell off their stools as the Cuban ran. He ran out of the bar, actually bolting out from under his hat, leaving it on the floor. He ran down the street pursued (but not for long) by a flouncing tormentor, now transformed into Isadora Duncan pirouetting with her veil, leaving his *machismo* behind him never to be reclaimed, never to be seen in the Renaissance again.

Stanley set up drinks on the house. The bar fell into an uproar, with Rod Munday the lion. Later I offered a toast to Fred Rackley. Excepting Stanley and Munday, no one had any idea whom I meant, but the comedian shouted wahoo and drank to that.

8. THE POLICEMAN'S TALE

"Intelligence?" the detective said. "You sure you know what you're talking about?" Dominic Rugolo is close to his real name.

We were on his front porch, looking out on a shady street. A damp summer afternoon made the Connecticut shoreline hazy. The policeman now serves on the force of a small town near New London, but for many years he was attached to one of New Haven's high-crime precincts, where he had been shot up several times. As he lay back bare-armed on his porch hammock drinking Budweiser from the can, I saw that both biceps were heavily pitted: "Family fight, this crazy guy with a shotgun . . ."

A swarthy man, he spoke with cold, fleeting smiles that made every question put to him seem a little foolish. "All it comes down to is one thing. Survival . . . nothing else. Intelligence is how you handle yourself in whatever situation you get into. Well, the kind of psycho you mention practically always *survives*. The only thing that kills him is getting bored and taking too many chances, like jumping out of a car at sixty miles an hour or going off a bridge. And that's what makes him so dangerous. He's not afraid of pain as most people are. He won't hold back. Once an impulse gets hold of him, a guy like this is capable of practically anything. Go up against him in an emergency, unless you're trained for it, he'll wipe you out. He may be ignorant compared to you. If you sat down together and took one of those tests you might finish way ahead of him. But how can you measure the animal cunning some of these people have? The way they can calculate the kind of person you are, and make a fool of you?

"I guarantee that even in this town here I can produce a half-dozen psychos, men *and* women, who if the average Yale professor was left alone with them, you know, head to head, for any length of time, they would destroy him. I don't just mean beat him up either. Mentally too! They would know how to confuse and frighten him until he'd break down. So in a scene like that, what good is your education and all the books you've read? I'll give you one example. We saw it happen, about a year ago. Another beer?"

He came back from the refrigerator with two cans, and stretching out again on the hammock, he began his story.

We had this Ivy League shrink who worked with us. He lectured around New England but lived here, and last winter he came down to headquarters and gave a series of talks on "The Psychology of the Habitual Criminal." It was kind of pathetic really. He could tell us, you know, that "children whose oral desires haven't been gratified are marked for life," and heavy information like that. Then he worked as a consultant on some of our cases at the hospital.

I always thought he should have stayed over on his own side of the tracks and made himself into one of those society doctors. He had the perfect name for it. Ian Plummer Ames! How do you like that? Actually I liked him all right. Kind of a nice guy, rosy, fresh-faced, conscientious, very sincere. Married, three kids, churchgoer. He really wanted to do good. Some of our guys laugh at this, but I don't. The trouble was that even though he had his Ivy League Ph.D. and M.D. and had worked in the psycho ward at Bellevue in New York, none of us felt that he had ever really absorbed any real knowledge of what he called "disadvantaged people." On the level of theory he could turn out papers for the *Journal of Psychology*, or whatever it's called, but I don't know, something was wrong. He was just too nice to come anywhere near understanding some of the bastards we have to deal with.

What got him into trouble was this theory he had picked up along the way. He'd started to write a book about it. "Participation With the Patient." One time he lectured us on his idea: "Gentlemen, the day is past when the psychiatrist can pose as an authority figure. He must get down on the same level with his patient and *share* and *compare* experience. Treat your patient like a friend. *Go out and do things together.*" Would you believe it? I knew then he was headed for a bad time, and it wasn't long in coming. You could say that Dr. Ian Plummer Ames got himself locked in a cage with exactly the wrong animal.

Of all the bastards we have in this town, he had to run into Ron Kossi. I think of people as factories. Each one has a product he turns out most of the time. Some, like Kossi, turn out trouble. That's his product. I've been here eight years. From the beginning Kossi has given me personally more trouble than all the rest put together. I don't know how many times I've locked him up. But he always comes back. We've had him part way committed three times. But he has some kind of genius for talking himself out of trouble. Shrinks, probation officers, even a judge who'd had him in his courtroom twice before—they swallow that phony line of his. Oh, sincerely, with tears in his eyes, he's reformed. A different man. Sees the error of his ways. Going back to his family. Won't take another drink. All that crap, over and over again. You wouldn't believe they'd accept it, but they do.

He's a big redheaded bastard, a supersalesman. When he works, that's what he does for a living. He sells used cars, and he's terrific—for a short time. Being a con man, he has a real talent for it. You could say Kossi was a roving salesman. He goes from one lot to another up and down the shoreline. All the dealers know that he's good to sell a dozen cars or so—he's an expert at unloading lemons—before he gets drunk again and quits. That's all right with them, so Kossi has a job anytime he wants it.

Kossi's in his late twenties now. His wife just divorced him, but that doesn't make any difference to a son of a bitch like this. He comes "home"—he still thinks of it that way—whenever the mood strikes him, meaning when he's drunk enough. He yells at her and the kids, breaks the furniture. By the time we arrive there's a wild cop-fighter in there. You have to belt him out. There's no other way.

Where does he live otherwise? Who knows? He keeps changing his address. In a furnished room somewhere. Overnight with whores. So long as the bars are open you can find him somewhere on Vine Street. Or maybe in a bowling alley. Another thing about Kossi. He's got telephonitis. Just for a lark, he'll phone in to headquarters: "I'm crazy! I'm going to kill everybody! Better come and find me!" So the call goes out: Kossi again. Oh, Christ . . . No, he hardly ever does anything that's really terrible. Just the same, somebody like that gets to you. All this troublemaking is some kind of *horseplay* with him. As if his life depends on getting attention, even if it's from the cops, or else he'll die.

He's always threatening suicide. Sometimes he actually carries out the attempt, in a phony way, of course. Getting up on top of buildings, and you have to talk him down. Swallows a hundred aspirins, so you have to get his stomach pumped out. One time he slashed his wrists in a bar. We come in with the doctor. There's blood all over the place. What does he do when our backs are turned but slug the medico and escape in the night.

You know the amusement park near here. He gets in a bar fight. We corner him. He runs out along a big long wharf and dives forty feet into the water. It's night. Everything's black. Man overboard! He's going to drown. "Let him, for Christ's sake," I said, but, of course, we couldn't do that. So we have search-lights sweeping the area. Two of us get in a rowboat. I guessed he might be hiding there among the pilings. There he was, laughing like hell. And I blew my top then and yelled at him: "Kossi! Leave me alone! Drown, you bastard!" Naturally when we hauled him aboard, don't you suppose he tried to capsize us?

That's Ron Kossi, except for one thing. He may be a wild, uneducated son of a bitch, but when he wants to be, this guy is very, very intelligent. He's got a smooth speech and a pleasing voice when he's selling you something. He can put on a sincere act better than anyone I've ever met in my life. And you know what? When he's not giving us trouble, I even like him. I can't explain it.

Anyway, this is the guy that Dr. Ian Plummer Ames has to pick out for "outpatient rehabilitation." This is the guy who the doctor is going to *share* and *compare* experience with. Treat your patient like a friend. "Go out and do things together!"

It was the beginning of summer. Ames had just sent his wife and kids to Maine for two months. Weekends he would generally commute up there. We had pulled Kossi in again. I forget what for. I wasn't in on the arrest. He had been sent to the hospital, as usual. There he managed to get in the women's part and seduce three of them, I think it was, within forty-eight hours. So he was in trouble for that too.

This may have been what first drew Ames's attention to him. I think that Ames secretly, without even knowing it, admired Kossi's success. Kossi was always very good at scoring with a woman right off. He just turned on that used-car-salesman vitality and they would open their legs. Even with his reputation. Everybody knew about him. But he still scored just the same. Maybe he's a great lover for a night or two, until he gets drunk and beats her her up. I wouldn't doubt it.

So Dr. Ian Plummer Ames got himself assigned to Kossi's case. Now watch Kossi work on him. Here are your two intelligences—a psychiatrist M.D. and Ph.D. up against a phony used-car salesman and bar fighter who quit school in the tenth grade. Think of that match-up. No contest, right?

From the first minute, Kossi must have seen he had a live one. An earnest inexperienced mental sort of guy who admired him. He would get outpatient clinical care instead of being confined. This meant, from his standpoint, going to the shrink's office and bullshitting for a few sessions. He was used to that. But he discovered that he also had something else going this time. The doctor wanted to *get to know him.* "What's your favorite sport, Ron? Bowling? Hey, let's go bowling together." Did you ever hear of anything like that? First the couch session; then doctor and patient go to the alleys.

Some of our guys thought it was a faggot thing, but I don't believe that. What Ames hoped to do was to get another case history for his book. Also he felt that following a tough, wild, incorrigible guy onto his own home grounds would somehow be good for him as a man as well as a psychiatrist. Test his courage or something. And beyond that, idealistically, he really cared. He felt it was his job to help Kossi because, he said, "the man has so much potential." You know who explained most of this to me? Kossi himself. Later, after it was over. He was laughing. "Rugolo, Little Doc wanted to feel like a real man!"

So they had three sessions in Ames's office, and nothing much happened, but "all the time," Kossi said, "I was probing for his weakness." It was easy for him because built right into Ames's system of getting down on the same level with the patient was this technique of *mutual confession.* The doctor would admit his own weaknesses and fears in exchange for an admission from the patient. Ames's idea was that in this way brotherhood could work where authority failed.

I don't say Ames's system is all wrong, but with somebody like Kossi it's got to be insane. Because Kossi doesn't feel guilty or ashamed or distressed about anything, and he's not afraid of anything. So you've got no mutual confession. You've got a put-on. You, the doctor, are being sincere and revealing yourself to a cold, lying bastard who's laughing at you all the time. "I made up all kinds of sad stories about when I was a kid," Kossi said. "It used to kill me, the serious look he would get on his face when he wrote them all down."

And so they went bowling together, and went to bars. The mousy little M.D. and the big cat playing with him. As a matter of fact, for a few weeks Kossi got so interested in the game that he stayed out of trouble. But very slowly and carefully he was building up trouble for Ames.

The first thing he did was to sell Ames a used car that the doctor didn't need. I've got to admit it was kind of funny. Ames thought that as part of Kossi's therapy he ought to go out and get a job as soon as possible. Not realizing that Kossi only needed to walk into any lot and the dealer would put him to work. So Kossi, pretending to be proud and grateful, called up Ames saying: "You were right! I've got a job. Come on down and watch me work!"

So Ames went down to Maloney's near the turnpike, and, "Boy," Kossi said, "did I sell him a wreck!" It was an old MG. "Everything was wrong with it. Oil leaks. Clutch practically worn out, brakes out of line." But even if the car had been in good shape, an MG was exactly wrong for Ames, with his family of five. For him to go tooling around in a two-seater was ridiculous. He wasn't that kind of a swinger at all, and he kept saying to Kossi: "But how am I going to explain buying this to my family?" And Kossi, his patient, remember, grabbed him by the arm, stared into his eyes, and told him: "So you and the old lady can get away by *yourselves* once in a while. Make her feel *young* again!"

By now you can see how things were going. Kossi knew his customer. "I could tell he'd buy that 'young again' idea!" Their roles were already beginning to be reversed. At the bowling alley, Kossi was the instructor and he doubled Ames's score after three evenings. They got into that close, sweaty relationship. You can just see the doctor standing back to watch Kossi thundering up to the line and firing his ball like a cannon, with his leg kicking in the air, hitting close to two hundred most of the time. It's got to be both exciting and intimidating, if you see what I mean. And then afterward, the beers and fraternizing with Kossi's bar

companions. "Meet my friend, the doc. I'm in his *custody!*" And
Kossi said to me: "I'd always get him to be the one to put quarters
in the jukebox. You'd see Little Doc, serious, you know, standing
there, picking out the rock numbers he thought we'd like!"

I saw them together once, in one of Kossi's favorite places,
Irene's on Vine Street. Kossi was loud as usual but not drunk.
Ames sat at the bar, making himself small, with a beer in front
of him. He didn't exactly look frightened but more unsure, a
little mystified, trying to pretend that he didn't feel out of place.
Kossi looked at me and winked, jerking his head in Ames's direction.

One weekend when Ames was in Maine with his family,
Kossi got drunk and ended up in jail again. By his standards, the
charges against him weren't so bad. He hadn't hit anybody, just
bad-mouthed an officer. When Ames came back and heard about
it, he was hurt and depressed. He had hoped that his mutual confessions and friendship treatment of Kossi would pay off. Naturally Kossi got out on low bail with his usual routine. It would
never happen again. He'd got drunk because he felt lonely. He
guessed he needed the doctor's shoulder to lean on. A friendly
hand at the right time. If he could only have called up his psychiatrist on the phone . . .

Evidently Ames believed this, and made his stupidest mistake.
He gave Kossi his private night phone number and told him to
call anytime. Meanwhile, though we didn't know it and Ames
certainly had no idea of what was happening, Kossi had completed his inventory of the doctor's weaknesses. Actually it was
one main vulnerable point that Kossi had located. Ames was
terrified of physical violence. Now, free again and ready for some
fun, Kossi began to get on Ames little by little.

What happened was that Ames started to realize he was out
of his depth. He tried to withdraw from bowling and nights in the
Vine Street bars—but Kossi wasn't about to let him withdraw. No,
he didn't have any especially important reason for this. It just
pleased his sense of humor and that cat-and-mouse cruelty he
has. Now he decided to call up Ames in the middle of the night.
We'd been getting these calls at headquarters for years. Now it
was the doctor's turn. "I'm desperate, Doc! I'm going to cut my

wrists!" The first time Ames got dressed and went down to the
bar and found Kossi in no trouble at all, except a little drunk.
Kossi grabbed his arm and forced him up to the bar and made
Ames drink a couple of beers before letting him go home.

Kossi explained to me later that he had started slowly to build
up the level of (for him) playful violence during their regular
sessions. He would suddenly grab the doctor's wrist or his arm,
or grip his shoulder, and stare at him. Each time Ames would
jump back with a look of panic, and then Kossi would let go, at
the same time making his stare more intense and fierce. Then,
after leaning back for a while, he would slowly move closer and
closer to the doctor and suddenly grab him again.

"He'd piss in his pants!" Kossi said.

By this time the doctor knew he was in a trap and started
struggling to get out. Answering the midnight phone calls, he
refused to come down and join Kossi in the bar, or wherever he
was. Then he had the therapy sessions transferred from his office
to the hospital. As he guessed, Kossi began not to show up, which
was now all right with Ames. But Kossi guessed that too. His
answer was to arrive on time every other session, just to keep
Ames off balance.

The sessions got worse and worse from the standpoint of
playful physical violence. Kossi now took to punching Ames in
the ribs or on the shoulder during his phony "confessions." It
was obvious even to Ames that Kossi was showing up only for
fun. Ames then did something that he would never have done a
few months before. Sacrificing his principles, he offered to declare Kossi competent and responsible and to certify to the court
that he no longer needed to remain in psychiatric custody. You
have to know Ames to understand what a blow that would be
to his self-respect. Because whatever else you'd want to say
about him, he was sincere in his beliefs and had really believed
in the technique of sharing and comparing experience with the
patient and treating him like a brother. He must have known that
to recommend releasing Kossi was dishonest on his part and was
something he was doing only because he was afraid.

Now watch Kossi. This is true evil. He refused to be released!

No, he wouldn't feel right about that. No, sir. "I need more treatment!" I saw Ames a couple of times then. He walked around
trembling, with his head down. His family would be coming back
soon. What would they think of these night calls that now were
getting to be meaner and more threatening? And looking at him
I thought: Who's the shrinker now? Who's getting therapy? Who's
being educated?

You wouldn't believe what Kossi tried next. He got on Ames
to sell him another used car! Ames, I heard, had driven the MG
only once and then hid it in his back yard. Not knowing how to
explain this second car to his family, he had decided one night
to drive it off the highway, take off all identifying marks, and
abandon it, and he did this. As I said, you have to know Ames
to appreciate what kind of a moral defeat that was. He's the type
who would walk across the street to put a candy-bar wrapping
in the litter basket. And yet now out of fear of what his family
would think he'd secretly litter the roadside with that wreck of
an MG he had wanted to refuse in the first place but hadn't dared.

Then Kossi came after him again. By this stage all pretense
was gone. Kossi was out to humiliate Ames and drive him crazy.
Ames had his private number changed. But Kossi started to drive
his car back and forth in front of Ames's house late at night, honking his horn. And the doctor's family was coming home in a
week.

One morning when I reported in at eight, there was Ames
whimpering in the station house. The doctor was a wreck. There
were big gray circles under his eyes. Kossi, he said, had come by
his house and insisted that he buy another car from him.

"I refused, and he tried to run me down!"

Kossi had got back in the car, started it up, and headed
straight for the doctor, who had to jump behind a tree.

"You've got to protect me from him!"

I talked to Kossi, and he laughed: "Aw, Doc's imagining
things. He's just nervous . . ."

We warned Kossi not to bother Ames anymore, but there
was nothing we could do unless we actually caught him in some
kind of harassment.

But Dr. Ian Plummer Ames was finished. Not only did he quit as Kossi's counselor, but overnight, without telling anybody, he dropped all counseling work with us and at the hospital. For a couple of weeks nobody saw him. Shortly after his family came back, he had some kind of breakdown. The whole business with Kossi had ruined his confidence and the picture he had of himself. You know what? They moved. The Ames family put up their house for sale and left town. I don't know where they went.

Kossi? He's here. The other day we almost got rid of him. He crashed in on his ex-wife again and said he'd swallowed a bottle of pills, this time having washed them down with a pint of rum. He showed her the pint of Bacardi, smashed it on the floor, and passed out.

Usually when something like this happened she'd get on the phone, you know, hysterically, and we'd shoot the ambulance over there and pump him out. But this time she just sat by the phone, looking at him sprawled on the rug, and did nothing. She said her hand felt paralyzed and that she couldn't move it to lift up the phone. She thought how nobody would blame her, and how good it would be for the world if the son of a bitch would just die. But then being a good Catholic girl, she couldn't go through with it, and phoned in. As it turned out, this time he might have died, the rum and pills having a synergistic effect. But you know sometimes I get the feeling that it isn't luck; that Kossi is meant to survive forever; that for some reason beyond me the Lord puts these bastards on earth to make the rest of us pay for our sins.

I saw him yesterday in the bowling alley. He gives me this big grin, as if I hadn't busted him on the jaw and locked him up six or seven times. "Hi, Chief!" He likes to call me that. And I thought of Little Doc Ames and all his good intentions off somewhere hiding in another town, trying to pull himself together.

You know, I don't scare much, but Kossi spooks me. I swear he does. I keep thinking he knows something I don't. It's that kind of animal understanding he has, of what life's all about when you strip it down. Of course, he's wrong. If this man isn't pure evil, there is no evil. By the way, could that be possible?

9. THERE NEVER WAS A MOMENT
WHEN EVIL WAS REAL

Near the end of the 1960's a twenty-one-year-old boy with a name like Johnny Jameson, going nowhere, got behind the wheel of his car. Driving through four western states with his girl by his side, he shot to death in various towns three men and two women. With one possible exception, the killings had no motive. "Just target practice," a highway patrolman said. Johnny shot a man and wife on their front lawn; the second man in a parking lot; the third, a filling-station attendant (the only victim for whom an explanation was offered), because he had been too slow putting gasoline into the car; and the second woman, a young girl of twenty, was struck down like all the others by a single bullet as she came out of a lavatory in the park.

Psychiatrists examining the skinny blond boy found him to be a sociopath but not psychotic, hence fully responsible in his head for the cross-country homicides. After a two-day trial he was judged guilty and sentenced to death.

He had never been conventionally religious. None of the orthodox faiths held out any meaning for him, and he rejected the comfort offered by prison chaplains. But in the United States, especially in the western part, we have scores of itinerant evangelists, self-ordained preachers of the Word of God, determined not to abandon a doomed boy like Johnny. And they arrive at the gates demanding to see the prisoner.

These preachers are often ignorant, craggy-faced men with blazing eyes that project frightening authority. Wild souls, they tramp across the landscape, holding down a job here and there before moving on. Their congregations assemble in skid rows or free-speech areas in a city park. But they have an eye out for the damned. With any credentials at all, sometimes with none, they enter our jails and console lost men.

Such a preacher was Stewart Hunt, a bank guard most of the day, who became a regular caller on Johnny Jameson while his sentence was under appeal. Almost immediately after these visits began, a change was noted in Johnny's behavior. His probation officer observed:

The defendant has been dallying into the study of metaphysics, or is suffering from a delusional system or both . . . Apparently [he] at this time accepts the fact that the soul can leave the body and then return, and, therefore, if he is "away" when the court takes action against him, such action would be irrelevant.

Pending a discussion with Mr. Hunt there will be no opportunity to know what is the nature of the relationship between Johnny Jameson and Mr. Hunt. Does Mr. Hunt believe him to be innocent and is [he] teaching him out of a motive of mercy or is there collusion between the two to mislead the psychiatrists? . . .

From evidence that can be observed at this time, Johnny is definitely attempting to escape the reality of his dilemma with the law by means of a form of *astral projection* . . . While the defendant wishes to make the "trip" before final sentencing, he is not at this time sure whether his body will die.

Suspicion grew that Stewart Hunt was dedicated, for whatever reason, to helping Johnny Jameson feign madness. To determine what was going on between the two, the following conversation was surreptitiously taped.

To avoid mockery, the preacher's references to "Gawd" haven't been transcribed as they are pronounced. Still, this is exactly the way Hunt says it, and the pronunciation—pounded home over and over again—achieves, on the tape, a certain hypnotic effect.

Questions . . . Who in the world are these people? Is this only a dialogue between two madmen and nothing more? May we detect a brotherhood of psychopaths? What stage of enlightenment has the country reached to produce a man and a boy such as the two speaking in Johnny Jameson's cell?

PREACHER: Okay, look now, you listen. What you have to maintain is this awareness that you are the One Infinite Intelligence.

PRISONER: People keep coming in and ordering, and ordering and ordering. But they're just images and I keep telling them that. Just the same they keep trying to get in, so I just lock them out completely, and I can do it.

PREACHER: All right, how do you do it? How do you lock them out?

PRISONER: I just go into the Light, that's all. And it's with me all the time. It just gets stronger and stronger, and they don't exist anymore. It's like a fragmentation of the mind: arms, legs, and bodies disappear, and finally there's nothing.

PREACHER: Yes, and now you're in this Great Void. Good. You're the first student I've ever had that's done so well in so short a time. You're doing perfectly. But don't forget now that *everything is an image*—whether it appears to you as mental or it's the one you're looking at. They're all mere images, and the only life they have is the life that *you* give them.

PRISONER: Uh hnn.

PREACHER: The only place that any appearance can claim to be is right there in your awareness. It's not actually out there. *There is no one out there.* When you stay in the Infinite Light as the Infinite Light, you have not let in one dark image of mortal thought. And that kind of thought, you must understand, is absolutely unreal. If you believe you are seeing something real out there, it is only that you have let the Devil come in and take over your God-Awareness of Light and Glory.

We live in the City of God. We dwell there. You as man image, and a false image at that, *never existed*. Nothing and nobody and God never made that false image body. But you as Infinite Spirit-Light, God dwelling in Infinite Light and Glory that you are, are the being of God. Not Johnny Jameson being God, but God Being Himself. The human sense of existence must be entirely eliminated from awareness, and we give up, surrender wholly to God. God is living and being Himself. He lives you. So working, we must see that in ourselves there never was anything but God, Spirit, Light, dwelling in its own brightness and glory.

Then that appearance of aggressive suggestion, the one that is saying to you that there is something out there, and people out there, is all a lie, just a bad dream. The One Infinite Intelligence cannot go, or do anything. It cannot have hallucinations or anything of that sort. You see. It just isn't so. You have to be God to the extent that you can look right at any so-called appearance and see its own Light and Glory. For you can never see anything but Yourself, so what are you identifying as?

PRISONER: You have Infinite Spirit. Nothing but you. That's it.

PREACHER: Right! There is a Path that the fowls have not known. The vulture's eye has not seen it. The young lions have not discovered it. Nor the roaring lion gone over it.

PRISONER: Uh hnn. But, you know, whenever I begin to feel this, I seem to reduce my degree of awareness. That's the only way I can effectively explain it to you. This boiling in my ears, and it's very, very sensitive. The top of my head is very sensitive, like it's boiling. Even now I can't touch it.

PREACHER: That's all right. Just remember that the body and the top of the head and all is just a concept.

PRISONER: These images . . . They just want to talk. But as soon as I try to talk to them—you know, like I would talk to you right now—then it seems like something was punishing me. It just follows me around and says: "Don't do it. Don't do it."

PREACHER: Can God be punished?

PRISONER: No.

PREACHER: All right. Now you have to wipe out those images, and I think it would be easier for you to do this if you'll say what I tell you. *You are Nothing and Nobody and God never made you.* God Spirit dwelling in Infinite Light and Glory is all there is. Work it out completely, and go into your Light and stay in the Light as Light. Regardless of what those images tell you. Don't forget that *there are no people.* Nothing to poison you, as you wrote in your letter. There is no poison. All these are dark images coming into your mind. Reality. What is reality? *You* are the only reality. This mundane business is a concept, you see.

PRISONER: Yes, well it does seem extremely mundane, as if there was a world and something existed, but then now it seems to have gone away. Everything is imaginary. Everything is just floating around.

PREACHER: All right. Everything *is* diaphanous. There is no solidity. Every wall you see is diaphanous. Now I got the gist in your letter of some thought about "eliminating this grotesque form named Johnny . . ."

PRISONER: I just wanted to get rid of the body, you know. It seems like it's hindering me. I just want to destroy it. And if I couldn't do it mentally, then do it physically, just to get rid of it.

PREACHER: No. You don't do this, because then you are playing right along with your images. You are God. Can God destroy Himself?

PRISONER: No. Well, that was what I was trying to do. I thought maybe if I just—

PREACHER: There is no Johnny Jameson. You are denying the Allness of God by even thinking like that. Now, I know that you trust me completely, and understand that I wouldn't lead you astray, not for one iota.

PRISONER: Yeah, I do.

PREACHER: Not for any reason at all.

PRISONER: Right.

PREACHER: So I will stick with you come hell or high water. Even to the end of the world. Now you must, must, stick with this.

PRISONER: But then something . . . like when I talk to somebody, they just feel like tiny little voices. I don't know what they're saying really. And they tell me . . . people I'm supposed to remember, and I really don't, truly . . . they think I'm nuts. But it really doesn't matter because they're just images, and I tell them this, and I—

PREACHER: Yes, well can you distinguish people that come and visit you? Like me? Do you know when they come to you?

PRISONER: Yes, sort of, but they—

PREACHER: Right. See, you are the One Infinite Intelligence, Johnny, and we do not throw our pearls before the swine. In other words, we don't tell them what we inside know. Act like they do. If they ask you questions, answer them on their level.

PRISONER: Yeah, but I just don't know their level anymore. I just can't make any correlation between them. There's just nothing. I can't explain; I can't be articulate.

PREACHER: There *is* nothing. I agree with you one hundred per cent. But at the same time, since they are so stupid, and so nothing, that we come down to their . . . remember that God is dimensionless. He can take any dimension. High or low. You are this one Supreme Being. It is *they* who are insane, not we. They don't know this, so we play along with them. But inwardly we maintain that poise. We are God, Spirit, and—

PRISONER: But when it comes out, it *seems* as if it were a physical reaction. My ears are ringing terribly, and I hurt all over, and I can hear every organ, like screaming little caterpillars, screaming to get out. But of course, I realize, I know it doesn't exist and I'll just ignore it. And it only happens when I try to talk to these people. Like it's really painful to talk—

PREACHER: Now, I want to read you a couple of sentences. There are no persons. Live in the City of God where Light and Glory everywhere meet with Light and Glory. There never has been anything else. No humans. There is no world out there. It is what you live, as your own God-Being. And everything is within you. You see, there is no Out There. There are no solid walls anywhere. All is diaphanous, pure mist. Pure light.

PRISONER: I see.

PREACHER: You see, *there never was a moment when evil was real.*

PRISONER: Then obviously I couldn't have forgot anything, because I never remembered anything to forget. Because I know everything.

PREACHER: You are the One Infinite Intelligence. Stay in that awareness all the time, regardless of—

PRISONER: Because I was beginning to think maybe something was wrong, but I don't think so now. Because—

PREACHER: What is wrong? You see, these are all appearances coming to you. Aggressive expressions. This is the only Devil there is, you see, the mind. And it will take any form to try to induce you to believe that you are not God.

PRISONER: I'd like to get along with all these appearances. I don't bother them, but when they start to bother me, try to bother me like get inside . . . it just seems then that like the physical reaction is so strong that— What I think is that I would rather just destroy my physical self just as soon as I can.

PREACHER: Now don't you dare, because then where will you be?

PRISONER: There will be nothing.

PREACHER: You will be one of them. You will be one of them! Yessir. You do not destroy the physical appearance because there is none.

PRISONER: But why then would it be so extremely painful, the other?

PREACHER: What do you mean?

PRISONER: It just seems painful that . . . like right now everything bothers me. I don't know why. I mean talking to you . . . it's not as much as with other people, but—

PREACHER: This is again the human mind trying to get you to do away with this somebody that thinks there are things besides the One Infinite Intelligence and One Infinite Light that you are. The glory of your being is radiating light all the time. And this is what you have to maintain. This awareness. All the time. And before I forget, I will come any time you call, so don't hesitate. Did the doctor come last night?

PRISONER: No, I don't know. Nobody saw me. Somebody came. Somebody by the name of Milton or something.

PREACHER: He was the doctor, I think. Your mother thought you were ill.

PRISONER: No, I was just afraid of him for some reason. But then I just went into my Light and ignored him. And you know, there just wasn't anything there. He asked me some strange questions, but beyond that it was nothing. I told him I wasn't eating. You know, if somebody was trying to poison me I still have this physical thing. And it's true. They were trying to poison me, and—

PREACHER: Now see. Who's saying this?

PRISONER: Well, nothing. That's what I thought.

PREACHER: Was God thinking this?

PRISONER: No.

PREACHER: Is there anything besides God?

PRISONER: No.

PREACHER: See, that has to be your first question every time. Is this God? Can God be saying this? Can He be thinking this? Is there anyone to poison me? God is All means God is All. There are no ifs, ands, buts, or maybes. No exceptions. Not an image. And you are this All. Could God poison Himself?

PRISONER: No.

PREACHER: Could God destroy Himself?

PRISONER: No.

PREACHER: You are God-Being, you see. Oh, the devil-sent mind will come to you. You don't know how it's played hell with me. I've had warfare many, many times where I've stayed up night and day battling. But you've got to battle, fight, fight, fight. You are God. Bearing the Light. That's all. You're going through the initiation right now. That's all this is. An initiation. And you've got to walk straight on ahead in this Light. As the Light, nothing can touch you. Oil flames may lick your boots and you might feel a twinge, but it will all be nothing, nothing. You will walk through victoriously, as the pure Morning Light that you are. God-Being. So don't flinch for a second. Nobody is poisoning you. Nobody can poison you. Is there anybody else? Is there anybody else? So who can be doing this?

PRISONER: I'm beginning to see it all clear.

PREACHER: These are images, all images. Whether they seem to be out there or inside, they're images. The mind is a mirror and it's reflecting images. And Image is nothing.

PRISONER: Uhnn. Sometimes in myself, I throw things around and around. But it's like a mental gymnastics, and I think that just because it's something that I've never done before I would enjoy it. Like another route . . .

PREACHER: Do you remember our discussions about *The Wall Street Journal* and so forth?

PRISONER: Yeah.

PREACHER: Would you like a *Journal*?

PRISONER: They won't let me have it.

PREACHER: They won't? I didn't know that. Have you asked?

PRISONER: Uh hnn.

PREACHER: Well, it doesn't matter anyhow. Do you have any reading material or do you want any?

PRISONER: No, I've got my *Fortune*s and some financial books, and I'm writing. Just writing a lot.

PREACHER: Well, keep writing to me. I got your letter and it was real good. I'm real proud. You've got the theory and you're practicing real good. But your only problem now is these images. You're having a hard time distinguishing between the real and the unreal. *You* are the only reality there is. If they prepared a meal for you with four or five pounds of arsenic, it would still be an image, you see. Absolutely. They couldn't do that to you. How could a shadow touch God?

PRISONER: But last night, you know, I talked to somebody. I don't know who he was. I don't know if he was real or not. It sounds funny, I know, and paranoiac and schizophrenic and everything else. But in paranoia it's only an illusion, and in schizophrenia it's only a fantasy, but this was something I knew to be real.

PREACHER: Now, wait a minute, remember—

PRISONER: Yeah, but, just like I'm talking to you, I was talking to this thing in my cell. They were all saying that I was crazy, but I wasn't, because I saw this thing. It wasn't my fault that they couldn't see it. Because, you know, it doesn't exist anyway, so I thought it was just a mice-chattering noise.

PREACHER: Like I told you earlier, you must be able to go in and out of the various dimensions so far as people are concerned. *You* know that there is only one dimension, which is the dimensionless dimension, so when you are talking to people, come down to their level and act like other people. God never makes a jackass out of Himself.

PRISONER: What am I here for right now? Do you know?

PREACHER: Where?

PRISONER: Just like, what am I doing right now?

PREACHER: Where are you now? You are in this clear, dazzling, transparent Light. You see. You have never left it. All I see is this pure, clear, transparent Light when I see you.

PRISONER: Yes, but what should I say when they ask me questions like that? When they ask me what am I doing? Because I really and truly don't know.

PREACHER: What am I doing? Say you put me in here. "Who am I?" Say to them: "Do you want my name?"

PRISONER: Yeah, but I really don't have a name, now, so how can I give them a name?

PREACHER: I know that, but they don't. You see?

PRISONER: Just make up a name or something?

PREACHER: Your name is Johnny Jameson. Give 'em that.

PRISONER: But I mean, is it really?

PREACHER: No. But don't forget that you're dropping to their level. You know that and *I* know that. I am your awareness and you are my awareness, and this is God. Awareness is all we are. So get down to their level and answer their questions. Even though they're idiotic. You know this and I know this. So you, the One Infinite Intelligence, would actually be helping them to find their own glory by coming down to them, playing their game. Of course, *they* are the ones who should be locked up in strait jackets, but they don't know this.

PRISONER: Yeah, but it really sounds awful and paradoxical, but I really don't know when I'm talking to somebody. It's just like I don't know if I'm talking to you right now. I just don't believe it. It's very hard to believe.

PREACHER: Well, that's right, you see, because Beauty and Light is infinite and Beauty and Light is all there is. We're in it all the time, and the more you do this, the more you develop as you are doing. The more you stay in this Light-Awareness, because this is all there is, you see.

PRISONER: Yeah, but as soon as I come down to a level, I guess you would say, it's very painful and I don't know why. Why would that be?

PREACHER: Again it's a mental thing.

PRISONER: Like just now?

PREACHER: Sure . . . you're Light, transparent Light, joy, freshness, numbness, vitality. This is all that you are. But your physical appearance as a form and a mind are going to battle you every inch of the way.

PRISONER: The physical part feels lethargic, you know.

PREACHER: Feels what?

PRISONER: Lethargic, blasé.

PREACHER: Well, it's absolutely nothing.

PRISONER: It feels like it's trying to contain something. I feel like if I'm cut open it will get out. You know what I mean? I can't explain it other than that.

PREACHER: There is no *out*. Remember, everything *is* already, everything coexisting simultaneously now, and it's all within you. There is no form and there never was any. Never. No Johnny Jameson. So if you were to feel that you would dissolve this form, physical form, you would just be part of it. It wouldn't do that much for you. You see, you would be enmeshed in it more than ever. You cannot become a shadow. You are Infinite Spirit-Light. Don't you dare think of anything like that. No, no! You're *pure*. These are your images. This is the battle you're fighting right here.

PRISONER: Yes, but just the whole world. The whole universe. Everything seems like that tiny little speck there compared to—

PREACHER: That's true . . .

PRISONER: And it means just exactly that much, that little, to me, but they don't seem to understand—

PREACHER: Naturally they don't. But don't forget that you have to play their little game, so that we can go on from here, you see. Play their game, but inwardly stay poised. Hey, let me see you smile.

PRISONER: Oh, I can smile.

PREACHER: But I haven't seen ya. There you go. (*Laughter.*) There you go! Because it's just a big joke!

PRISONER: Well, it seems like it really because—

PREACHER: It is, it's really funny. Remember what I told you all along. It's the same as reading the funny papers.

PRISONER: Yeah, that's it exactly. Everyone is walking about so serious about everything, and just sometimes their legs go walking one place and their bodies go off another place, and . . .

PREACHER: That's right, because you see, everything is diaphanous.

PRISONER: And I want to look at them and laugh. I don't want to offend them or anything, but—

PREACHER: They're nothing and nobody. God never made any forms.

PRISONER: You know, it's strange. I was talking to this man, and I felt like laughing because his posterior, you know, was where his face should be. All jumbled up, and I wanted to laugh at him because it seemed funny.

PREACHER: True, because there are no forms. In fact, in the physical form, as it seems to be, there is more space between the cells than solidity. But it's all diaphanous, these walls, everything. It's a pure, transparent essence. This Light and Glory that you are is all there is.

PRISONER: I sort of felt this way on LSD one time, but not as strongly. It's like the difference between a cigarette and heroin.

PREACHER: What did you say?

PRISONER: I said I felt this way on LSD one time, a long time ago.

PREACHER: Well, this even transcends that. I know, because I've had some too, and it can't even be compared. Because it's still a mental-physical combination—the LSD or marijuana, or whatever you take. But this transcends all. It doesn't take a physical form. This is forever. There was never a beginning and never an end. No birth ever, and no death. Ever. You see, even if a man was taken to an electric chair and they strapped him in there, they couldn't harm him if he stayed in this awareness. They couldn't possibly harm that man, but he would have to stay in that awareness. And how can God be done anything to? Now . . . I have never gotten around to giving you a number of books I wanted you to read. Especially about the man who had to go through this cave, and there were snakes and earthquakes and everything, and he—

PRISONER: Hey, I'm beginning to see these things. They're bad. Wow . . .

PREACHER: You what?

PRISONER: I say I see these things around all the time, but they're no different than anything else . . .

PREACHER: You have to wipe them out. This is your initiation like I told you. Every student goes through this initiation. Remember, Saint George knocked down every single dragon.

PRISONER: I have to go, I think.

PREACHER: Call me or get in touch with me, and write me.

PRISONER: Okay.

PREACHER: Thanks a lot, and remember that you are the One Infinite Light. I'm with you. Smile . . .

PRISONER: Okay.

Partly as a result of this recorded conversation with Stewart Hunt, Johnny Jameson, upon appeal, was later determined to be legally insane. He was committed to the State Hospital rather than to the penitentiary, and the gas chamber. Mr. Hunt has left his job as bank guard and moved on elsewhere.

III

Bridge to the
New Psychopathy

We have a new situation. In the past year, perhaps two years, it seems almost overnight, events caught up with medical and sociological expertise: the psychopathic style has become epidemic around the country.

Hence, we have no quarry. There's no need to hunt for psychopaths, identify, classify, isolate them. The style has infiltrated everywhere. And in trying to pin it down, the single-minded pursuit of a mysterious mental illness or defect in the nervous system turns out to be not nearly informative enough. Certainly to deny psychopathy as an aberration of some sort would be foolish. But today psychopathic behavior can no longer be described *only* in terms of a disease. Rather it should be explored also as something else: a release of newly developed impulses in late-twentieth-century heads.

The style, for many, appears to have evolved away from its destructive and criminal sources. Of course, the antisocial model persists. The moral moron is loose. His atrocities (as, say, with the loan shark's savagery) have become institutionalized. But today we have a new phenomenon: a milder, often drug-induced psychopathy in which many outlaw values—relating, for instance, to time, responsibility, and the reach for immediate pleasure— remain, but not necessarily in destructive form. Thus, criminal as well as revolutionary sociopaths and free-form psychopaths of varying persuasions exist side by side, sharing many characteristics, but even so they can't fairly be judged the same.

Probation Officer Dan Sakall of Tucson remarks that most sociopaths coming under his jurisdiction "would be better suited for frontier living than the complex living of our modern society." One hundred years ago in the American Southwest, he pointed out, gunslinging psychopaths like Billy the Kid arrived in such numbers that no one thought to describe them as mentally ill. Dodge City, Roswell, and Las Cruces more or less accepted these adventurers as bad news but not crazy, to be hanged or shot if it

came to that, but otherwise put up with as the kind of actors you
would expect to find in a violent theater.

Medical libraries contain scores of authoritative papers on the
mystery of the psychopath. Most of these work as well-documen-
ted and illuminating presentations, but even so, as we have seen,
they tend to project conventional middle-class values. The psychopath is unhesitatingly identified as an absolute misfit, and sick.

But suppose one day that the mild family man, brilliant
Ph.D., the expert on psychopathy, who knows nothing of menace
in his own life, wakes up, looks around in alarm to discover that
his middle-class security guard has vanished—one son perhaps in
jail for assaulting a dean, another on heroin, his daughter pregnant in a commune, and even his wife giggling over her first
illegal smoke. Stripped, no longer safe, he finds himself living on
the edge of a freaky, violent frontier he never knew existed. The
analytical techniques that have served him so efficiently seem all
at once useless. What then becomes of his carefully constructed
understanding of the psychopath's behavior patterns? For he
himself, sitting at home, in his classroom or laboratory, may
shortly be engulfed by the very psychopathy he presumes to
investigate.

Not surprisingly, a great many of the analytical studies con-
ducted by such authorities come across as old hat now. The
prevalence of what was once comfortably defined as deviant behavior has turned the game around. Indeed, the psychopath now
pursues, defies, and may be bent on remaking *us*. Whether violent or passive, he seems concerned only with today, and this
way of living has grown into a philosophical or even spiritual
force that seriously (or laughing) threatens all that we have
been taught to believe in.

Tattered people calling themselves saints gently put us on
with weird questions from the Orient. Boisterous ones on motorcycles or riding in painted buses roar through town grabbing
for our daughters. Sharp, swaggering men buy, sell, and cheat
us. The polluter yawns, making his home elsewhere. Obviously
these individuals must be abnormal in one respect or another,
either softly irresponsible, promiscuously and goofily gentle, or
impulsive as children, raffish, brutes, bastards much too cool,
often criminals and crazy. We maintain. But for millions who

don't agree with us, the traditional (rational) criteria defining mental health no longer hold good. Many such new heads feel certain that we—the straight, decently restrained people—are the ones with disordered psyches.

So medical diagnosis of the aberration understood as psychopathy could soon become not very important. What else, if not the illness itself but a headlong free-form style derived from it may be about to *turn into the norm?* And in this sort of predominantly psychopathic society, the sober, rational examiners who devise such classifications would be judged abnormal. Worse, we could be laughed at, with our learned pages used as paper airplanes. Dispassionate scientific inquiry—spending days and nights indoors, tabulating statistics, poking patients, animals, or both with precision instruments, subjecting them to tests, electric shock, etc.—might then itself come to be imagined as weird.

Fantastic projection? No, this prospect may fade or suddenly change, but at the moment the outline of such a society has already emerged. Although originally founded on an antisocial condition, it offers exciting new alternatives to the way we have lived until now.

Certainly an evil side of the condition persists. Establishment and outlaw psychopathy come together at My Lai. Anyone who has a satchel to carry it away can buy dynamite. Everybody who wants one has a gun, possesses a needle, with psychopathy of gun, torch, bomb, and needle all routine now, and the notion of an impending apocalypse long since old news except to the old.

We have all the crazy ones, diabolists, savage bikers, wild racists of all colors, skyjackers, and also dumpers of nerve gas into the ocean, poisoners of the atmosphere, water, and earth, war-blinded temporarily driven psychopathic gunners of slant-eyed women and babies, writers of filthy letters to war widows, dialers of obscene phone calls to wives of airmen shot down over North Vietnam, those who insert razor blades in Halloween apples for trick-or-treating children, and the one who threw pepper in the eyes of the zoo donkey.

But the violent style produces, too, an uprising of, according to certain new standards, *responsible* people who refuse to live within the law when they believe the law to be stupid or unreal. Those, for instance, who, tired of arguing against the war, fling themselves in front of tanks and trains, bomb draft-board headquarters, and smash and burn draft files. Or those dedicated to saving the environment by such action as chopping down billboards and dousing the board of directors' room with muck and refuse from the company's own products.

Psychopaths? Extremists cast up from the varied American undergrounds? Where do these people come from—the emerging worlds of dope, rock, mystical vision achieved with or without acid, communes inspired by the suddenly fervent adoration of Jesus? The categories into which we once fitted them seem so much more difficult to apply than they formerly were.

What matters is that the outlaws we so carefully classified according to one theory or another as borderline mental cases, if not crazy, have arrived massively on our scene, and now confront us. A host of rebel souls, some clinically psychopathic, others not, run loose around the country untreated—and they have begun en masse defying and invading the citadels of those who traditionally sit in judgment of them. These headlong people in all their exciting variations not only live by different moral standards but have actually started to change the rules that once governed our conceptions of mental health. Are they abnormal? Who is to be the authority for saying so? Can we make the old classifications stick?

Even now, to label someone a psychopath and try to treat him psychiatrically seldom works. It's hard, almost ridiculously so, to treat somebody who is laughing at you and, as Dylan sang, drawing crazy patterns on your sheets. Medical authority has little or no luck with such an individual, and there are so many of him. He doesn't care what diagnosis we hand down. He simply will have no respect for it.

Outlaw attacks on bourgeois complacency and innocence, such as those described in Section II, no longer serve as startling examples of anything. They've become almost routine. For among large elements of the population, symptoms of psychopathy as illness and style *have now merged.* You can hardly, if at all, tell them apart anymore. Walk out on the street, read the paper, watch television, and nothing formerly described as psychopathic seems out of the ordinary. Thus, the researcher can find no relief. He scarcely knows where to look next, as the distinction blurs hopelessly between present-day psychopathic patterns as observed in prisons, institutions, and clinics, and equivalent behavior, which may often be put to use in good causes, outside these places.

Imagine a psychologist of whatever old school confronted, say, by Jerry Rubin—author, among other things, of the Yippie manifesto *Do It!* This manual for insurrection grooves strangely with Zen humor, as Jerry preaches the inevitability of a new apocalypse to smash the outgoing society and make the world ready for love. He also proclaims measurements of sanity as well as moral standards all but unthinkable a few years ago. Like this: "What's needed is a new generation of nuisances. A new generation of people who are freaky, crazy, irrational, sexy, angry, irreligious, childish and mad . . ."

Or for example: "All money represents theft. To steal from the rich is a sacred and religious act. To take what you need is an act of self-love, self-liberation. While looting, a man to his own self is true."

And with such humor as: "Are the Kennedys Assassination-Prone?"

And his program: "Our tactic is to send niggers and longhair scum invading white middle-class homes, fucking on the living room floor, crashing on the chandeliers, spewing sperm on the Jesus pictures, breaking the furniture and smashing Sunday school napalm-blood Amerika forever."

Now then, is Jerry Rubin crazy? Pretending to be? Psychopathic, at least? Fuck, yes! he would shout. All those! Like Allen Ginsberg, who in *Howl* first brought rejected and despised madmen off the streets to confront a complacent culture, Jerry would be glad to embrace identification by middle-class label as any kind of a lunatic.

What good then are our old labels? How will civilized reformers deal with such people? Even more urgently, what may these people be about to do to us—and just possibly, *for* us?

Assume then (though it may abort) that something like an uprising of psychopaths is under way. In the beginning, we have supposed, the reflexes that produce such an uprising may be observed in the nervous systems of brain-damaged, neglected, or badly treated children. They also come (we concede this all too easily) from slum ferocity generated out of injustice and squalor. Dutifully we have traced, studied, watched out for, tried to control these dangerous reflexes, locked them up, tranquilized them, provided them with odd jobs. But at last there are too many damaged souls, including those of dropout privileged middle-class children, for us to keep in order. They have broken free—and the psychopathic spirit infiltrates everywhere, appearing simultaneously as illness, style, and new consciousness.

Again, the free-form style may fade out, be repressed, or change in some unforeseen way. Not only has this tremendous psychic shift just begun, but the long-range effects on it, for instance, of LSD and other such materials, not to mention the inroads of the despised aging process, won't be revealed for years.

Just the same, our new trip promises to be a long one. Already the breakaway spirit in its two forms—(1) headlong, pitiless action, and (2) quiescent dropping out, abandonment of the whole idea of leading a competitive life—is beginning to change over many of our supposedly civilized procedures.

Inquiring into this, perhaps every speculation should be allowed. Even ask, say, whether, in evolutionary terms, if the psychopath's time has come, there may be a world-wide need for him. Could the Coming of the Psychopath be a natural and inevitable result of our drastically deteriorating environment (which helps fling him up) as well as one answer to it and, who knows, a potential remedy for such deterioration?

Conceivably, without attempting a clever inversion of values, the race may be calling upon uncivilized, antirational, antiscientific, nihilistic violence as a last-ditch effort to save us from destruction. Following this line, evolutionary man may have come up with psychopaths by the millions just in time to blow up air-polluting smelters and rescue our species, and all species, from the cloud of evil we ourselves produced. Then we may be struggling toward something not necessarily all bad, not necessarily death. In the midst of our slow-motion apocalypse we dimly perceive this. Could our kind be passing through a plague of the spirit that, destructive as it may seem, might purge the over-crowded, clouded, gassed, smog-stricken society and somehow make it better?

IV

Psychopathic Journal

1

In the Asylum at Danvers State Hospital, Hathorne, Massachusetts, Dr. Tomislav Zargaj, director. The subject of part-psychopaths comes up, and Dr. Zargaj refers to "lacunae in the superego." Such individuals sometimes show selective consideration for the people who run across them. But how does this work? Under certain conditions can they shed their psychopathy at will—say, by whim or if someone appeals to them aesthetically?

A quick, big man who practiced in Yugoslavia not many years ago, he smiles and looks out the window. A dozen or so inmates may be seen on the lawn.

"We're calling names, you know," Dr. Zargaj observes. "It's for the bourgeoisie to label others . . ."

And most of the patients here have long since drifted hopelessly beyond label. These are the ones who will never make it back to the sidewalk. There seems to be a terrible stillness at the center of the withdrawn soul. The greater number of inmates allowed on the lawn remain silent and motionless. They could be so many dismal statues. Whoever walks, moves very slowly. Tranquilized, they march around an enclosed area known as the bull pen. A path has been worn around the edge of the rectangle alongside the buildings with barred windows. For some reason, not one inmate wants or dares to make his way to the bright, grassy center.

Indoors, the smells of Lysol, urine, and wet laundry infiltrate everywhere. The attendants carry huge bunches of keys. Unwatched television images dance in the deserted game rooms. Silence. I remember the fashionable idea of going mad; with what foolishness insanity has been glamorized as an interesting

203

condition, a sort of nearer-to-God way station. I see again the
young black poet, wasted on speed, twitching in the back of a
North Beach bar in San Francisco. But among the crushed, so
many toothless, slow-moving survivors here, who are the artists?

I am in for a shock. In the arts and crafts studio, an eruption
of protest denied to daily consciousness has taken form in flames
leaping out of a dozen canvases. The representation of fire everywhere. Frightened faces, hands upraised. "Look what you've done
to me!" these works all seem to cry out. You walk among devils,
fantastic dragon mothers, stunted little father images with lop-
sided faces. Swooping cutouts of great, menacing birds. Mandalas
from each little hell. Huge, terrible eyes. And a number of in-
tricate, guillotinelike devices remarkably similar to the back-yard
machine Lewis Hoagland displayed to me in the moonlight.

One can't help but be shaken, even intimidated and made
ashamed, by this outburst of reproach, unanswerable as it is, and
the visitor wants somehow to apologize.

I like one mad boy. He looks out on the world bravely
enough when his family isn't around, but when they come to visit
something always happens. They nag and chide him, in spite of
being warned by the doctors not to do this. A week before, they
dutifully visited, surrounding him and pecking away at his obligations and the behavior expected of a good son. He excused
himself, they thought to the bathroom. But he went to the workshop, and came back minutes later to a fearful chatter of consternation, with his glasses painted black, gazing at them impas-
sively.

The few inmates called psychopaths here seem crumby and
second-rate. Mostly they appear to be small-time con men. One,
known among staff members and patients alike as the subtlest of
manipulators, spends much of his time trying to persuade somebody else to do his laundry. Another comes across as particularly
unimpressive, a flighty undersized person with a talent for stupid
jokes and horseplay. He contrives now and then to be discovered
in closets giggling with a girl patient. Later I'm told that he has
been booked several times for rape and attempted rape, and on
no fewer than four occasions was picked up "in the area" at the
time of killings attributed to the Boston Strangler.

He may not stay long. Psychopaths know how to beat this game and are not about to be indefinitely trapped here. They return home, and somebody, whomever they fall in with, will start to pay for the outlaw's damaged childhood.

But we're seeing that the criminal model is only one expression of psychopathy. Psychopaths aren't all evil: the condition and style may also express themselves, if often violently, in positive, useful action. Now a paradox. Imagine psychopathic behavior as a protective device of the nervous system designed to *fight off* madness, resulting from but also offering resistance to early brain damage.

2

Brain Damage. Permanent alteration of the head, new people. The catastrophically injured live out their disordered years in places like Danvers. But the partially damaged, psychopaths who survive, somehow overcome childhood disorder, sorrow, and terror, are the ones who return and shatter the neighborhood calm. Criminals, preachers, innovators—their heads are different.

Apparently the one who strikes back, putting everyone around him through changes if he can, nearly always begins with, or incurs by early accident, interrupted or frightened reflexes. William and Joan McCord, for example, cite the strong probability of "a greater proportion of abnormal EEG patterns among psychopaths than among the normal population." Early deprivation of tenderness in childhood, said Harry Stack Sullivan, produces "the *basic malevolent attitude* [my italics], the attitude that one really lives among enemies . . ." The McCords also believe: "If love is too weak to countermand brain lesions, which makes socialization difficult, the child becomes a psychopath."

Possibly the damaged psyche has—without knowing it—from the beginning felt closer to nonexistence; pre-experienced the approach of death in a way that can never be understood by those treated with consistent early tenderness. This could be the reason for the psychopath's impatience with mortal linear referents (time, history, responsibility) and his need to stay excited (reassurance that he's alive) by keeping his neighborhood, town, world, everyone about him in constant turmoil.

And like a mended growing bone or branch, surviving, say, whatever shattered the inmates at Danvers, he has healed over in some ways stronger. But this may have been accomplished at the cost of falling into altered brain rhythms, the kind—according to Dr. Lauretta Bender—that result in "diffusely unpatterned impulsive behavior." Or among the psychopathic winners, pure disassociation: cold, remorseless maneuvering. But look again at the surroundings that our healed-over children have to grow up and survive in. Conceivably the new rhythms driving them, abnormal as they appear on an encephalographic chart, may be useful for getting along in an abrupt, staccato, polluted, and noisy world of simultaneous happenings, especially in our cities. If so, rhythms that arise out of repaired brain damage may be neurologically in phase with increasingly psychopathic environmental rhythms.

Question also the nature of damage. Is the oyster damaged by its pearl? Does a damaged brain concede its injury? So frequently damage seems to *evolve,* emerging in the form of power drives not experienced by healthy people whom early love has left more contented.

Imagine the early lesions in Hemingway's head, all the misfiring reflexes that recombined and were converted into genius. Greater geniuses—Tolstoy, Gandhi, Eugene O'Neill—with erratic brain waves, wretched in the treatment of their own children, creating misery as well as miraculous works on all sides. The damage done by saints.

Dr. Bruno Bettelheim: "I have no use for saints. They are *impossible* people; they destroy everyone around them. The sooner they go to heaven the better, because that is where they belong."

Again the continuing and mysterious association between the saint and psychopath. Also the increased vulnerability of decent people. What about a castoff aerospace engineer—the one who committed himself to the vision of reaching the moon, only to be let go job hunting in a recession as soon as the dream was realized? Has he suffered a brain insult a little late in the game?

What did decency and loyalty earn for him? Possibly broken rhythms of confidence making him susceptible to an early stroke. The psychopath won't be fooled like this. He experiences no loss of faith when dreams start to go bad. If he himself can't be the lunar hero, such long-term commitment bores him, which is why you'll find very few psychopaths among the anonymous technicians.

The psychopathic style involves *no waiting.*

In 1969 the chapel at Logan Airport near Boston had to be closed for the reason that travelers were dumping refuse inside, using it as a urinal and also for sex.

3

Psychopaths can't love. Promiscuous, gratifying their transient urges on whim, they give themselves perhaps charmingly but only on the surface. We are confidently told this by one medical authority after another. But as Dr. Michael Glenn pointed out in his *Village Voice* essay, the outlaw men and women who report to clinics and doctors' offices—because they have to, or else be jailed or institutionalized—are the "disadvantaged losers." They may well come on as shallow individuals, offhand in sex and love—though if this holds good it becomes hard to account for the "astonishing power" cited by Dr. Cleckley (p. 19) that male psychopaths apparently have to "bind forever the devotion of women." (Or, for example, over the short course, the magnetism and power commonly exercised by pimps over the girls who work for them.)

But what about the more respectable psychopathic winner whom the therapist never sees as a patient?

"Winner or loser—why wouldn't he be a great lover!" the police detective answers. "With a woman, the psychopath is saying: 'I'm complete in myself.' He takes her. The woman feels like a possession. When he beats her, he's like a little boy. She admires his not needing her understanding. A neurotic may love her out of weakness, being nice, or because he thinks he should. But in this situation the psychopath . . . for once he's absolutely genuine. When he's happy, in the right mood, he'll love you like nobody else does, completely, all the way, nothing held back, because he *wants to*—until he's through or gets bored. This is what gives him the kind of authority women crave. It's the reason women go for cops, by the way. Did you know that?"

The psychiatrist laughs. "By definition they're bad husbands and wives. Sure, but they were *once* interested in their partner. Never doubt that. Perhaps only for an hour. But for that one hour they were so interested that even I couldn't get that interested."

And it's precisely the neurotic's heritage of sexual inhibition that psychopaths deny, assault, and transcend. In a businesslike way, they provide services performed by no one else. All over the world we have a tribe of sexual manipulators—whores for both sexes, madams, pimps, utterly amoral hustlers and exhibitionists of every description, *psychopaths ministering to neurotics*. We experience the outlaw as uncaring, cynical healer. Indifferent psychopaths performing their tricks at will—in brothels, secret apartments, rooming houses, and chic hotel rooms—help the sad neurotic act out his fantasies.

And do not current therapeutic techniques follow the psychopathic style? Since the middle 1960's, theatrical acting-out has begun to supersede remembrance of things past in the doctor's office. In place of tortured reflections on the couch, Masters and Johnson wire sexual play to recording instruments and teach pleasure by means of live-action models and partners.

Or the troubled, overcivilized neurotic may join encounter groups whose members not only confess and cry out but push, shove, insult, fondle, and wrestle with one another. Never mind mulling over your problem in unhealthy privacy. Go public with your frustration and fear, allow everyone a share in it; no, *insist* that they share; take your hostility and terror to the group, and in exchange receive theirs. In the Esalen sessions at Big Sur: "People touch, hold hands, kiss, throw each other up in the air, fight, use all the dirty words, tell each other cruel truths. Every aspect of so-called proper behavior is discarded. Every emotion is out in the open—everybody's property."*

Encounter thus aims often in a positive and helpful way at *controlled psychopathy,* putting outlaw impulses to good use, captured within a framework of games and rituals. It offers psychopathic baptism enclosed in new (though neopagan) sacraments with Christian self-abasement and confession tacked on to it. Psychopathy and Christianity mingle. Dignity is deliberately lost; identity is diffused among strangers naked together in the womb pool. Only frustration and anxiety are felt as evil. Everything else goes. We have no postponed gratification—excepting in most such groups the specifically sexual, and this is simulated in numerous ways. The encounter session then frequently becomes a psychopathic playground and presumably helpful torture chamber, in which socially disapproved "emotional immaturity," sometimes brutal behavior, callousness, irresponsibility, "impulsivity," and explosive assaults on others become the norm.

So the theater for damaged souls has emerged from little shame-filled rooms to arenas in which members of the involved group maul, embrace, and excoriate one another, reaching out for a new kind of love that surely must be there.

4

In 1955 Dr. David Lykken administered electric shock and other tests to inmates from reformatories and a state hospital in Minnesota. These subjects had earlier been classified as primary sociopaths, and Lykken compared their test reactions with those of a control group: high-school and college students in the area judged normal.†

All of eight tests confirmed his hypothesis that "the entire syndrome of primary sociopathy" could be attributed to "the absence of one quality alone, *anxiety.* The lack of guilt, of conscience or superego function, the failure to learn from personal

* Andrea Svedberg, *Time,* Nov. 9, 1970.
† *A Study of Anxiety in the Sociopathic Personality,* University of Minnesota.

210   *Psychopaths . . .*

experience, the bizarre and sensational indulgences; all these fall neatly into place . . ."

In comparison with the control group, Lykken's test subjects didn't seem to care much if at all about his warning buzzer and the shock that followed. They showed themselves to be "clearly defective" in their ability to develop anxiety in the test situation and therefore "relatively incapable of *avoidance learning . . .*"

Thus, anxiety, called by Harry Stack Sullivan "the one thing on earth no one wants," emerges from Lykken's study as positively useful, all but required for staying out of trouble and pursuing a reasonable and productive life. We can even imagine moderate anxiety, in proper amounts, being essential to the kind of civilization we've built up—yet the psychopath refuses to accept this. He won't have it. Regardless of tests and electric shocks, the mystery remains: what makes him persist in upsetting our comfortable routines?

Lykken found *lack of fear* to be characteristic of primary sociopaths. Nine years later, with this conception as a starting point, psychologists Stanley Schachter and Bibb Latané subjected inmates—paid volunteers—at the Stillwater, Minnesota, state prison and the Bordentown Reformatory in New Jersey to another maze-learning test ("punishing certain errors with electric shock").

They were surprised to discover that sociopaths who couldn't manage to avoid painful shocks when injected with placebo learned "dramatically well" under the influence of adrenalin. Under placebo, as expected, avoidance learning decreased as sociopathy increased. But following adrenalin injections (completely unhelpful to members of the control group), the more pronounced the sociopathy the more avoidance learning *increased.*[*]

"The effects of adrenalin . . . are dramatic and almost startling . . . This astonishing relationship . . . would certainly seem to indicate that adrenalin sensitivity is involved in the sociopathic complex . . . At this point adrenalin appears to be a remedy, but a remedy for what?"

[*] *Crime, Cognition, and the Autonomic Nervous System,* Nebraska Symposium on Motivation, 1964.

Schacter and Latané suggested that psychopaths live in a nervous high much of the time, subject to fevers of indiscriminate excitement. They "appear to be more responsive [than others] to virtually every titillating event, whether only mildly provoking or dangerously threatening. In the Valins study, the heart rate of sociopathic subjects increases as much during word association as when they are anticipating giving blood." Such indiscriminate activity seemed "almost the equivalent of *no reactivity at all.*"

What then do the adrenalin injections accomplish? Possibly, according to this approach, they boost the psychopathic subjects out of their usual state of random and diffuse searching for excitement to a level of not being bored. The shots substitute for adrenalin-raising explosions, crises, and aggressive action disruptive to others. With the adrenalin in his blood stream, the sociopath no longer needs to create disturbances in order to feel alive and unbored. He even worries a little, pays closer attention to electric shock games, and thus scores higher on the psychologists' avoidance-learning charts. So we achieve the restoration of anxiety, temporarily socializing the outlaw.

5

These seem impeccable experiments, yet something must be left out. Namely the question of why, given his apparent instability and craziness, this Pied Piper has so many millions following him and dancing in his style.

They are people who have the capacity to bring excitement, fun and even love into the lives of others . . .

The charm of the psychopath, his bewildering comfort in stressful situations and the observation that we at times envy, admire or even hate him are clarified if we consider his behavior in the light of a search for freedom . . .

While we may personally deplore the behavior of certain entertainers, business people, or even psychiatrists who live excitingly above and beyond the codes most of us hold

to be dear, we would be dishonest if we did not consider
the possibility that "these people have something" . . .

Also:

> . . . *the confusion which can arise when deviant behavior is*
> *considered as part of a medical model* [my italics]. Psychop-
> athy is an illness, but only in the sense that it seeks a basi-
> cally inhuman kind of existence which if allowed to prevail
> in a great number of people would make the continuation
> of organized society impossible.*

> Poetry, too, provoked—poetic—disagreement. Mona
> Van Duyn's "To See, To Take" won, but dissenting judge
> Allen Ginsberg presented his minority decision for beat
> poet Gregory Corso's "Elegiac Feelings American" with a
> Vedantic howl of anguish: "Om, om, om!/ Gregory Corso's
> genius despised./ Muses bored./ Mediocrity is prized./
> Bull- - - - the award!/ Om, om, om!" Ginsberg then lit a
> stick of incense and attached it to a microphone on the
> podium.†

6

Isn't "avoidance learning" a test based on purely middle-
class values? Perhaps the bourgeoisie receive too much instruction in avoidance. Many of us avoid all too well, and some—so as
not to run the risk of being hurt—shrink from any sort of chance-
taking as they would a disease.

Mailer said a few years ago that the university-trained intellectual has been protected from violence—and therefore from
existential experience. This is

> experience sufficiently unusual so that you don't know how
> it is going to turn out. You don't know whether you're going

* From "Psychopathy and Related Traits" in *Psychiatry and the Dilemmas of Crime,* by Seymour L. Halleck, M.D. Harper & Row, New York,
1967.
    † *Newsweek,* Mar. 15, 1971.

to be dead or alive at the end of it, wanted or rejected, cheered or derided . . . Something happens in the act of violence which is beyond one's measure . . . when violence is larger than one's ability to dominate, it is existential and one is living in an instantaneous world of revelations. The SAINT and PSYCHOPATH [my caps] share the same kind of experience. It is just that the saint has the mysterious virtue of being able to transcend this experience and the psychopath is broken or made murderous.*

Mailer's psychopath, yes. But the lighter-weight primary sociopath to whom Lykken and Schachter and Latané have been administering electric shocks may not be so drastically changed by violent moments. The truth is that he thrives on them, much as the middle-class masses thrive on avoiding trouble.

Sometimes the researcher can become imprisoned in his own vocabulary. For instance, what we diagnose as the antisocial subject's "emotional flatness" could just as well be translated by the psychopath as "Don't give a damn about your boring world!" We say the outlaw fails to learn from personal experience. Of course, it would be useful, from our standpoint, for him to learn. But isn't it also possible to learn *too much* from experience, especially second hand from the experience of others? Deliberately deaden oneself, try once and retreat, decide, say, not to dare anymore and instead keep to the narrowest routines, letting all kinds of risks and sensations pass by. In contrast, the sociopath undergoing our tests "learns from personal experience" that he's utterly *bored* with safe routine, doesn't mind danger, including, from where he impatiently sits, those silly electric shocks, and will do almost anything, never mind the pain, to experience some new thrill in order to get out from under the monotony. Perhaps for the psychopath *pain is interesting*—both to bestow on others and to receive. It could be that the consternation of others is interesting, or at least not boring.

None of the foregoing brings down two ingenious experiments. The uses of adrenalin especially, as projected by Schachter

* "Talking of Violence." Norman Mailer interviewed by W. J. Weatherby. From *Violence in the Streets,* edited by and with an introduction by Shalom Endleman. Quadrangle Books, Chicago, 1968.

and Latané, must give pause to all psychopaths. Also, no one can seriously question the advantages of at least rudimentary skill in avoiding trouble. The little boy who keeps putting his hand on the hot stove has a fool's future. (Remember, though, that clowns, who delight the world, live in a rambunctious, foolish, eternal *now*.) Still, can avoidance learning serve as the be-all and end-all in tests of psychopathy *vs.* sanity?

Suppose in our disturbing dream that psychopaths came to be in charge. What kind of tests would be laid on *us*? Might we be accused, for instance, of not having enough fun? The times I hurried past the girl beckoning in the doorway, and sensibly so, might be held against me. Might they sit me down in front of a huge Guilt-Calculating Machine and laugh at my soaring score? Conceivably, too, in another test devised by ascendant psychopaths, the cautious middle-class person might be riddled with electric shocks every time he *failed* to take a risk.

<h1 style="text-align:center">7</h1>

Dr. Thomas P. Detre: Hungarian-born; Professor of Psychiatry (Yale); Psychiatrist-in-Chief, Yale-New Haven Hospital; author with Dr. Henry Jarecki of *Modern Psychiatric Treatment*. From a conversation, July 1970 . . .

Violence is in all of us. Are we not talking about a multiple continuum of thresholds? Namely, what is each man's and each woman's threshold of violence at any given time?

For instance, you and I would never organize a lynching party. But I'm not sure that we would never *attend* any such party. Because I remember after the Second World War, a colleague of mine went to the hanging of a man who was not adjudicated by the courts, but who tortured I don't know how many thousands of people, a collaborator. He went to the public square and watched the man being hanged, and enjoyed it thoroughly.

I suppose one aspect of your thesis is that we are building a society in which people who otherwise wouldn't have a low threshold of psychopathic activity now *can have* the freedom to behave in such a manner. Such as students. But we must be careful here. There is a difference between a violent person who has very strict moral values but who responds very easily, or becomes provoked easily, and during these temper tantrums behaves in an antisocial manner, and someone else whom we would diagnose as a psychopath.

A key element to psychopathy, as Dr. M. H. Miller pointed out, is a profoundly disturbed *time sense*. They never see their behavior in the context of tomorrow. An example: You and I could be unfaithful to our wives and so could a psychopath be. You and I might have as much of an irresistible desire as he. What would differentiate the two of us from him is that we would rather carefully calculate the dangers involved . . . to minimize the pain as well as to reduce the social risks. All this requires is a number of steps. The psychopath, on the other hand, never adjudicates the situation with reference to the future. He just plunges ahead. In other words, if I'm a psychopath and I have an appointment to meet you but—all at once, unexpectedly—I run into an old friend on the street I might spend my afternoon with him, and simply not show up for our meeting.

People who are psychopathic in their youth quite often *mature out* of sociopathic behavior later in life. We don't know how to predict quite when or to whom it will happen, but for many what you might call psychopathic morality, or the lack of it, will be replaced by the most rigid codes of behavior. Often priggish, actually. Very rigid, scrupulous scrutinizing of others: they can turn into pillars of society. This is the former psychopath who spontaneously converts. You know, the country preacher who gets up to shout about hell and damnation and tells about his past.

I have known many psychopaths coming from relatively happy families. And I've also seen many straight people whose mothers and fathers show criminal or sociopathic tendencies. The second is easy to understand. It's because the models identified with society's current values are available outside the home. They come to the child on television, radio, from friends, the schoolteacher. Someone like the Lone Ranger, if that model attracts you. Television provides far more models for normal than abnormal behavior. I don't believe in this nonsense about TV being so bad for young children. The more naïve the model, the more likely the child will be to identify with the good hero or heroine.

A characteristic of all psychopaths is that there's no set of values by which they can live. Take some of your present-day revolutionaries. I don't mean the leaders. The followers in any such movement are likely to include a large number of psychopaths. That's in the beginning. But the psychopath will drop out soon. He'll be bored and feel too many demands on him. He may even turn informer.

He can't feel isolated or lonely for long. In order for him to experience loneliness, it would require that he do nothing about it. But that just doesn't occur. He immediately goes to a bar, or a drag race. He's always going somewhere. Perhaps we sometimes envy the diversity of his experience. I do believe that psychopaths, men or women, are going to be *less frustrated* by the discrepancy between fantasy life and real activity, but they will also be *more bored* than the average person. They have to constantly escalate in order to get a kick out of life. And at times they escalate to the point of being arrested. Have you ever seen a psychopath sitting down quietly in a chair? They always wiggle. Sure, they dissipate tension with greater ease. They get what they want more quickly. But though they dissipate tension, it recurs faster than in normal people.

Come back again to the matter of threshold. It's very important. I've never had a convulsion in my life, nor have my wife

and children. But there are children with a high fever who develop convulsions, and I guarantee that I can do something to
your organism to make *you* convulse. Now this depends on
threshold. And individuals in our society are placed somewhere,
each of them, along this continuum, having a very high threshold
of resistance to agitation in some areas and a very low threshold
in others. When someone starts preaching about something, or
intervenes dramatically in our society, then there are numbers of
people who are *marginal* in their ability to resist certain pressures.
And when that happens they can act erratically in a dangerous
way—to themselves and others . . . If we have a massive lowering
of emotional thresholds so that there is instability, for one reason
or another, all along the continuum, then you might have the start
of your revolution of psychopaths. I don't believe we have reached
this active stage. Still, some kind of upheaval can't be completely
ruled out and may, as you suggest, without our realizing it, be
taking place now.

8

Dr. Thomas Steele: "Psychopaths are very good at flattering
people. Others usually believe them, even those (myself included)
who know better. Physically they're inclined to be glowing, glittering people. You can't ignore them. They have a kind of aura.
They often dress in bright colors. I've noticed that you won't
usually find them to be drab. Bright red and yellow shirts. Strut-
ting around with a breezy: 'Hiya, doc!' Somehow they always
manage to grab your attention.

"But so many psychopaths have bad judgment. There was
Lester in California, a small redheaded guy with a wispy beard.
An electrician, bad-tempered, belligerent, but he was always losing fights. He looked like a member of a motorcycle gang, although he was a loner. One example of his propensity for getting
himself into trouble was his carrying a gun to an interview with
his probation officer. Another time he was picked up for driving
his Renault down the freeway with the lights out, 'so that the
cops couldn't see me.' One day Lester got mad at his wife and

told me that he had just wired the front doorknob so that when she came back and tried to get in she would receive a shock of one hundred and ten volts. It was during the rainy season. 'Christ,' I told him, 'don't you realize how dangerous that is? You could electrocute her.' 'Oh,' he said, 'she usually wears tennis shoes.' "

Dr. Gary Tucker: "You know, the psychopath who comes to us is someone who gets caught. Billie Sol Estes was a 'financial genius' until he was found out. You've got to consider American society as a whole, all the maneuvering, the selfishness. We say psychopaths can't delay gratification. The paradox you mention: that they can manipulate but not sympathize, can't put themselves in the other person's place. But what's so unusual about that today among so-called normal people?

"Most revolutionary kids aren't merely adopting a new style. The patina comes from society. In a riot they not only scream at the pigs but at the phoniness of their parents. Business duplicity, greed. But most of all at the hypocritical attitudes around them. The strange numbness . . . Do you know America is the only country in the world where you can watch three wars a night on television?

"Yes, psychopaths are acting out various kinds of protest, but they get tired. You don't see many old psychopaths . . ."

Dr. David Kupfer: "The very nature of modern organizations encourages this kind of behavior. The most effective administrative style encourages manipulation. So you can say that organization, increasingly as we see it today, generates psychopathy.

"Follow the urban style, you tend to become hyperalert. You develop eyes behind your head . . . The successful revolutionary employs the same style, in extreme form, as the psychopath who makes it in business. Look at Jerry Rubin and Abbie Hoffman. They believe what they're doing, but they also *score*. You know who can be pathetic, the ones in the crowd, their followers, trying unsuccessfully to imitate the revolutionary style. Jerry and Abbie and all the famous ones, they'll make their ego trips pay. The followers are the ones brought to this hospital. Stoned, hysterical, out of their heads for one reason or another. We get *them*. After that May Day rally for Bobby Seale and the Panthers, a lot of them came in. Hallucinating. On drugs? Not all of them. They were just high and scared. One I remember couldn't go to the toilet. Every time he sat down he hallucinated that there was a bomb under him.

"Psychopaths find vulnerability in other people . . .

"They require feedback, and to an extent they can be identified by the numbers of people around them. This is how they define their identity, and how they make it. The lonesome psychopaths are the ones we get here. Will a sociopath ever be found going off and fishing by himself? Never!

"Being shy, quiet, a nice guy, doesn't work in America. The nice guy is the postman, the milkman.

"Why did Manson turn on so many young people? Adventure, romance, against the Establishment, beating the system, excitement, charisma. The *need* . . . I see it in little doses all around me."

Dr. Jerry Maxmen: "Technocracy creates this. Banality leads to insanity. It's a psychopath's world. Everybody's after power. In this clinic, for instance. In all clinics. I've never seen such power-hungry places. And in a bureaucracy you've got to be sociopathic in order to get action.

"Unlike the daily round of most people, Manson's life was exciting. There's so much blandness . . .

"It's practically impossible to treat them. You know psychopaths always get the nurses fighting the doctors and the doctors fighting the social workers. 'Hey,' I ask, 'why are we always fighting over this guy?' It's a diagnostic indicator!"

Carol Anderson, social worker: "You know, psychopathy can be attractive. [*Smile.*] There's a challenge to tame it . . . The psychopath gives others what they need and want to hear. If you're less emotionally involved and uncommitted, you can play to the needs of your audience.

"At first he's charming, especially the successful one. He's going to show you the world, and he knows what it's all about. I sometimes enjoy watching a psychopath operate when he's trying to put something over. You like to see society put on—things you wouldn't dare do yourself. It's their style that's attractive, and with the successful ones it's not offensive.

"Everything's so uncertain now. You're not sure. You don't know . . . The attraction of the successful psychopath is that he seems to be *in control of the world around him.* But if he's not, if he plays a losing game, we show him how he can make himself into a more successful psychopath. Say 'If you're going to manipulate, learn to do it better.'

"Teach him to become a better psychopath. Then he can become an insurance-company president.

"Even so far as the losers go, you can appreciate their approach to life . . ."

She handed me a poem from Don Marquis' *archy and mehitabel.*

the lesson of the moth

i was talking to a moth
the other evening
he was trying to break into
an electric light bulb
and fry himself on the wires

why do you fellows
pull this stunt i asked him
because it is the conventional
thing for moths or why
if that had been an uncovered
candle instead of an electric
light bulb you would
now be a small unsightly cinder
have you no sense

plenty of it he answered
but at times we get tired

of using it
we get bored with the routine
and crave beauty
and excitement

fire is beautiful
and we know that if we get
too close it will kill us
but what does that matter
it is better to be happy
for a moment
and be burned up with beauty
than to live a long time
and be bored all the while
so we wad all our life up
into one little roll
and then we shoot the roll
that is what life is for
it is better to be a part of beauty
for one instant and then cease to
exist than to exist forever
and never be a part of beauty
our attitude toward life
is come easy go easy
we are like human beings
used to be before they became
too civilized to enjoy themselves

and before I could argue him
out of his philosophy
he went and immolated himself
on a patent cigar lighter
i do not agree with him
myself i would rather have
half the happiness and twice
the longevity

but at the same time i wish
there was something i wanted
as badly as he wanted to fry himself
                    archy

                 Yale-New Haven Hospital
                 July 23-24, 1970

9

Dan Sakall, adult probation officer attached to State Superior Court, Tucson, Arizona. In eight years more than a thousand convicted men and women have been referred to him. His assignment is to recommend the length and severity of sentences. In mitigating circumstances he will ask that the court suspend sentence and grant probation. If probation is granted, he must keep track of those ordered regularly to report to him, and will be held responsible for their conduct during the probationary period.

Varied pressures weigh on him. The probation officer's exploration and appraisal of a convicted person's crime, hope, moral awareness, likelihood of being rehabilitated or broken in prison, must be carried out in locked quarters, in jail, under stress and duress. Also the officer may have to play an ambiguous role. Serving as the accused individual's official friend, he will not necessarily turn out to be his advocate. He will sympathize, care, usually want to help. But as often as not he can be driven by law, a prisoner's temperament, or the need to protect the community to call for extreme punishment—then perhaps go home to dream uneasily about the kind of justice he has measured out for some desperate man to whom he may have been nodding and smiling sympathetically a few hours before. And these troubling dreams may often persist for months and years, until they are replaced by others—even though he feels that the sentences recommended to the court were appropriate and right.

A substantial number of those who come under his jurisdiction will be one-time offenders not likely to come back. The businessman picked up for drunken driving, the temporarily mad cowboy who breaks up a bar, the student rioter, or the young people involved in Tucson's heavy drug traffic—these give him no great amount of trouble.

But a group of others—frequently in trouble and repeatedly diagnosed as psychopaths—nearly always prove to be the emotionally exhausting cases. Because so often in dealing with them the probation officer is put on, had, deceived. From the start he finds himself involved with an aggressive, tricky, generally for-

midable person fighting to go free. Bogus sweetness, guile, intimi-
dation, and an enormously insistent persuasiveness—all the tricks
in the psychopath's repertoire—will be brought to bear on him.
    Yet he'll often be attracted to his sociopaths and do the best
he can for them. Sakall believes that many can be reached and
successfully treated, but only if handled in a certain way. He
says, like this:

    ••• The sociopath has no capacity for self-appraisal. *Ap-
proval* is what he wants most. The greatest dread he feels has to
do with loneliness and isolation, and being rejected. Most sociopaths want to admit how terrible they are, if they can be sure
that rejection won't follow. Psychopaths are always desperate.
Live with them; see things as objectively as they do. Treat them
harshly if they force you to—as long as you don't reject them.

    ••• The psychopath is only something in his own eyes when
he's gotten you "pregnant" after a confrontation.

    ••• Their moral sense can throw you. Typical sociopathic
comment: "Why should I have to die in the gas chamber because
my lawyer has a speech impediment?"

    ••• The psychopath never shows active self-restraint.

    ••• They are utilities moving over the land. Animated utili-
ties.

    ••• There is infantilism in all insanity. The charisma of the
psychopath is an appeal of the infantile uncluttered self. We have
also a biological yearning for absolute freedom of action. Sociopaths know no deferred reward. If I am a sociopath I'm not clut-
tered by the fact that you're in the chair I want to be in. No, the
psychopath isn't complicated. In treating him, there's no synthe-
sis. It's all there, very simple. He's much like lower forms of life
where survival is almost innate. He's *purely operative,* the most
efficient human organism alive.

• • • The socialized person is complicated by the fact of not being able to throw you out of the chair he wants. The socialized person doesn't want you out badly enough.

• • • Most psychopaths don't differentiate much when it comes to sex. They'll take whatever is around, if possible without waiting. Now you or I looking at a woman as a sexual objective won't immediately, with no preliminaries, expect to take her— because she's a cultural subject as well. But the sociopath is either untrained in social values or they mean nothing to him, so why pause? He'll not hesitate to go after her and immediately try to seduce her. That, of course, in some cases will mean rape. The culturized man pauses basically from fear and to avoid danger. Psychopaths aren't put off by that kind of fear.

• • • All socialization slows us down. The psychopath is most effective because only he can give his whole self to any situation. A man conditioned by history remains a man conditioned by history in any situation. The psychopath has never been in history. He just isn't a time-oriented animal.

• • • No one can detect fraud like a psychopath. He's the most objective person on earth.

• • • We have to look at the psychopath in many ways as a child, and the most irresistible charm is the charm of children.

• • • Two psychopaths will never be together for long.

• • • The psychopath is terribly fearful inside. He has to know by constantly reinforced experience that he's capable of affecting the world of objects, the most important being other people. He can't get along without people, even for a short time, because when he has no one available, close to him, in his manipulatory net, he feels dead, falls into inertia and even critical depression. His only life, his only identity, comes from moving other people around. Without that he's dead.

••• The sociopath can't make it between the speed-limit signs. He needs constant cues.

••• They trust what they control. The achievement of a psychopath is contingent on a trusting individual.

••• The psychopath swings from spectator to manipulator.

••• If a psychopath does something for you, he expects you to be forever indebted.

••• We had the insurance executive's son who kept giving his parents so much grief that they moved into progressively smaller apartments until they found one with no room for him. This boy finally got a young girl pregnant. We had a conference, the parents on both sides and the girl. They, of course, wanted marriage, which would be a disaster for her. She said she was sensitive to his needs and could help him. "Look, Alice," the counselor said, "the only part of him sensitive to you is the end of his penis!" The girl's mother leaped up. "You dirty man! What kind of an officer are you?" All this time the boy had somehow been hiding undetected in the bathroom, and was there listening. When the counselor said this about him he burst out of the bathroom laughing, and hugged the counselor around the neck, saying: "Here's one man in the world who knows me and doesn't put me down!" There was no marriage. She had the baby and put him up for adoption. Since then she's been married to an understanding guy, a good Joe who knows all this.

••• Watch his need for achievement! The boy arsonist was completely delighted with what he had done. His biggest thrill was the firemen and police, all the guardians of society he had brought to the scene. With ecstasy he watched them sift through the ashes. He said to me: "I lit that last fire with one ounce of lighter fluid. *One ounce!* And then, there they were—all those people and machines! I couldn't sleep. I had to go back and see if the fire was really mine, or whether it had just been a dream."

• • • The great psychiatric sin is that of not identifying with humanity. The psychopath plays God, which separates him.

• • • They can program into another person's conscience at will, then imitate it until *your* thoughts are taken over by *them.* Many times I've come awake just in time to realize: "Hey, that's not you speaking. Those aren't your ideas. They're mine!"

• • • This young man—a former probationer—went out hunting with me. He got behind me and said: "Dan, you know if I killed you now, if I shot you in the back, I wouldn't have any feeling for you." I said to him: "Ben, I knew that when we came hunting, but we came to hunt and let's hunt."

• • • You've first got to strip sociopaths of their veneer, their fraud, and then show them that they aren't rejected without it. Get hold of the bark and work it off them. This fraud begins with objective cunning. It turns your most humane qualities against you and uses them to whip you. He uses them to trip and control you. The real psychopath will take your finest qualities and shoot you down with them. Turn them into weapons for your own destruction. It's sort of *chutzpathic*—to make you feel guilty because you don't feel sorry for the orphan.

• • • Basically all mental illness is disconnection of the heart and mind. In other words, the feelings are wrong or inappropriate or nonexistent. So the callousness we think we see in the sociopath may be understood as an inappropriate emotional reaction to the scene, or no emotion at all. My friend Ed Morgan, a lawyer, feels that the sociopath knows only one appropriate emotion, hostility.

Ed feels that what I do is to set up a *compatible emotion* at the start between myself and the psychopath by creating a terrible hostility in him, toward me, because I start by making him feel worthless and degraded. And this feeling will be genuine. Then we can hope to get somewhere, from that base. This may not seem kind, but there's a reason for it.

I think that, without meaning to, we can *destroy the psychopath with kindness.* For this reason: We take away from him the chance to understand due reciprocity and consequences. We all emit in kind, whether we like it or not. Now, for a moment, imagine yourself from the psychopath's point of view. You have initiated behavior contrary to your own welfare as well as mine, and then—out of kindness—I arrange things so that you don't have to pay; if *I* always pick up your tab, lift you up, don't let you lose, what am I doing to you? I am saying, no, whatever you emit, you can't change the outside environment. Out of kindness I am telling you: "You have no identity, not even the identity of a bastard, because I won't let you be a bastard. I will be divine and truly forgive you." But it's not true. I'm human, and by forgiving you too readily I destroy your achievement, even your bastardly achievement, and in doing so destroy your integrity, and practically guarantee that you will go out and do something worse in order to prove yourself.

Therefore, the psychopath must be made to pay in kind. Not out of vengeance. No! Pay the coin of suffering. This is why kindness is lost on him. I'm not a cruel man. I hate it; I feel terribly depressed every time I recommend prison. But if he never has to pick up the tab after repeated antisocial actions, how is he going to find true reciprocity with other human beings? So I'm not talking about punishment. What he has to learn is the true ecology of things.

• • • These people feel terribly, but not compatibly. That's the problem. It's displaced emotion. What has caused this? The nearest explanation I know is that idea from the Bible of having our conscience seared with hot irons. In other words, at some point their compatible emotions have been calloused by a branding iron, and experience has numbed them.

• • • A psychopath can't keep a murder silent.

• • • The sociopath of this kind immediately transmits his impulses into action. Naturally then, people guard against him.

They avoid him. The result is that he becomes more isolated than ever, and a vicious cycle recurs. He may be, as the psychologists say, emotionally "flat" with regard to the consequences of his actions. But he's not free of anxiety. The anxiety relates to his isolation. He may not feel guilt but he does feel shame. Particularly over not amounting to anything. So he requires the feedback, and must at all times have external recognition in order to know who and where he is.

So *give him feedback*. Begin with the hypothesis of frustration. In dealing with the psychopath, we too often ignore the basic need for achievement. The answer is to kick him in the pants, and then make him productive so that he can show off. Don't so much try to change his head as to fit him into a reinforcing environment. Measurable, demonstrable success plus, I would say, excitement and variety in his life—with as little routine as possible—these can keep the psychopath in line. Forget the abstract philosophical treatment and the deep analysis. This kind of person requires a sense of dominance. So we have to create conditions that give him, or give her, constant action and reinforcing feedback. Keep them very busy. Make them tired. Introduce fatigue into their fight and flight systems. Shove the psychopath out of your protective care. He doesn't want it or need it. Make him walk alone. Never think you've changed him. I mean accept him, but still watch out!

••• You have to learn to laugh on my job, or you crack up. The longer I've wrestled with these people, the more I understand them in terms of simplicity. They don't have subtle needs. But understanding them is only a small part of the battle. The thing to remember is that they never let up.

I'm humane, I suppose. Sure, but it's not entirely from humaneness that I've got to straighten them out if I can. In my job . . . they'll get to you. They will wear you out and bury you if you don't come to grips with them. I've got to anesthetize myself or they would strip my psyche and leave me bare. Combat fatigue is never far away. You have just got to hang on— and every once in a while you really help somebody, turn a lost life around. That's what keeps you going.

10

The prisoners of Florence, Arizona, State Penitentiary, March 10, 1971. Members of our fourteen-man tour group line up as instructed, two by two, behind the huge cheerful Chicano who will guide us, Sergeant Joaquin, a leader of the guards. The visitors from outside joke, anxiously looking around. Straights we are, all appearing abashed, even apologetic for being free. Also watchful. A massive jailbreak attempt took place here a few years ago and several guards were seized. The warden countered this threat by personally herding all of them, rebels and hostages together, into the occupied cellblocks. Then he sat back, and the rebellion collapsed.

We have just heard a talk by the warden, Mr. Frank Eyman, congratulating us for having decided to enter the field of law enforcement. The majority of our group will go into police or probation work, most having been military police at Fort Huachuca. I am accompanying Dan Sakall as some kind of observer.

Now we step forward in a ragged formation behind Sergeant Joaquin. The prisoners gathered in corners have been covertly watching us. Later somebody explains that visits like ours are scheduled infrequently because they arouse so much resentment. From the start we feel this. At our approach all the prisoners stop work; they even stop lounging, and we are invisibly riddled and shafted.

One of our people, an older man for whom probation work will be a second career, previously visited Folsom and San Quentin and whispers that compared to these places Florence is a country club. It may be. The surroundings here in the courtyard don't seem horrendous, perhaps because of Arizona's bright air and sun. The yards are filled with sunshine. Banks of orange and yellow African daisies extend along the pathways. Birds chirp everywhere, fluttering for crumbs, and pet cats dart between the cellblocks and play in the flower beds. But then on top of their wall the guards stare down at us. I have an impression of big Polaroid eyes. Shades hide their scrutiny, and all that sunshine is ringed with guns.

Now we disappear into a cellblock and the tour begins.

Nothing much will be held back; we peer at practically all there is to see. Mess hall, kitchen, the menu for today (fried chicken, peas, mashed potatoes for lunch), study areas, library; emerge again, visit the outdoor gym, observe prisoners hoisting huge weights. One-on-one basketball goes on around us. The officers and guards in charge of these areas give brief talks. Leading us, Sergeant Joaquin beams good will, not insensitive, not unfeeling, just cheerful. We look in on vocational facilities, people being tested. Young men are fitting blocks together. Several greet Dan Sakall. He put them there, but evidently with leniency. There are quick handshakes and a smile or two. A psychiatrist with a little brown moustache passes by smoking the smallest pipe I've ever seen.

We begin now to move deeper into the insides of the prison. The guards patrol our passage more alertly. Many prisoners are out of their cages working. They're all around us. The closed-circuit TV cameras that can explore what may be going on in every cell pick up the incoming tour group. These must be the only dispassionate eyes inspecting our safe-conduct. There is a pulse, beat and shuffle all around, energy moving in these dank cells and corridors. We hear whispers, the clang of a fallen bucket, unexpectedly loud whistles, a faint song, and the television watch barely protects our innocence.

Sergeant Joaquin cheerfully calls us to a halt, saying: "In front of you is the homosexual wing. We believe that homosexuals should be together and not disturb the other prisoners."

"Notice," the man who visited Folsom and San Quentin whispers, "how nicely the fags fix up their cells compared to the other ones."

Filing down a spiral staircase, we descend deeper among the dungeons, passing by prisoners under maximum security who have done atrocious things. There are those who when let out almost immediately assault the others.

Some of these are very bad, a guard explains. Incorrigibles among them sometimes have to be put in the hole. There they remain in blackness with a toilet, fed once a day for from five to fifteen days. "Sergeant Joaquin," the guard calls out, "there's one unoccupied, I think!"

We look stupidly at the four windowless cells, realizing that there are men actually in there now, squatting on their toilets as we pause. "Oh, Lord!" a voice suddenly intones out of one black space. "I'm goin' to glory!"

The sergeant asks whether we would like to experience the blackness of solitary confinement. With a few others I step into the cell. The door slams with an unexpectedly catastrophic muffling sound.

"Jesus, it's like being in a coffin!"

After a few moments one law-enforcement candidate starts to hammer on the door. Grinning, the guards open up. Shamefacedly we emerge, having been rendered foolish by the playful little force-feeding of death.

A laugh from one of the other cells makes a guard turn quickly. After the echoing slam of a door and a jingle of keys, we move on, heading toward the depths. At last, on Death Row, the famous face comes as a shock.

On his twenty-first birthday, Charles Schmid, Jr., "the Pied Piper of Tucson," later convicted of murdering three teen-age girls and burying their bodies in remote desert areas, learned that the Schmids weren't really his parents. He traveled to Phoenix for the first time to meet his true mother, socially prominent there, who reportedly said to him: "I didn't acknowledge you when you were born. What makes you think I would recognize you now?"

This happened a week before the first murder, of Alleen Rowe. On the last day of May 1964 ("I want to kill a girl!") he executed the fragile fifteen-year-old. True, walking down the arroyo before smashing her head with a rock he said to one of his collaborators: "Tell me not to do it and I won't." But she said nothing. And when Alleen cried out at the last moment: "Oh God, Charlie, why me?" he couldn't answer then or later.

This was the first of three murders. The Schmid story was picked up by every wire service. He became the most detested boy in America, but fascinating too: his trials were covered nationally, and two reporters wrote a book about him. F. Lee Bailey arrived to take on the hopeless case, forcing him, according to

Schmid, to plead guilty to the murder of Alleen Rowe against his will. But then, over his denials, Schmid was also convicted of having choked to death and buried two teen-age sisters, Gretchen and Wendy Fritz (Gretchen his more or less steady girl in an angry yearlong love affair), and was sentenced to the gas chamber. Thereafter, along with more than six hundred other men in cells around the country, he waited for the Supreme Court decision on the legality of the death sentence.

He showed no sorrow, never stopped claiming innocence, demanded the right to plead his own argument for a retrial (an appeal since lost, April 1971). What could be felt for Schmid? Practically everyone wanted him dead. His horribly smudged, unshaven, glaring countenance, eye make-up, and tinted hair seemed impossible ever to forgive. Smitty, the prowler of Speedway, Tucson's trashy extension into the desert, heartless, menacing, dropout gymnast, five feet three, the one who walked with crushed tin cans in his boots to make him look taller. There was something about him. The evil he stood for fascinated not only the young hoods, waifs, and even rich girls of Tucson, but also those who combined to send him to the gas chamber. His probation officer, who recommended life for him, felt this.

"It's the first time I ever saw the police really *spooked* by a murderer. Charlie frightened everybody, cops, lawyers, judges. But you know, if for a minute or two at a time you can somehow put those murders out of your head, it's possible to like him. For instance, the way he changed in jail, helped the other prisoners, read to them, showed them how to draft pleas, and taught the Chicanos English."

Now six years afterward, on Death Row, seeming hardly any older than when he was convicted, a radiant condemned boy bounds toward us crying: "Dan!" He reaches between the bars to clasp the probation officer's hand. The blue eyes shine. A startlingly clean-cut attractive young man gazes out at us.

"Wait!"

He runs to his shrouded cell. Members of our tour group stand off to one side murmuring.

"Look!" He's back, thrusting a piece of paper between the bars for his probation officer to see: a certificate from one of Arizona's state universities. This correspondence-school student has passed five subjects with straight A's.

An ill-tempered young drifter currently doing time in the Pima County jail will serve only one year more for theft. Bets are made that he'll almost surely kill someone as soon as he gets out. How much more dangerous he seemed last week than the one here on Death Row waiting for our praise.

"Yes," nodded the probation officer, "he hasn't yet cut his statues out of the marble. Charlie did."

Three statues. Girls under the earth. Can this be the Pied Piper of Tucson, so like a child holding out his report card? It's impossible not to feel sorry; then a rush of promiscuous tenderness toward the incarcerated. Their future, a breath of cyanide or eternity in this shrouded place. Cruel deeds endlessly expiated. Irresponsible sympathy runs in the visitor's head. Open the gates. Let this flesh out. Or keep the crazed repeaters in, but let the others go. The boy has gone through his savagely destructive trip. Anyone can see now, there's no doubt about it, all his evil is behind him. Isn't it possible, whether we want to admit it or not, for the most wicked, wholly inexcusable psychopath to murder his way into a state of grace? Achieve a sort of purity by terrible means? (And again the comparison made by so many: morality and decency aside, the saint and the psychopath can be seen as freed men. It's Burroughs' "animal innocence of lithe movement" confronting us on the other side of the bars.)

"Great, Charlie!"

The irrational moment passes. Hand back his college report card with the straight A's and judgment returns to normal. Grant that agony given and received may bring out a vivid humanity unknown to decent people. Say the prisoner has been transformed by his ordeal, and the ordeals he imposed on others, into a different person, his spirit cleansed by theater, publicity, fame, terror. From here on in, who knows, utterly harmless. Explain this to the families of the three girls.

We say good-bye to him. Clutching the bars, Schmid watches us move off. Now for the gas chamber.

Outdoors, we pass by the exercise court for the condemned; then only a few steps from Death Row, arrive at a small brick cottage in the sun. "It's always at five o'clock in the morning," explains Sergeant Joaquin. "The bag of cyanide opens. Twenty-nine pellets drop right down on the money. He takes a breath and it's all over."

Does it hurt?

No.

"Who says?"

One by one members of our group are drawn to sit down in the chair, testing the straps. Along with several others, I decline, just can't do it. In the room where witnesses gather, we see on the walls photographs of all the men and one woman executed here. Before gas, by hanging. A gallery of wild, staring faces. Some deaths have been officially confirmed at 5:02 A.M. But others haven't been certified until 5:06 and 5:07, and one not until 5:11. And each hanged person's picture on the wall is wreathed by the executioner's knot that killed him.

We come back to the sunny courtyard where the cats and birds are, daisies, hostile stares, and an occasional shout and whistle. Guards walk along the parapet, following us on our way out. Sergeant Joaquin arranges us again, two by two. We move toward the gate, our footsteps quickening. The sun is going down over the wall, and the prisoners in the yard have started to cast longer shadows.

11

RESIDUAL MAN
by Charles Schmid, Jr.

And so the days ask to the years . . . in multiples of pain . . .
caring about the tears of men who hurt—from dying hearts . . .
for something they cannot find . . . and so I stand with the
  blind . . .
not meaning in the eye . . . but those that seek and cry.

As I look into your face . . . seeing depths of sadness, struggle
  and

sorrow . . . I wish I could suffer . . . in your place—yet, I don't believe in sacrifice . . . one has already paid the price.

But just to share the things . . . that hurt you—replacing the agony . . . with something new—

The struggle to see . . . and touch . . . invisible blind souls . . . screaming for mercy—into deaf ears . . . can know and feel the inherited awareness of isolation . . . the mockery and fright . . . the icicled kiss—of fear.

What price . . . a place of honor—demands from a man . . . who
cannot speak and fight or find a place to stand?—The
deadliness of time . . . And this is his right—the virginity
of blossoms . . . begging furry love . . . are born with the wisdom
he will never know.

A suffocating wall . . . crushes his will . . . still, yet he screams . . .

gasping breath . . . dying . . . trying to believe . . . a reason . . . denying the apparent anachronism . . . accepting the lie.—

Quiescent weighty secrets . . . drift up from a tomb—still
begging for compassion . . . finding only doom . . . devours a life . . .
without a sense of meaning—or reason—except greed and
fear . . . that he may know the struggle to grasp . . .
tangibilities
was not in vain.

And so he sometimes flirts with death—pushing Quixotic
abandon—attuning ego to reality . . . yet knowing he can never
win . . . but trying anyway . . . against all reason and odds . . .
except his own . . . this creative complex enigma—integrity—
innate—born within because he is a man.

Lost within the shadows of mystic magic moons—lives the parasitic atrocity . . . that defies all probes.

A twisted satchel . . . of crumbled bones . . . peers out—from
iron jaws . . . to ask why . . . but never knowing . . . lost to error . . .
forgotten . . . alone . . . dead.

12

[He shows] a complete disrespect for the truth . . .
It is evident that the psychopath does not play by the rules.
He makes a mockery not only of the truth but also of all
authority and institutions.

> —Dr. Arnold Buss
> *Psychopathology*

People have asked me why I did what I did at the
station house and I told them a story similar to the one I
just told here, but it was all bullshit. I really did it because it
was fun. That's what I tell my friends. To my brothers I tell
the real truth, which is that I don't know why I did it. They
smile because they know any explanation I give is made up.

> —Abbie Hoffman
> *Revolution for the Hell of It*

The problem of truth ought also to be considered. In
every age, among the people, truth is the property of the
national cause. No absolute verity, no discourse on the
purity of the soul, can shake this position. The native replies
to the living lie of the colonial situation by an equal false-
hood . . . Truth is that which hurries on the break-up of
the colonialist regime: it is that which promotes the emer-
gence of the nation; it is all that protects the natives, and
ruins the foreigners. In this colonialist context there is no
truthful behavior: and the good is quite simply that which
is evil for "them."

> —Frantz Fanon
> *The Wretched of the Earth*

13

In New York, along Lexington Avenue, I see a man hauling
his heavy laundry bag. It's Saturday morning, with relatively few
people around. I know where he's going. To the laundry, and it

will be fascinating to watch. Because there is no longer a laundry. The same thing happened to me two days ago. He's plodding, with his head down, and across the street I follow him.

He stands before an empty lot on which the Chinese laundry stood only a week before. It has been bulldozed and swept flat. All the buildings are gone, and they have even taken the rubble away. The man finally turns about with a numbed look. He actually begins turning in circles, dragging his laundry bag along the sidewalk.

I can see his face, dumb and desolate. For years perhaps he has made the weekly trip to Shan Lee's, from his apartment or rooming house to this steamy hole in the wall. Without fail the spry mysteriously unsweating Cantonese, like animated punctuation marks, grinned and bobbed their heads and handed him a bright red or yellow ticket. Now, with no warning, all at once they've vanished. Somebody might have told him. Not that it really matters. A block or two away another laundry will do the same job. Still, how dejected and lost he appears as he heaves the bag over his shoulder and trudges down a side street.

The psychopath escapes all such nostalgia and loss. Stupid, repetitious journeys are not for him. The disappearance or mutilation of a landmark, a row of chestnuts in blossom like those chopped down by rioting Parisian students, let alone the vanishing of a dear familiar laundry, will give him no feeling of disorientation or pain. He's accustomed to disorientation. He experiences time in frames, disposable units, and lives in a traveling compartment of the present. History is what he sees before him now, lived in. Because with all other history banished, the prospect of deterioration and slow loss of energy through the years, which he can't work with, is forcibly ruled out. (But the possibility of violent, explosive death doesn't appall the psychopath; indeed, he often courts it.)

Followers of the psychopathic style, above all else, mortally fear aging and exist in opposition to it. Refusal of linear continuity—the idea of planning, studying for the future (which doesn't exist)—serves as a temporarily effective denial that one will grow older. Stop time by means of randomness. A portable, impulsive present dictates the day. Throw out all clocks and calendars.

Again and again students have told me that they take it for granted they will not survive the next 10 years. This is not an attitude with which to prepare for a career or bring up a family.

—PAUL GOODMAN
"The New Reformation"*

"When a doctor told [Janis Joplin] she should slow down, she replied: 'Man, I'd rather have 10 years of superhypermost than live to be 70 sitting in some goddam chair watching TV. Right now is where you are. How can you wait?' "†

. . . Dylan's problem is one of time. He is older than most of us and it's beginning to show in his music. That isn't necessarily bad, but who can say that it is necessarily good . . . The question facing him is whether or not the students still need their teacher.

—JON LANDAU
"Rock 1970 It's Too Late to Stop Now"‡

I don't plan to be singing that long. There's nothing more ridiculous-looking than old people on the stage . . . When I was young, around ten, and my parents' friends would come over and try to be real chummy, like be your friend or peer, and you just thought they were assholes. And people who continue to perform on stage figure everybody really thinks they're neat, and they don't. They think, "look at that old jerk."§

—GRACE SLICK (age 31)

* *The New York Times Magazine,* Sept. 14, 1969.
† New York *Daily News,* Oct. 6, 1970.
‡ *Rolling Stone,* Dec. 2, 1970.
§ From a *Rolling Stone* interview, Nov. 12, 1970.

Psychiatrists regularly speak of the psychopath's disordered time sense—as phrased, for instance, by Detre and Jarecki in *Modern Psychiatric Treatment*: his "inability to appreciate the passage of time." The authors refer also to his "peculiar sense of nothingness" without a "busy sense of excitement" to fill up each new day. But psychopaths' excitement rapidly diminishes and must soon be revived by a fresh enthusiasm. Thus, among those following the style, we see a relentless breaking down of past models, and a profusion of fleeting, disposable new models, constantly changing.

Yet possibly the ones, older, scared of chance, who have lived out decades the opposite way—hanging on to outworn commandments, eternally postponing pleasure, counting on the hope of deferred reward—have had an equally disordered time sense. For these, "now" hardly ever exists. Pleasure is waived, so long as the insurance policy can be kept up. Time passes until they collect their pensions, and they have been decent and done their duty and wasted the years, and you see them in tour groups at air terminals starting to have fun at age sixty-five. This is only feasible if you believe in a good God. For the new breed of religionless man (psychopath, rolling stone, grasshopper), no pension plan covers withholding of the libido, and the leap for this moment's pleasure makes all the sense in the world.

Someone independent of time remains independent of government, and not as respectful as he formerly was. Therefore all authorities in whatever country fear the citizen's removal from time (and any drug that helps accomplish it) because this means removal from emotional responsibility and loyalty, such as to a war.

Psychopaths forget the clock. They're not only late: they frequently pass bad checks, ignoring deferred punishment. Cash is what they understand. The idea that time is money makes them laugh. A band of psychopaths recently burned money in the stock exchange, and the vagrant who once lived in a similar style was the first to drive the money-changers from the temple.

In music the new style has taken form in pop and rock. It

too rejects long-term duration, excellence for the ages, monu-
ments. As stressed by Richard Goldstein in *The New York Times*
(Nov. 2, 1969), Pop "should willingly succumb to obsolescence.
. . . Good rock is a collision of surfaces, producing immediate
energy the way an explosion does. What you listen for is the bang,
and when that impact vanishes, so does the experience."

Again the denial of aging: "Pop doesn't age gracefully because it's meant to disappear." Rock music has no intention of
lasting through the years. "Some people consider mobility a sign
of decadence, as though an artist's prime duty were to devise a
system and then hold it, like a fort. But in Pop, any artist who
doesn't move becomes imbedded in his moment and institutionalized as nostalgia. . . . This tumult of constant change is what
gives rock its vitality."

Goldstein asks: "Must something last to be art?" No, not for
"an entire generation to whom 'now' is an essential quality, not
a descriptive one."

14

Just beyond the rim of the throbbing present lies boredom—
pursuing the psychopath and all who emulate him.

The *Antioch Record* (July 24, 1970) featured a dispatch from
a commune with this paragraph:

> Beth told me. "You know, I can't stay anywhere too
> long. I get up to Vermont, I hang around for a week or two.
> By then I'm going crazy, stir-crazy, so I split (NOTE: by
> the way, what split really means: "Become somebody else"
> —"Am reborn"). I hitch down to the City. In the City
> there's a million things to do, so I run around all the time,
> not getting any sleep, not eating right. After two or three
> days I'm exhausted, worn out, burned up, full of city dirt.
> So I split, I hitch up to Vermont, back home again. So it
> goes."

The true psychopath can go on in this way, has no alternative,
knows no other. His imitators are the ones who may suffer ter-

ribly, not because the random way of living is inherently wrong but for the reason that it's hard to manage.

"Judy" interviewed in *The New York Times* (Aug. 25, 1969) after coming back down from Woodstock.

> Q. Do you want a family?
> Judy. "One child. Just, you know, to procreate. But I don't want a family because I don't want to get into that much responsibility. I want to be able to move. I want to be able to leave at any time. I don't want that much restriction."

But in the next breath:

> Judy. "We're more oriented to the present. It's like do what you want to do now. It's almost a rushing thing. And it's bad. . . . Because it seems like, well, you can never stay one place very long. The kids that you know go off. If you stay anywhere very long you get into a planning thing. If you get a job, if you keep it, it seems like, Oh hell, what am I going to do? You know, I've been here this long and I've got money—what am I going to do? Save it? What for? So you just move on."

Years ago I knew Neal Cassady, even stood up as a witness at one of his marriages before a gloomy justice of the peace in Newark. In 1957 he would become famous as Dean Moriarty, racing, pot-smoking, jazz-digging, continent-splitting hero of Jack Kerouac's *On the Road*. According to any medical model ever devised, Cassady, or Moriarty (they are virtually identical, with hardly any fictional difference), qualified as a complete psychopath. There can be no way to get around this label. He fits every description.

This was Moriarty:

> . . . In a matter of days they were dickering with Camille in San Francisco by long-distance telephone for the necessary divorce papers so they could get married. Not only that, but a few months later Camille gave birth to Dean's

second baby, the result of a few nights' rapport early in the
year. And another matter of months and Inez had a baby.
With one illegitimate child in the West somewhere, Dean
then had four little ones and not a cent, and was all troubles
and ecstasy and speed as ever. . . .

In one of the novel's best-known passages Moriarty and Sal
Paradise (Cassady and Kerouac), at all times living ecstatically
in the present, have hitchhiked a ride with a dull couple, and
Moriarty cries out:

> ". . . Sal, think of it, we'll dig Denver together and see
> what everybody's doing although that matters little to us,
> the point being that we know what IT is and we know
> TIME and we know that everything is really FINE. . . .
> Now you just dig them in front. They have worries, they're
> counting the miles, they're thinking about where to sleep
> tonight, how much money for gas, the weather, how they'll
> get there—and all the time they'll get there anyway, you
> see. But they need to worry and betray time with urgencies
> false and otherwise . . ."

Today's psychopathic style (as opposed to the certifiable illness, if it can be certified) began, at least in the United States,
with the romance of the Beat Generation. The wild demigod
Moriarty called to the trapped conformists of the Eisenhower
years: "Come on! I'll show you how to live!" Rushing from place
to place, back and forth across the country, Kerouac and his
friends opened up the possibilities of a crazy, exciting new way
to take hold of life. "He makes you want to go to Albuquerque!"
sighed a young girl at that time, just after finishing *On the Road.*

But what does not come through in Beat Generation writing
is this: with the exception of ecstatic moments flagellated out of
them by speed (at that time, of automobiles), hit-and-run sex,
and wild new bebop music, the beats, always living in the present, were much of the time catastrophically bored. From the literature, one has the impression of unending excitement, rushing
here and there, one ecstasy after another, this tempo being broken
now and then by periods of holy meditation. But in reality the

days were for the most part directionless. There were long, long stretches of boredom during which I remember the heroes of this generation simply not knowing what to do with themselves and sitting around with hangovers, smoking, and wondering what now.

The writers report only the high points. So we have ecstasy, and some great and almost-great writing founded on boredom. Boredom pursued the beats like a cloud of gnats and they ran from it. But then—the paradox and wonder—a handful of them managed to produce out of this littering of time, and the waste of days, enormously creative work arising mysteriously from the banal hours they actually lived through.

And Cassady, head psychopath, was the most bored of all. Never a bore himself; no, he was exciting, but bored nearly to death. To save himself he kept constantly in motion. Physically, he never stopped moving, hustling, lighting up, moving on. Even his jobs had to move: railway brakeman, car jockey in parking lots. Yet sophisticate and fetishist of hip that he was, Cassady would always make the wrong move at a critical time—selling marijuana to narcs, mistakes of that sort. The glamor of living by the moment, digging only the moment, impaired his judgment. He was incautious as the rawest rookie. Neal should long since— with his experience and time in jail for the same offense—have had a sense of the narc and how to avoid him. But he had to have whatever he wanted *now*, and dealt now, if that was his impulse. He lay down to sleep *now* with too many drugs in him on a night in Mexico that was too cold, and that was the foolish and unnecessary way he died.

15

Are saints bored?

16

In "The Anatomy of Violence," from *Violence in the Streets*, John Paul Scott wonders:

. . . what is the cure for the person who has developed a strong habit of violent behavior over a period of years? This kind of person is often described as a psychopathic personality . . . At present there is no conspicuously successful method of dealing with the psychopath. Psychiatrists agree that their chances of improvement are poor, and since they are highly dangerous, few people wish to work with them except under the conditions of physical restraint provided by prisons and detention centers. We can only conclude that prevention of violence is far more effective than its cure.

Yes, but perhaps we're much too late for that, since violence has now become respectable, condoned, even honored, certainly (the outraged response to Lieutenant Calley's conviction) taken for granted. Everywhere we have apologies for violence, as well as violence without apology. Again the medical and sociological model lags behind, for this is no longer an aberration; it's virtually the rule. True, the ascendancy of the psychopath's game has been swift. Only a few years ago in civilized quarters, smashing the other person along with what he intellectually stands for was considered wrong or at least regrettable. But polite dialogue, courteous persuasion, agreement to disagree, have abruptly become outmoded.

Arguments now have an intensely physical base. (Fanon notes approvingly "the inaptitude of the native intellectual to carry on a two-sided discussion; for he cannot eliminate himself when confronted with an object or an idea.") Hence, at this time the civilized man must be alive to the chance that—once involved in even relatively mild controversy—he may be physically shut up, pushed, or hit.

A letter has just arrived from an old college roommate, quiet, scholarly, pacifist, math professor. He has been working with the White Panthers, and writes: "I think that at the same time my horror of violence is growing my acceptance of it as reasonable is growing too. That is, my acceptance of the necessity for it."

My young friend Arnold announces scornfully: "Bourgeois

culture has been organized to *avoid pain!*" He believes that pain should be sought out, mastered, given, received. To be intimidated is to die a little. This fourth-year college student agrees with Mailer that a psychic backdown is equivalent to sustaining a bodily insult, with biological deterioration in store for the insulted person. Now, to avoid this, he's going for his black belt in karate. He wants to be able to stand up to almost any conceivable assault or put-down, even the slightest abridgement of his self-esteem; win, or do better than hold his own, in whatever face-to-face situation may present itself, whether dangerous or trivial. For him, the ideal of nonviolence amounts to nothing more than the refuge of the weak elevated to a moral position.

Arnold has deliberately made himself paranoid. Even on a sunny suburban sidewalk he carries himself alertly, as if in a swamp or jungle, darting glances here and there, aware at all times of the impression he's making on passersby. He has no patience with weakness of any sort, knowing as he does the pain of endless push-ups from the knuckles, the shock of smashes to the kidney, a twice-broken nose, all endured with a smile.

He was trained by a mean Korean who finally told him: "All right, you've gone far enough in the gym. Now take your knowledge into the streets . . ." Arnold went to the worst part of several towns, shouldering his way along the sidewalk, going from one honky-tonk to another in search of trouble. In a garage he challenged a hairy motorcyclist, but the man backed off, muttering: "Excuse me . . ."

He reads aloud passages from Mailer, and explains: "The bourgeois will always fold up. But the psychopath—he's ready to die!"

Arnold tries to stay cool. "Karate's not the ultimate release, sex is. But karate makes you feel good and look good. What it does is release your natural anxiety. It gives you the ability to relax so that your natural powers, if you have any, can take over and function properly. You say 'Fuck everything or fuck nothing.' If I can't fuck everything I feel frustrated. I feel the venom of hatred. If this happens, hatred turns inward and consumes you, if you can't turn it toward the enemy."

He believes also that the bourgeoisie have tried to take the violence out of sex. "Another thing that blocks people. The idea that sex is like a warm puppy. No! Sex *is* violent. It's good to be violent. The kissy-faced love like a warm puppy takes the pure animalism out of it. A certain kind of sadism isn't unhealthy. Like karate, crude balls-y. *Uuuh!* Why can't karate release tension like sex? They both relieve it—but in different ways. Sex is a man-woman thing. Karate is man-man."

Then Arnold said: *"If this was a woman's world and they were running things, I wouldn't feel the same kind of anxiety."*

He comes, of course, from a middle-class background, and feels the self-contempt, or rather contempt for his class, from which children of the bourgeoisie were once exempted, but not now. In the war between the bourgeois and the psychopath he senses that the rough invaders will win. Wasn't it the bourgeoisie, he asks contemptuously, that *abolished dueling?*

The bourgeois then is afraid for his own skin, and the dignity he thinks he owns. The psychopath finds himself, his identity, in violence and in theater. Adopting the style, in revolutionary terms, Jerry Rubin has the rebel coming on as a "longhaired, bearded, hairy, crazy motherfucker whose life is theater, every moment creating the new society as he destroys the old."

Arnold is no revolutionary, wears no beard. His hair is a bushy blond mop but not especially long. Not an outlaw either, he still finds it essential—anyhow at this point in his life—to make use of the psychopathic model. Arnold's father told me five years ago that a psychiatrist had advised: "He'll grow out of it. Give him five years." Perhaps so, he's now twenty-two. *"Mature* out of it . . ." That was what Dr. Detre said about many young psychopaths. If transported back in time, a psychiatrist might judge Genghis Khan close to insane—certainly by European standards. Yet the man's murderous cavalry overran much of Europe. Perhaps the psychopaths among us are our Mongols.

Systematic brutality seems to work especially well against the bourgeoisie. In Nazi concentration camps, according to Dr. Bettelheim in *The Informed Heart:*

    Non-political middle class prisoners . . . were those least able to withstand the initial shock. They were utterly unable to understand what had happened to them and why. More than ever they clung to what had given them self-respect up to that moment. Even while being abused, they would assure the SS that they had never opposed Nazism. They could not understand why they, who had always obeyed the law without question, were being persecuted . . . All they could do was plead, and many groveled . . .

    No consistent philosophy, either moral, political, or social, protected their integrity or gave them strength for an inner stand against Nazism. They had little or no resources to fall back on when subject to the shock of imprisonment. Their self esteem had rested on a status and respect that came with their positions, depended on their jobs, on being head of a family, or similar external factors . . .

    Up to then they had never realized just how much extraneous and superficial props had served them in place of self respect and inner strength. Then all of a sudden everything that made them feel good about themselves for so long was knocked out from under them.

    . . . they disintegrated as autonomous persons . . . Nearly all of them lost their desirable middle class characteristics, such as their sense of propriety and self respect. They became shiftless, and developed to an exaggerated degree the undesirable characteristics of their group: pettiness, quarrelsomeness, self pity . . .

The absence of paranoia in innocent bourgeois faces: I notice this particularly as they wait, only a moment or two, for one of the restaurant's best tables.

Saul Bellow finds the bourgeoisie often responding with secret admiration to the psychopath's attacks. From *Mr. Sammler's Planet:*

    And for the middle part of society there was envy and worship of this power to kill . . . How they loved the man strong enough to take blood guilt on himself. For them an elite must prove itself in this ability to murder. For such people a saint must be understood as one who was equal in spirit to the fiery twisting of crime in the inmost fibers of his heart. The superman testing himself with an ax, crushing the skulls of old women . . .

I know a privileged man of sixty, who, in to New York from his Maryland farm, whacked a taxicab with his umbrella when— moving against a red light—it almost ran over him. He was horri- fied when the driver leaped out and gripped his throat, forcing him over a fender, shaking and cursing him. Until recently coach- men didn't act that way.

Our train passed through New Haven with the blinds down. The blacks were rioting and throwing boulders down from the bridges. These had crashed through the diesel's shield, cutting the engineer. Now we waited. Police cleared the bridges. The conductor wouldn't let the train proceed until every blind was down and all lights out. Sound precautions, at once calming and alerting the passengers. But they also blinded us to the as- sault being carried out against our estate. The train crept out of town. Twilight was falling and we smoked in our unreal cabin. Not until New Haven was a mile behind us did the word come to lift our shades.

A summer before, the revolutionaries rocked my taxi. Trapped mid-block in Harlem on that sweltering night I thought I was gone. I had a black driver whose especially sullen and brutal face I had marked when innocently stepping into the cab at the 125th Street station. This man cursed and bellowed at the rioters sur- rounding us and forced his taxi against the crowds. A stream directed from a fire hydrant hit the car, making it shudder. Teen- age boys capered and mugged in front of us.

We got through. My tip was high, and he scowled on re- ceiving it.

This happened last year in a western state. An unemployed handyman of Norwegian extraction, call him Lars Gunderson, his wife Mary, and their eight children were traveling west in an old pickup truck on the way to California, where he hoped to find a job. The truck broke down. They ran out of money, and foraging for odd jobs yielded nothing. For two weeks they spent cold autumn days and nights in an unheated wilderness cabin. Then with the last of his money Gunderson paid for a small motel room, good for one night only, and, in the words of a newspaper account, "attempted to sneak his eight children in."

The motel manager, say Henry Royce, was outraged. He wouldn't put up with such a fraud. Besides, so many occupants in a single room was against the law. Royce then ordered Gunderson to get out.

Gunderson fell on the manager, stabbing him *ten times*. Royce was taken to the hospital and Gunderson to jail. The story excited immediate newspaper and television interest, and the plight of the Gundersons became a lead story.

Lars was released on probation, and within two weeks . . .

Contributions to the beleaguered family amounted to $1,543.75.

A temporary home was donated to the Gundersons in the best part of town.

Free groceries filled the kitchen cupboards. Mounds of donated clothing piled up in every room.

A garage repaired the broken-down pickup truck, and put new tires on it.

A Gunderson Assistance Fund was established at the local bank, with Mrs. Gunderson and the real estate developer who had provided the family with their house designated as co-signers.

Contributions kept on pouring in.

The Gundersons sorted out the donated clothing and in their turn passed along to charity what they couldn't use.

17

The psychopathic ethic can be summed up in one word. Perform! Or perhaps two, in a positive revolutionary context, Jerry Rubin's *Do It!* Gunderson did it, and saved his family. Nothing else he might have done would have served him so well. Had he quietly departed, as ordered by the motel manager—had he been law-abiding—the family would probably have gone under.

Again psychopathy and Christian fable curiously combine. The black sheep more beloved than the ones who never strayed; the manager administering the motel and only doing his job, ends up in the hospital with multiple stab wounds. No outpouring of love and gifts, no collection, no fan mail.

Though he himself may be one, the outlaw has no patience with losers. Get with it, or die. Nonperformance is the sin, especially, for example, when it takes the form of illness. See Kerouac abandoned with dysentery and blazing fever by Neal Cassady in Mexico City. Sal Paradise: "I looked up out of the dark swirl of my mind . . . and I saw Dean bending over the kitchen table. It was several nights later and he was leaving Mexico City already."

The enchanting psychopath speaks: " 'Poor Sal, poor Sal, got sick. Stan'll take care of you. Now listen to hear if you can in your sickness: I got my divorce from Camille down here and I'm driving back to Inez in New York tonight if the car holds out. . . . Gotta get back to my life. Wish I could stay with you. Pray I can come back. . . . Yes, yes, yes, I've got to go now. Old fever Sal, good-by.' "

Later, Kerouac: "When I got better I realized what a rat he was, but then I had to understand the impossible complexity of his life, how he had to leave me there, sick, to get on with his wives and woes. 'Okay, old Dean, I'll say nothing.' "

. . . the only morality a matter of how far out you're brave enough and demented enough to go . . .*

—MICHAEL THOMAS,
Rolling Stone writer

With the bankers and things like that . . . I did a job on this banker that we were using, and on a few other people, and on the

---

* From review of Mick Jagger in the film *Performance*.

Beatles. How do you describe the job? . . . I maneuver people.
That's what leaders do, and I sit and make situations which will
be of benefit to me with other people, it's as simple as that . . .
Maneuvering is what it is, let's not be coy about it. It is a deliberate and thought-out maneuver of how to get a situation the way
we want it. That's how life's about, isn't it, is it not? . . . it's maneuvering. There's nothing ashamed about it. We all do it, it's
just owning up, you know, not going around saying "God bless
you, Brother" pretending there is no vested interest . . .

You have to be a bastard to make it, that's a fact, and the
Beatles are the biggest bastards on earth.*

—JOHN LENNON

I mean to say, if I really want to do something, I don't particularly care if it's legal, illegal, moral, immoral or amoral. I
want to do it, so I do it.†

—WILLIAM POWELL,
author of *The Anarchist Cookbook*

The revolution has replaced the church as the country's moral
authority.

—JERRY RUBIN
Do It!

In a *Newsweek* interview Erik Erikson foresees the emer-
gence of "a worldwide ethic superseding traditional moralities."

"I would call ethical," he writes, "such guidelines and inter-
dicts as are based not on what is arbitrarily permitted or supersti-
tiously forbidden but on what *liberated experience and informed
intuition can agree on* [my italics]."

Erikson goes no deeper than this. But what he must be heading toward, at the very least, is a realistic ethic based on life as it
actually happens, works out, from day to day (see John Len-

Rolling Stone interview, Jan. 7, 1971.
† Quoted in *Newsweek*, April 12, 1971 (p. 98).

non), rather than what ought to be. Ethics without an ought. And ethics, it's not too much to say, constructed—with improvements—from the psychopathic model.

Wherein lies the improvement? Simply in awareness. The certifiable psychopath (if such a person may be assumed to walk around) has been projected by Dr. Cleckley and many others as a sort of imitation human being. Despite his ability to maneuver people, he doesn't really know what he's doing because he can't experience the opposite of maneuvering, that is, innocence. He can make the sounds of love, but has no idea what others feel when they are affectionate together. He has heard of compassion. But he doesn't know what it is; it's not there for him, zero. We might say the sociopath of this kind remains innocent of compassion. Therefore, he's forever innocent of others' emotional rights.

But those who freely *adopt* the psychopath's ways know what they are doing. They're acting not reflexively but on the thought-out conviction that all previous moral codes, however useful they are intended to be, simply end up dishonest, hypocritical, and don't work besides, since if you believe them and really live by them (as opposed to faking it), others not so innocent and inhibited will victimize you and put you down over and over again.

Everyone his own revolutionary, his own artist; his own Gunderson, Lennon, and Rubin, the new man will no longer even pretend old-fashioned fairness and moral restraint. Such followers of the psychopath have openly let us know that they will reduce and destroy us with no apologies if we get in the way, and feel no shame whatever. Could Gunderson afford not to stab the motel keeper?

But in contrast to the psychopath, their mentally ill model, they are not loveless men (Gunderson fiercely protects his family; John's devotion to Yoko couldn't be better known). They practice selective psychopathy, like gangsters, sometimes tender with wife, girl, friend, family, but then cold, ferocious, in calculating the exploitation or downfall of another person inconvenient for them, and (different from the past)—except at the time of the surprise action or maneuver—not for a moment pretending otherwise.

Pursue this hard new ethic, here, with us. What is it based

on? First, disrespect for law. Dr. Karl Menninger writes of the psychopath: ". . . he breaks the rules as if he had a presumed immunity from the consequences which affect other people." Now come back to the probation officer's remark that a sociopath is the most realistic person on earth. Unsurprisingly then, his ethics relate to power. If he feels that a conventional, obedient, decent response to the rules, the law, custom, will bring him down, cause him to lose, suffer, not get what he wants—or if the rules bore him—he will violate them. No general principles apply. If they exist, which they don't, such rules and principles should be cited only to bend things your way. From this standpoint, for example, Eldridge Cleaver was able to say that violence can be judged wrong when employed by the authorities and morally right when used to advance the revolution. In any event, if you're going to be violent, ruthless, fight, maneuver—like, say, Jerry Rubin, like Gunderson—the psychopathic ethic tells you to *do it well*.

Psychopath and sociopath make it their business to intrude on the moral assumptions of the middle class. My wife was twice attacked by purse snatchers in Central Park while she was holding our baby, once while changing his diaper. "With a baby in her arms!" Inhuman! . . . By whose rules? Mine, laid down by the privileged who can afford to be civilized.

In these circumstances, when the quarry can't strike back, outlaw and psychopath care only that the prospects for success will be all the better. Nor can we imagine this as in the least inconsistent, or from the invader's point of view remotely unethical. For have not rules of the game, fair play, courtesy, etc., always protected privilege and injustice? Grace of all kinds protects the status quo. Neat hair, dress, and deportment, the well-rounded syllable, clipped speech, savoir-faire, knowledge of the menu and the dance, separate the privileged from those who ought to know their places. And good manners, the beau geste gentlemanliness, refusal to take advantage, fairness to the adversary, all are means of forcing the underdog to play proper croquet.

How can rebels and the psychopaths among them be convinced that violent rule-breaking is really delinquent—if adherence to the game rules means defeat for them, *or boredom*? If we play fair and I always win, and the sociopath finds himself either hungry, furious, or bored, why should I be surprised when he tries to disrupt my game in any way possible for him?

Though it remains unclear, try to make out the structure of the ethic now emerging. It seems to be founded on a conception of grace involving sheer performance. This has many aspects— success, wielding power, being funny (bullying comedian), frightening, beautiful, or theatrical. The ethic of thou shalt dominate the space around you, come on in style, never stumbling, looking awkward, or being caught in an unattractive moment. Thou shalt not feel unsure of yourself, or if you do feel unsure, never reveal it, and never explain.

This new grace has to do with beauty of performance and contempt for nonperformance. Unfortunately, the almost barbaric worship of performance can turn cruel when it encounters the ludicrous, defenseless and inept, such deficiencies being considered crimes. We have then the vile side of beauty, an aesthetics of cruelty. Zen sadism. I have felt in myself, though nonviolently, a number of times, this giggling time-stopping cruelty while smoking marijuana. It's the kind of feeling that in bad company can produce gang rapes and torture deaths—the victim's fate being experienced as aesthetically appropriate for one reason or another.

Beyond the commandments to perform well and be attractive, the outline of another absolute virtue may be detected. More than any other quality, the new ethic values *speed* in varied forms. Far more than impatience, the need for instantaneous action comes out of the psychopathic style. Instant being, not laboring to become. Moving into what you want immediately, no delay. Free-form, even serene maneuvering, not slowed by sentiment. Thus violence is speed. Motorcycles. Brutal directness, speed on the uptake. Getting there effortlessly from one place to another, from one thought to another. Telling the exact truth is speed. Even more, silence is speed, electric understanding too swift for words, moving on.

And then, stasis in flight, a sort of strung-out motionlessness, as seen in the drawings of genius by Saul Steinberg (who remarked, grinning, one night that the most important thing in life is speed; also that life's most exciting exchanges and best moments occur "tangentially," passing in a flash, not to be dwelt on, gone before you can think about them).

Drugs provide this sensation of speed and at the same time motionlessness, some compounds being named after the state of bliss desired. Even marijuana helps in a smaller way to achieve the goal of the psychopath and his imitators, which couldn't be more understandable, to remain forever young at the speed of light.

18

Each human being is a spaceship. No, each human being is a galaxy spinning lonely in space, and the only contacts we have with other galaxies (light years, really) are the flimsy flickerings of our sense organs.

And what an ontological, epistemological leap of faith it is, really, to believe in the existence of each other.

—Timothy Leary
The Politics of Ecstasy

Years ago, in the spring of 1963, Timothy Leary and Dick Alpert turned me on in a Manhattan apartment with what I've always felt, but never can prove, was a gigantic overdose of pure Sandoz LSD. What must have been between 600 and 1,000 micrograms sent the neophyte on a wild death-rebirth trip. The universe shivered in pieces. He became a speck, nothing, an item of terror, like an astronaut flung out too far, with the apparent certainty at one grievous moment that he would never make it back. This meant going laughing, crying, sobbing crazy for the greater part of ten hours. The journey was difficult and terrible, albeit with some ecstatic moments. Recovery from it even now seems miraculous.

As Leary has always said, and believes now—wherever he may be—the journey through inner space couldn't help but change the voyager's psyche forever. This is no exaggeration: one will never again be quite the same after experiencing the simulation of death and being reborn. It's practically impossible not to see life in a new way.

Looking back, I realize that, for me, LSD trips required a formal structure involving some kind of worship, and were too unbearably shattering without it. More on this shortly, but for the moment consider the likelihood that acid may someday be taken religiously, like Communion, on formal and regular occasions, especially after age forty—a time when a man, a woman, often desperately needs to review the years and select paths of renascence. (As a part of a *rite de passage*, how beautifully LSD could work within a religious framework: the wafer and wine of middle-aged renewal.)

Leary and Alpert put many of us through such spectacular head changes. This may have been medically irresponsible but it wasn't a matter of negligence. They had absolute faith in the material and seemed almost to feel that there couldn't be an overdose. They also believed that the voyager ought not to be led gradually into the consciousness-expanding trip, with small doses. Rather he should really be hit over the head with a heavy cluster of mikes so that the "temporary therapeutic psychosis" would surely break him apart and put him together, shatter him so that he would feel truly reborn.

Leary was relatively buttoned down then, and appeared sometimes in business suits, but began shortly to go into white robes. Those were exuberant times for anyone involved in the early LSD movement, comparable to the early days of communism or psychoanalysis. We met in cells, initiating one newcomer after another in an atmosphere of love and holiness that for a long time didn't sicken and become too sweet. But the food often was. Psychedelic fudge, brownies. We lay about sacramentally by candlelight. Each voyage was a holy trip; we waited, arms out, for the newly initiated brother or sister to come down. We

cradled the terrified soul, and laughed with the joyously returning pioneer, and people lay naked and peacefully together.

Later we were to witness (or ourselves experience) broken
marriages, abandonment of jobs and families, careers changed
and forgotten, sex preferences altered, some energies increased
and others given over to sloth, all resulting from the LSD voyages. For many, idleness became a virtue, and all forms of work
—except for projects like gardening and drawing buckets of water
from the well—spiritually distasteful. And then, as I've mentioned, torpor set in. After a while our parties became dull and
droopy-eyed, all friends and disciples with our music, incense,
and candles, and no one with much to say. A stranger might
have thought he was in a loony bin populated exclusively by the
zapped, ghosts and zombies—and this was to become the standard
set for acid gatherings on campuses and in cities and villages all
over the country. Later, as acid was indiscriminately combined
with speed and other compounds, came the violence. As Leary
said: "I didn't anticipate speed . . ."

But unquestionably, back in 1963, we knew a spiritual revolution would soon follow. We were the lucky advance people. A
few thousand of us shared an enormous secret that would and
did start undermining the society we had grown up in. Godless
America would become religious again, and as their employees
turned on secretly and remained—no longer believing in com-
merce—stoned for much of the day, the citadels of capitalism
would shiver (and this is happening!). We passed one another
with knowing glances, the equivalent of secret handshakes. At
any gathering among those who hadn't yet tripped out, we went
mysteriously among the ignorant like missionaries, whispering
news of the voyage into inner space that could transform them
utterly and the world too.

Leary and Alpert were exultant. In a pamphlet, "The Politics
of Consciousness Expansion" (also 1963), they wrote:

> Make no mistake: the effect of consciousness-expanding
> drugs will be to transform our conception of human nature,
> of human potentialities, of existence. The game is about to
> be changed, ladies and gentlemen. Man is about to make use

of that fabulous electrical network he carries around in his skull. Present social establishments had better be prepared for the change. Our favorite concepts are standing in the way of a floodtide, two billion years building up. The verbal dam is collapsing. Head for the hills, or prepare your intellectual craft to flow with the current.

And it largely proved to be true. The psychedelic drugs *have* permanently changed millions of heads—and there isn't any question that they helped produce a number of the multiple revolutions now sweeping the old world away. Correctly again, Leary predicted the arrival on the scene of a band of "mutants." Even reformed heads who don't trip out anymore have been marked. They're simply not the same people they once were, and the change is qualitative. They have had glimpses into, and been stunned by, an infinitude of cellular movies. Whoever travels back into the Collective Unconscious Jung told us about long ago —even the most ordinary individual—comes back with the memory of wonders that make his ambitions, worries, and hang-ups here, in this particular span, appear small and trivial.

In this frame of mind, linear life-planning becomes much more difficult to follow. It's hard to go back to the agency and put your heart into the promotion of chewing gum except—we will see—as a lark. Any kind of crusade seems ridiculous, business crusades most of all, and if undertaken can only be faked as an as-if, "the crusading game." For while the sales manager is talking, your mind returns to the Jungian voyage, the jungles, swamps, and caves of ice, the enormous inner world of your own cells.

(Diving through an enormous lotus flower in the void, at the shuddering climax before rebirth, I beheld a great electric power station in space, like a jungle gym consisting of naked bodies all joined together, and that was [is?] the sum of all existence.)

Playing the prophet game, Leary did then, as he promised, help corrupt millions of a generation that might otherwise have carried on as dutiful young conformists. He managed this by enveloping LSD in magic mists, celebrating the material as sacred food ("the religious trip," he now calls this phase), and holding it out, issuing it to the young for use as ammunition in the war between generations.

For a decade or more, experimental work with LSD had been going on in laboratories around the country. What Leary did was to steal this sacred food from the gods (laboratory scientists) and, clad in his white robes, cast it among the children of the 1960's. Did he enlighten, temporarily stupefy, or damage them? Possibly all these. And in pursuit of our theme, ask whether Dr. Leary didn't also help to create and glamorize a new psychopathic model for the youth of the country to follow.

Psychopathic? A word, a label. Still, it tries to describe a condition. Going back to 1963, I remember lying across a couch exhausted after my trip. Leary came in joking: "Now you know what it feels to suffer ego loss!" He gave me a bite of his apple and a swallow of ginger beer. (He's the only person I ever met who drank Scotch with Schweppes tonic.) Then he picked up a needle that looked as big as a dirigible filled with DMT, offering me the half-hour up-and-down still wilder and farther-out trip that this instant mushroom could provide. I said: "No, no!" pushing it away, and he only laughed and everybody was kind.

I was vaguely elated, but afraid too. All the people around me had such huge (from the drug, dilated) eyes. Leary clapped me on the shoulder. I could see him, facing me on the couch, a bright, well-wishing, and perhaps, yes, a holy man, but—it's hard to express, making allowances for acid-induced paranoia—I felt in the presence of a monstrous tenderness. Later, stumbling home in the dark, with automobiles still seeming to swim by, I rang the doorbell in renewed doubt and panic, and bursting in on my wife I told her: "It's a nest of psychopaths over there!"

Ever since, I've wondered what vibrations these were. Why did such likable people, Leary, Alpert, and the others, seem vaguely menacing? Had I intended to say that they didn't know right from wrong, or anymore care to distinguish between the two? Were they perhaps telling me that right and wrong were obsolete, merely part of a Justice Game?

They seemed from another world, out of time. That long ago the psychopathic concept meant little to me. Yet the word came out: "Psychopaths . . ." It was the precise word. I felt I had just come from a cell of new people, and I thought then that there was a controlled madness among them. They would soon be able to overturn the world. The substance at their disposal made sure of that. I sensed smiling danger. They were going to put my world into shock. At the same time I was asking myself why not, why shouldn't they? They had been bright, affectionate companions and instructors during my voyage. Again, why not? Because that disturbing first impression kept returning: *they're crazy!*

Perhaps as one of the crowd in Galilee, on the hillside, by the lake, listening to the New Man preach, I would have experienced the same shiver of paranoia; sensed a new idea being born and wanted to stamp it out. Like Leary and Alpert, that one would have seemed (as, of course, he did) the bearer of a sinister new message, an overly democratic, disastrous conception of love; someone who ought to be shut up, because if he were allowed to continue preaching the doctrine he was coming on with, all the laws I lived by would crumble—and, ill-equipped, I'd have to start over again.

Alpert (Baba Ram Dass now) is said to have given up on the use of LSD and other drugs, achieving his spiritual highs without chemical help. Leary has been treated shamefully and cruelly, persecuted and imprisoned.

Signs appear that the drug revolution he did so much to create has passed him by. Students are reported to be turning off LSD, partly because you can hardly get hold of pure Sandoz or be sure of pure anything anymore, and the available material—sometimes laced by malevolent amateur chemists with amphetamine and strychnine—can produce horrible trips and scramble the user's brain for long periods.

19

In Algeria a year ago Eldridge Cleaver spoke scornfully of the "whole silly psychedelic drug culture." It may have become silly now, with the mind-changing foods abused and misused. But in the beginning it was anything but silly, and certainly its effect can't be put down as being in any way trivial. For it has produced a breed of mutant inner-space travelers, and a great many of these people, by medical definition or imitation (amounting almost to the same thing), may be judged psychopathic. I mean that among millions of acid-trippers LSD brings about lasting psychopathic symptoms that won't change. And Dr. Leary, underrated as a thinker, possibly a genius (*The Politics of Ecstasy*, for example, being a great book), may well have served as, played the role of, master psychopath, guiding his followers to a mysterious end that no one can yet predict. A warm, nice psychopath, wishing no man, no woman any harm. He could be remembered (depending on who writes the textbooks) for having done irreparable damage by turning loose a shattering substance on millions of children unready for it. He could also go down as some kind of stoned, ironical Prometheus.

The values and characteristics assumed by acid heads may be easily observable (though not necessarily in an evil aspect) as values and characteristics identified clinically with the psychopath. Marijuana, too, brings about limited psychopathy (flightiness, indifference to time, duty, assignments, responsibility, any kind of crusade). The hallucinogens, or whatever we prefer to call them, tend to result in more profound psychopathy extending beyond the experience. True, alcohol also can release similar tendencies, recklessness, irresponsibility, antisocial responses, as with the quiet man who turns into a dangerous drunk. But the alcoholic comes back down with hangover and remorse, making his fall acceptable to Christian authority. For this reason, hard alcohol is primarily a Christian drug. Cop-fighting and other resistance to authority may take place. But the fighter returns penitent. After the hangover and guilt, authority is recognized again.

Liquor makes things hazier. But marijuana clarifies and enhances a feeling of the ridiculousness of events, which doesn't go away. Authority becomes ridiculous, pompous, and irrelevant—and after the high, and with LSD after the trip, disrespect for this-worldly values will remain. No hangover, guilt, or comeuppance can be counted on to follow.

As indeed with the psychopath. And why may not this state of mind be imagined as healthy, all to the good? If LSD can help eliminate guilt, hang-ups, hatred, why be upset if a legion of mutants—even those who no longer or only rarely trip out but still have a residue of psychopathy eternally within them—may be taking over and drastically changing our present scene, which, after all, appears in many respects quite sick?

The answer naturally depends on what kind of world we prefer . . .

At the heart of all psychedelic philosophy you will always find the idea that life is made up of games and trips. Every activity should be seen as a game, and every extended experience as a trip. The Stations of the Cross, for example, would be a heavy trip. Putting Christians and lions together in the arena would be the persecution game.

From this point of view, a game, a trip, should be enjoyed, suffered, or gone through with the knowledge that it has been experienced millions of times before and will recur infinitely, and will pass. You can stand apart from it; another game, another trip will come along soon. Leary defines a game as a "learned cultural sequence," never to be taken with do-or-die seriousness. Thus, a Crusader off to the Holy Land should understand that he's into the crusading game.

At the 14th International Congress of Applied Psychology held in 1962 in Copenhagen, Leary, sharing the platform with Aldous Huxley, delivered a brilliant speech on "How to Change Behavior." Here are a few excerpts:

> All behavior involves learned games. But only that rare westerner we call "mystic" or who has had a visionary experience of some sort sees clearly the game structure of behavior. Most of the rest of us spend our time struggling with roles and rules and goals and concepts of games which are implicit and confusedly not seen as games. Trying to apply the roles and rules and rituals of one game to other games.
>
> Worst of all is the not knowing that it is a game. Baseball is a clean and successful game because it is seen as a

game. [But] the family game is treated by most cultures as far more than a game, with its implicit contracts, limited in time and space. The nationality game. It is treason not to play. The racial game. The religious game. And that most treacherous and tragic game of all, the game of individuality. The ego game. The Timothy Leary game. Ridiculous how we confuse this game, overplay it . . .

The currently popular method of behavior change is called psychotherapy. A medical game . . . Psychotherapy interprets confusion and inefficiency in game-playing as illness. We call it sickness and attempt to cure it employing the medical game.

Finally, "the most effective approach to the 'practical' games of life is that of applied mysticism," and "the most efficient way to cut through the game structure of western life is the use of drugs . . . Drug-induced *satori*. In three hours under the right circumstances the cortex can be cleared. The games that frustrate and torment can be seen in the cosmic dimension . . ."

Deriving as we know from the Buddha, this doctrine offers us a source of wisdom if we can handle it and disaster all around if we can't. The twins, saint and psychopath, can both make use of Game Theory for their own purposes. So can all losers. The difficulty today is that, with the availability of mind-opening drugs, every clod can come on as a mystic. Every idiot can go out on his own with no guidance whatever and experience the voyage through death and rebirth, and learn from it only this: that, games being all, *nothing is real* and everything is permitted —the psychopath's knowledge, which leads to the free-form model of living.

If everything's a game, if each sequential experience is just one more trip, then where are you, who are you, between games? If last night's experience, just some kind of riff, can be discarded and forgotten the next day, was it ever real? For a continuity of nothing but games can play tricks with time and truth. We become multiple selves, or as Leary would prefer, serial identities. Commitment to an idea, a cause, amounts cosmically to no more than a small hang-up that will pass just as you will pass. We can keep changing hats and changing philosophies at will because the scene will shift; the theater, game, characters, will shift and pass, dissolve.

All linear responsibility is deliberately abandoned. And ideally pain and hatred, envy, meanness will be evaded too. We achieve serenity—or is it detachment—as we pass from one game to another. Does not the game-player fall into the psychopath's "emotional flatness"? But this, who knows, may be desirable too. In *The Politics of Ecstasy*, Leary makes a leap:

> Emotions are the lowest form of consciousness. Emotional actions are the most contracted, narrowing, dangerous forms of behavior. The romantic poetry and fiction of the last 200 years has quite blinded us to the fact that emotions are an active and harmful form of stupor.
>
> . . . Beware of emotions . . . Watch out for the emotional person. He is a lurching lunatic.
>
> Do not trust anyone who comes on emotional . . .
>
> The emotional person cannot think; he cannot perform *any effective game action* . . . [my italics through the following passages] The emotional person is turned off sensually. His body is a churning robot; he has lost all connection with cellular wisdom or atomic revelation . . .
>
> What psychologists call love is emotional greed and self-enhancing gluttony based on fear.
>
> The only state in which we can learn, harmonize, grow, merge, join, understand is the *absence of emotion.* This is called bliss or ecstasy, attained through centering the emotions . . .
>
> Conscious love is not an emotion; it is serene merging with yourself, with other people, with new forms of energy. *Love cannot exist in an emotional state* . . .
>
> Did you imagine that there could be emotions in heaven? Emotions are closely tied to ego games. *Check your emotions at the door to paradise* . . .

20

Thus, Leary proposes the removal of emotion as a technique for surviving all trips. The psychopathic style again—and we may wonder whether in fact, as we have been told many times, the psychopath, by an approach still undiscovered, should be taught to *overcome* his inability to feel and relate, or whether as the world stands now, if it comes down to this, lack of feeling is a *boon* to him because it removes pain.

I smoke very seldom, but can best understand Leary's model from the memory of a marijuana high. Several months ago a number of us decided to have a breakfast smoke in the early morning, and then we went bowling—early bowling being common where we live, especially on Sundays. It's not my sport, and rare visits to the alleys have always brought on a vague headache and depression caused by the infinity of shattered pins and jumping numbers, and on all sides the plebeian shouts, groans, and applause, beer, hot dogs. But this time the game was different. In our alley, none of us cared about winning. We were at once removed from the scene and pleased to be there.

It was pleasing slowly to wind up and gradually let the ball go. Forever rolling down the alley and then, after minutes it seemed, there was the unbelievably beautiful *tock* as the ball hit the pins. And they flew slowly upward, spinning lazily in the air, and around us numbers would slowly jump. I could see colored lights blinking in every alley. Meanwhile—imagine those pins still in the air—on the other alleys they were all tense and striving, involved, hung up in their competitions. (We hardly even bothered very seriously to keep score.) They sweated, cheered, groaned, and twisted with body English. We just gamboled. Nothing could touch us. The moment slowly continued.

Then a picture slowly grew inside my head and projected itself on the wall. In my mind's eye a man's face appeared, and it was Vince Lombardi, who had died a few months before. Coach, who had said: "Winning isn't everything; it's the *only* thing!" And drove and tormented his players, making them care beyond pain (caring *vs.* digging), and died a legend. And I wanted to say to his fabulous, brutal memory: "Look, *ours* is the real alley. You see now! It's only a *game* . . . all the pain, sacrifice, and heroism you loved was nothing more than a *preference* . . ." and then his image slowly faded.

Leary turns life into games. Lombardi symbolized games as life. Which magician is which? Who is right? Or both.

Removing pain, detachment paradoxically can sharpen pleasure. The unconnected person, feeling no responsibility, has nothing to inhibit him: we have heightened sensation achieved through indifference.

In a small, scattered way, feel the exciting vibrations among strangers, say, at an airport bar. Within minutes everybody will fly off in different directions, never to see one another again. Often talk breaks free, and people confess. Uninvolved, we touch each other.

And sex in motels. Motels are absolutely for use. There's no dear familiar. In the good ones, bed and thick rug seem to flow into one another. Every toilet fixture is sealed with rice paper, antiseptic beyond belief. A timeless place, the room is intended for nothing but rest, sleep, or sex. It offers not the slightest emotional possibility. Sex pit, paradise wholly without extraneous charm. Go to the automated ice bucket, get out your bottle of vodka, drink or smoke together; make coolly passionate, detailed love built out of marijuana or martinis. Or, a pro, carefully calculate and feel nothing, perform any trick the client wants within reason. Bourgeois swinger, into group sex, find refurbished ecstasies in the exciting absence of love.

But detachment can also bring on manipulation of others, taking form as some kind of sadism. Sometimes the victim doesn't even know it; the bored cruel view of life can be that remote. The other night I visited David in his penthouse. As usual, he had his high-powered telescope out and was making the rounds of lighted windows across the park. Nearly every clear night he enjoys this pastime. Whenever he gives a party, guests take turns hunting for naked couples, peering in on their privacy from a mile or two away. David gives a curious little laugh and focuses the telescope. He has found some action. I don't even disapprove of what he's doing (after all, no one is hurt by his inspection), but the onanistic cruelty of it . . . he finds the exposed lovers only ridiculous. Voyeur, eavesdropper, obscene phone caller, all game-players really. These are the areas in which psychopathy turns mean.

Why is cruelty so close to the detached observer and player of games? For instance, the manipulative art of blowing the other person's mind, so popular now. As we've said, Zen sadism, confusing the innocent one by means of (John Lennon) "only another mirror." There's only a short step from "blow his mind" to "Let's throw the VC out of the airplane and listen to him whistle on the way down." Because it's just a "throw the slope out the window" game.

BREAKS LEG TRIPPING

Mrs. Anna D——— tripped over a blind man's cane yesterday, breaking her leg...

That item broke up a party of smokers one evening. Also the story of a thirty-five-year-old claims adjuster in Brooklyn who lived with his mother. He had been out of work for a while and for various reasons decided to kill himself. What held him back was the disgrace and the shame his mother would feel. So he grabbed her around the waist and jumped out the window from four stories up and, landing on her, killed his mother but he himself survived.

"Mattress-cide!" cried one smoker.

Then this account, again with all names fictional, and time and location left out:

WRESTLER SEIZED LEAVING HOSPITAL WITH MOTHER'S BODY

Ken Barlow, 37, was arrested yesterday, as, police said, he ran from a hospital with the body of his mother over his shoulder.

[She] had died in the hospital a short time earlier, apparently of a heart attack. Hospital guard Michael Condon said Barlow . . . struck a nurse and fired a shot at Dr. L. K. Lucas as he wheeled his mother's body down a corridor on a hospital table.

Condon said that when he tried to stop the man Barlow picked up the body and put it over his shoulder. The guard continued to struggle with Barlow outside until police arrived . . .

For the smokers, detached game-watchers, these three stories offered unacceptable anguish, a drag if taken seriously, and were therefore hilarious. Ludicrous pain can only be laughed at. Suffering must never be condoned. "The games people play" appear ridiculous, stupid when they let misery get the best of them. Because they're taking themselves too seriously. Suffering is stupid, and an illusion besides. (Since nothing is that real, and will pass.) People are not ends in themselves, but reincarnations, reiterations of—not even a single self—an ever-dissolving, renewing, accidentally thrust-up life form each of us imagines as "myself." And this perception is what makes detached cruelty and laughter possible on such easy terms.

We even have detached, unbelieving, game-playing revolutionaries, and the psychedelic left's concept of theater as all. From *Revolution for the Hell of It,* Abbie Hoffman's laughing celebration of meaningless and violent games:

> We become communist-racist-acid-headed freaks, holding flowers in one hand and bombs in the other . . . So what the hell are we doing, you ask? We are dynamiting brain cells. We are putting people through changes. The key to the puzzle lies in the theater. We are theater in the streets: total and committed . . . The aim is not to earn the respect, admiration and love of everybody—it's to get people to do, to participate whether positively or negatively. *All is relevant, only the play's the thing* [my italics].
> Don't be for or against. Riots—environmental and psychological—are Holy, so don't screw around with explanations. It's dynamite . . . *By allowing all: loving, cheating, anger, violence, stealing, trading,* you become situation-oriented and as such become more effective.

Thus, a virtue is made of what the straight world would call psychopathic irresponsibility—anathema to straight revolutionaries as well. Eldridge Cleaver: ". . . it is not realistic or serious to suggest that people try to deal with the situation in the United States by taking acid trips or other drugs [he exempts marijuana] . . . we are finished with relating to this madness, we are through tolerating this madness . . ."

So when Leary escaped from prison in California and briefly enjoyed an Algiers sanctuary under Cleaver's protection, the Panther leader soon personally arrested him for a few days. (Leary and his many visitors—including, Cleaver made an educated guess, disguised CIA agents—were regularly turning on as usual.) From a revolutionary standpoint, the bust was necessary, and Leary's eventual departure from Algiers most welcome. In their own Algiers compound, the Panthers had to put a stop not only to LSD flights but to the destructive concept of Revolution as One More Game. For Cleaver, revolution is not a game or a trip but all that his life is about. For such a pure revolutionary, left-wing gamesmen are far more dangerous than the CIA. Because in contrast to the cold, professional revolutionary who lives out his fanatical years in one world only, the stoned "revolutionary" of the left inhabits any number of worlds, and can trip from one to the next at will. He can escape boredom, find himself, only in the adventure of theater, riot, and showing off. Through him Yeats's "mere anarchy" is loosed upon the world. And in this manner, as Dr. Detre and his colleagues pointed out, the true (perhaps not the imitative) psychopath can well become the irresponsible betrayer of all insurrections that he has promoted for fun.

Tim Leary's brains may have been addled by countless acid trips, as Cleaver charges, though this is uncertain—depending on what we count as brain damage. Repeated use of LSD has not yet been proved measurably deleterious in terms of actual cellular deterioration, as has alcohol. (Late research, though, may indicate the contrary.) But, just as important—again perhaps amounting to illness of the same severity—the more you trip out, the less sure you are of which world you're in, which trip you're on. A confusion of identity sets in. You forget the hat you're wearing. Nothing is real, and all is real. There is no truth, any truth will do. Hence, what Cleaver may be driving at is that an immediate and urgent situation—requiring practical answers—may have no more objective reality to Leary than any other of the trips he has taken and hopes to take.

Understandably then, we have Cleaver's rage, and black rage in general against psychedelic drugs. Removal of emotion means removal of commitment. Any commitment will be subject to revocation because identity is serial; it's really all a game, and, besides, the stoned individual, holy or otherwise, has become a different person now. Because—as all mutants, I, all of us, know from the flights taken inside our heads—the Collective Unconscious *is*. The events and sensations re-encountered there *were* and *are*, just as I *am* now typing, as real as that. Not only are these experiences in no sense unreal, but they can make the job at the agency, as well as the solemnity of revolution, seem unreal and even ridiculous, elsewhere, and in fact the job, the revolution, may perhaps—set against the cosmos—*be* so. This is a large and difficult order for any head to process. For many, trying to manage it, feckless and frequently destructive manifestations of psychopathy can be let loose, and never again put back in the box.

See now into the undisciplined acid head's confusion (I mean people who take it all the time), for he can be experiencing many frames of existence at once, and simultaneously living out a collection of many lives. In *The Village Voice,* Ron Rosenbaum remarked of Leary: "It may be that he is nothing more than a regression of roles within roles." It's not so much, no crime, that Leary has been inconsistent. He simply switches from one identity, one philosophy, to another, not in the least disconcerted, with no pain. But his casual abandonment of "the religious trip" ("It was a low level game to start a religion") exemplifies the irresponsibility of this free-floating style. He doesn't seem to care that he may have let down many disciples who believed in his game of worship, and thought he was taking it seriously all along. They must wonder: What will my master believe, what will he teach, tomorrow? Supremely manipulative, the guru seems only to be trying to stay alive in his own head through theatrical scene changes.

Holy man and psychopath may be seen as equally cynical, in

that they believe existence to be repetitive and circular, hence boring. For them, the wheel of being does not roll or life build toward anything. It just spins. They don't imagine that the evolutionary chariot might be moving in any direction, such as toward a higher civilization.

If we're just meaninglessly spinning, and each of us amounts to nothing but a spin-off, a flake, soon to disappear, then the solution offered by the holy man and psychopath makes perfect sense. Have fun. Forget about dragging responsibilities. Seize the moment, one frame at a time. Reject the linear. Discount history and any sort of long-range planning.

But if it's possible again to suppose that the chariot is careening somewhere, possibly toward a higher, more satisfying existence, then linear faith can be restored and what each one contributes may indeed have some meaning.

Holy man and psychopath are not new. Neither is the classic argument whether to respect the institutions handed down to us, our generation not owning them and therefore not lightly destroying them, and preserve the best of these for our children (Edmund Burke) *vs.* to hell with it, live now, fully, free, unshackled by the past (Thomas Paine).

But there *is* something new under the sun, an utterly new, unprecedented situation. This is the availability of chemicals that can perhaps help save all lost souls. For used intelligently and sacramentally, as Leary once intended (but a conception he turned his back on), these drugs can contribute toward teaching us to *combine* circular and linear being as well as to restore each shaken pilgrim's faith in the worthwhileness of being worthwhile, making it possible for psychopath and nonpsychopath to live together, and even become as one, we will see, periodically reborn.

V

Psychopathy
and Rebirth

Now to tie the strands of our theme together. What began as a condition identified, at least according to middle-class psychiatric diagnosis, as a form of mental illness has now moved beyond the medical model to a style of living followed by great numbers of people. A country-wide invasion or uprising of psychopaths has already taken place. But the psychopath's original "moral insanity" is being transmuted in revolutionary passage. Although he himself may remain sick, his imitators, adopting the sick man's spontaneous and theatrical mode of making out, seem to have broken through to new methods of mastering time and bringing new excitement to many of humanity's outworn games.

The new ethic foreseen by Erikson, though not visualized or described by him—an ethic based on grace and performance rather than good will only—has begun to take form. We find the psychopath and his followers refusing to accept rules of conduct based on the sacredness of time, responsibility, and long-term planning. Living for the day and for all immediate sensations and excitements, reaching for whatever simulations of rebirth they can discover, these invaders of the culture furnish perhaps not an answer but a crude working model of behavior through which we may eventually be able to approach some kind of salvation. What they have impressed upon us is a new sensibility relating to time, pleasure, and death.

Such behavior derived from psychopathy may be seen as medicine we have required. A form of illness produces a form of therapy. Disease has evolved into style, offering—all-important—repeated simulations of being reborn (a desperate need evidenced, for example, by the mystical 1971–72 return-to-Jesus movement).

For rebirth is the key. Unhappily, the old orthodoxies that once sustained us have lost it. Young priests, ministers, and rabbis are shaking the old structures, but more must be done, quickly; new ceremonies developed to overcome the now fully revealed drag of unadorned death and meaninglessness. And largely for this reason the massive imitation of psychopathy has arisen, as a palliative really.

Too often the alternative has been madness. Striving for rebirth has meant for thousands a headlong drive toward mental illness, as if to sweep death and meaninglessness away by going crazy. A deliberately sought crack-up is achieved, with fragmentation hopefully laying the groundwork for spiritual renaissance. We have the idea of fashionable madness, the soul's stormy progress, risking padded-cell disaster en route to tranquillity, propounded by Ronald Laing and others. As Leary put it: "Go out of your mind in order to use your head." Hit bottom before coming back to life. Nearly all therapeutic ceremonies at this time *seek breakdown* before reunification of the soul. Even political therapy. Jerry Rubin: "I support everything which puts people into motion, which creates disruption and controversy, which creates chaos and REBIRTH [my caps]."

Lack of meaningful rebirth ceremonies within a structure of religious faith has had a disastrous result in recent years: the epidemic use of heroin. Heroin addiction, of course, has grown out of many crises, all the familiar ones, social, economic, Vietnam blunder and betrayal, the continuing crisis of boredom. But it has grown very much out of a religious crisis as well: new ways of periodically feeling reborn are required. Drugs provide the illusion and promise of rebirth that increasing numbers of people can no longer find by orthodox religious means. Hence, whether we like it or not, they are used—tragically, in so many instances— to fill a religious need.

And another tragedy is that middle-class authority has almost willfully refused to concede any merit whatever to a selected few of these substances, as opposed to the purely destructive ones. LSD is lumped with heroin as essentially evil, only in a different way. True, LSD and kindred materials have been criminally misused, destroying thousands of souls, and LSD became a food for anarchy. But the abuse of a practice is no argument against the practice itself. The abuse of a drug (swallow a hundred aspirins) doesn't necessarily clinch the argument against that drug. And the abuses we recognize need not and must not put an end to these redeeming materials. For, used properly in the right set and setting, LSD has a power as great and useful as prayer. We will see that by refusing to make allowances for a church or temple, any religious structure, to contain and sanctify LSD trips into inner consciousness, we gave them over to anarchy, abuse, and gangsterism.

Do such drugs encourage psychopathy? Yes, LSD, psilocybin, and the other psychedelics (as opposed to the horror of heroin) have provided much of the energy for the psychopathic invasion, and can also help heal the wounds it has inflicted. Speaking mainly of the hallucinogens, and even of marijuana, such consciousness-expanding substances and their availability to the middle-class masses may be recognized as the irreversible force that has probably changed our scene forever. For these materials—if ingested in a sufficiently heavy dosage to simulate the experience of dying and being reborn—have *already*, in a permanent way, changed the psyches of most voyagers so that they can never again fully accept linear values involving acquisition, advancement, and amassing prestige. (That is, they may grow rich, advance, and become famous, but will have fun, not laboring humorlessly as though *obliged* to do so.)

Sylvia Porter in her syndicated column (May 18, 1971): "Mounting numbers—maybe millions—of our young people are rejecting our long-standing occupational values of money, security, success, challenge, position. They are turning their backs on the standard careers which are listed in the vocational counselors' handbooks . . . They are trading well-paying jobs they would be quite capable of performing excellently for non-paying volunteer work of all kinds . . ."

The cold, maneuvering psychopath has always pretended to accept the old standards, though, as Dr. Michael Glenn noted, laughing behind his mask. But the self-destructive knockabout village psychopath, refusing to hold down a steady job, bucking his respectable neighbors, has a consistent record of rejecting just such values. Today he is no longer the exception in town. A generation has joined him—or at least a notable percentage of the first generation exposed en masse to psychedelic materials.

For these—because of revelations experienced during LSD and other such voyages, or, at the minimum, marijuana-taught irreverence toward bourgeois complacency and show—middle-class values have simply collapsed. While most rebels and dropouts are by no means clinically psychopathic, values of the psychopath—mainly his denial of time and responsibility—have come to the fore. And the new psychopathy in a number of its manifestations could be helping us *not* go mad.

Salvation and rebirth by means of deliberately induced madness is a cruel and nutty solution to the problem of a man's, a woman's, fight to survive unbelieving in the face of the void. Psychopathy may be serving as a compromise state of mind, a mental halfway house between our old, outworn sanity (which can't properly confront the void) and fragmentation without rebirth (splitting before terror and meaninglessness). When a straight person can't make it anymore he goes to pieces. Since the psychopath never lingers over his fear but acts out whatever bothers him in precipitate, unreflective fashion, he's much less likely to break down.

Stress again that we are speaking mainly of the middle classes. The poor don't have to be taught psychopathic arts. The best, to struggle free in harsh cities, must employ them. Driving toward liberation, black revolutionaries, among others, work with violent sociopathic techniques, and these, as emphasized by Fanon in *The Wretched of the Earth,* absolutely can't be dispensed with:

> . . . muscular action must substitute itself for concepts . . .
> Violence is thus seen as comparable to a royal pardon. The colonized man finds his freedom in and through violence . . .
> So the pimps, the hooligans, the unemployed, and the petty criminals, urged on from behind, throw themselves

into the struggle for liberation like stout working men. These classless idlers will by militant and decisive action discover the path that leads to nationhood. They won't become re-formed characters to please colonial society, fitting in with the morality of its rulers; quite on the contrary, they take for granted the impossibility of their entering the city save by hand grenades and revolvers. These workless less-than-men are rehabilitated in their own eyes and in the eyes of history . . . all the hopeless dregs of humanity, all who turn in circles between suicide and madness, will recover their balance, once more go forward, and march proudly in the great procession of the awakened nation.

Again rebirth, this time by revolution. An uprising of people driven sociopathic, seeking justice, revenge (same thing), a legitimate, even holy aim for the oppressed, using their psychopathy as a fearful weapon.

The psychopath, we know, has been described as ideally suited to frontier life (roving gunfighter). In the Old West, as we've chosen to remember it, he became a romantic figure. We celebrated him, and still do. Now, in our time, most alert people find that they have reached another kind of frontier along which varieties of psychopathic behavior flourish and triumph. All souls maneuver in dangerous, contested territory. Some feel stifled, want to smash everything, urinate in your hallway, break your head. Others retire, hide, ask only to be left alone, almost certainly won't be. In this border country the soul longs not to be afraid. And for many children of the present time only outlaw behavior can overcome fear, only having fun or smashing things relieves the feeling that one is stifled and oppressed, if not by other men, then by the indifferent universe itself.

It seems that the Great Psychopath in the Sky has it in for all of us. The only thing to do is ride out from under his arbitrariness and indifference, get over the border and break free. No more meditation, musing over this doubt and that fear. No more plodding in earnest pursuit of a sober and responsible life plan. For the psychopath, and now his followers, this is a fool's game. Instead, for them, physically, spiritually, travel, move, make out, exploit, strike back, enjoy, unimpeded by any guilt whatever, compassionate only when aesthetically excited or on whim, cross all borders, made new after each illegal crossing, keep going.

Assume the ascension of psychopathic values among great numbers of us to be accomplished and irreversible. Somehow then, if we are not to reach an Armageddon involving psychopath and bourgeois, their conflicting approaches to life must be reconciled or manage to exist side by side. How can this be done? (The revolutionary, of course, believes that it positively should not be done. His path is open. He needs no suggestions.)

One fantasy: The psychopathic style is here, with us, we live with it, many by it; therefore, recognize this and formally teach it. Establish a curriculum of Psychopathic Studies in American schools and universities in which ramifications of the psychopathic arts would be *taught like a second language* side by side with the straight curriculum.

Such courses would teach both straight and psychopathic values, not in a spirit of advocacy or condemnation but rather recognition that what were formerly considered outlaw practices exist in force, grow in importance, and dominate an increasingly powerful minority of headlong, uninhibited people. Teach psychopathy to take the mystery out of it. Also open up for straight people, particularly inhibited conformists, the pleasures of breaking away from time and responsibility, and of enjoying guilt-free, non-dues-paying play.

Just as Machiavelli exposed the mysteries of power for the education of a prince, teach our children practices they will surely come up against in the world outside. Teach, for example, Psychopathic Ethics, contrasting them—not as recommended or evil, but as they work—with traditional systems.

Such a course of studies would expose, compare, advise. Its aim would be to release but perhaps also contain outlaw tendencies in everyone. Combining humanism with psychopathy, it would instruct students in the proper execution of the Psychopathic Arts. At the same time, by holding up these practices to the light, it would teach the innocent how to recognize and live with them.

But now imagine, not in fantasy, a development that may
well actually come to pass, for millions of psyches are moving in
this direction: the establishment (*yes*) of a nation-wide active
Drug-Church, or rather, better, a Spiritual Circus bringing together sacramentally under one main tent all known techniques
of simulating death and rebirth. The aim of this Church or Circus
would be to institute a kind of Reform Psychopathy, combining
the best, exuberant aspects of this transmuted mental illness with
linear hope and persistent striving, perhaps within the framework
of Games Taken Seriously.

Establish then a Church of Rebirth by Any Means, a Temple
for the Repeated Simulation of Dying and Being Reborn, a religious base making it possible to reconcile the linear and circular
views of life. Achieve a fusion of the straight and psychopathic.
Psychopaths and nonpsychopaths lie down together, and by sharing the death-rebirth experience learn to live with one another.

The psychopath protests linear responsibility. Straight people
resist the idea of a meaninglessly turning wheel. Their faith, for
many flagging now, is that the evolutionary chariot must be
rolling toward a higher state of being. How to combine these
approaches and live peaceably side by side? Again, by sacramentally dying and being reborn together; sharing trips in the new
temple within a sacred framework. In this way, produce the effect
of ceremonially taking time out, restore faith in the games we
live by, teach the obsessed as well as lapsed crusaders among us
to become searchers and voyagers instead of glory hunters—
enjoying each trip, game, quest for itself rather than being tyran-
nized by the obligation (vain hunt for God's approval) to rack
up an unforgettable score.

And gradually new Rebirth Temples around the country
would build a body of doctrine. Also charts of the infinitely
varied, yet also eternal, voyage whose progression through breakdown and revival never changes, so that the traveler can be more
readily comforted—depending on what stage he's passing through
—and have a spiritual map of his journey on hand. The chart
would make all phases of the trip recognizable, like Stations of
the Cross, with the body of doctrine available to help all guides

and companions involved to interpret and include within a sacred
order the transformation and renewal he's undergoing.

Thus, in uninhibited fashion lay the foundation for a new
orthodoxy. This would undoubtedly embrace, among many variations, the orgiastic, attempting to achieve the shuddering and
throbbing that comes up through the spine, solar plexus, center
of one's being, the continuing preorgasm that travelers on the
death-rebirth trip so frequently experience (with drugs or not);
the same experience that the psychopath randomly, often clumsily
seeks, and which, being out of control—except in bed, on pre-
scribed sexual occasions—frightens the bourgeois. The aim then,
in Temples of Rebirth: to drive out of control, regularly and
ceremonially break apart, kill and heal, reassemble the aggressive
and also fearful self, shrived, renewed—within ritualistic limits.

As Leary originally intended but later disavowed as a low-
level conception, substances such as LSD, if used with dignity
and care, can serve as the food of such a new faith—pursued in
temples, not alone—that so many of us, psychopath and nonpsychopath, desperately need, replacing eventually, perhaps very
soon, the wafer and the wine. The psychopath's predatory drives
may be softened by the experience of being shattered and healed
over during voyages inside his head. Bourgeois complacency and
blinkered fixation on linear advancement will similarly be stripped
away as the sales manager laughs and weeps and rolls naked.
Soften the psychopath's harsh, manipulative nature. Release the
conformist's blocked spontaneity and teach him playful violence.

Emerge refreshed from carefully spaced ceremonial explora-
tions into the common pool of memory. (In the temple, bank
presidents lying down with horse players.) The experience of
traveling together would link psychopath and nonpsychopath—as
in fact, whenever undertaken, it does—so that they would never
again completely misunderstand each other. Tame the psychopath; enliven the straight arrow in order that now and then he
can taste the delights of irresponsibility. And for the psychopath
and his followers, the next great religious leader, himself Bored
Master Psychopath, must teach a Divine As-If enabling them to
rise above the "just games" attitude that finally weakens the head

in the act of freeing it. At the same time avoid Vince Lombardi-
type games of torment.

The Church or Temple of Rebirth would by no means guide
the spirit to renewal exclusively through the sacramental use of
drugs. The Spiritual Circus put on by such a faith would celebrate
and give sacred authority to every form of the death-rebirth trip.
Such as through (if desired) ritualistic violence; orgies (bringing
sex and religion back together where they belong), every sort of
productive encounter session, fasting, sleeplessness, yoga, dancing, rolling, quaking, mystical calisthenics, multimedia bombard-
ment, all trips, and every one of the alternate nondrug highs now
being devised, would be welcome under the main tent. *Carnival*
is the secret, but not as farewell to the flesh. In simulation, a
carnival of dying with resurrection only a few hours away.

In a religious vacuum, the godless psychopath, our most
recent model and, it's said, emotionally disturbed advance man,
may turn out to be, as Robert Lindner described him, "the harbinger of social and political distress." We may experience him as
a sometimes charming, sometimes brutal antichrist multiplying
among us, a bored and reckless Pied Piper soon to make off not
only with our children but our very history and all the beliefs
we live by.

Yet could his coming also represent "the birth of the deliverer" projected by Jung, the event "equivalent to a great ca-
tastrophe since a new and powerful life issues forth just where
no life or force or new development was anticipated"?

Decades ago Jung warned:

> It streams forth out of the unconscious; i.e., from that
> part of the psyche which whether we desire it or not is un-
> known and therefore treated as nothing by all rationalists.
> From this discredited and rejected region come the new
> tributary of energy, the revivification of life. But what is
> this discredited and rejected region? It is the sum of all
> those psychic contents which are repressed on account of
> their incompatibility with conscious values, hence the ugly,
> immoral, wrong, irrelevant, useless, etc., which means every-

thing that at one time appeared so to the individual in question.

What may this new life force bring?

Now herein lies the danger that the very force with which these things reappear, as well as their new and wonderful brilliance, may so intrigue the individual that he either forgets or repudiates all former values. What he formerly despised is now a supreme principle, and what was formerly truth now becomes error. This reversal of values is tantamount to a destruction of previously accepted values; hence it resembles the devastation of a country by floods.

Are we then heading into a world of the deliverer or antichrist? Both? Whoever he is, will we necessarily be overwhelmed by him? Is he indeed delivering us? From what?

From death, surely, distracting himself and everyone by breaking apart time and filling our moments with aggression, tricks, games, pain. Distracting us from our linear path to the void, too desperately meaningless to bear now. This, if anything, must be the new man's evolutionary role. If not, he can only have come to teach us how to destroy ourselves.

Hence, it becomes urgent and essential that our new psychopathy be contained within the religious framework. There can be no way of accomplishing this except through fragmentation ceremonies, with or without drugs. Such Spiritual Circuses held in Churches or Temples of Rebirth would be designed to provoke therapeutic hallucinations, keep (in the head) all the colored lights going, and pinwheels, and crystalline explosions, terrifying apparitions and protective angels, all the paraphernalia and the visions of hell and heaven that attend the soul's renewing passage.

Psychopath and nonpsychopath retreat, mingle styles, are ritually shattered and reborn together. From this psychic collapse, renewal, and exchange there emerges a new kind of person, perhaps born free of time, whole again until the next visit to the temple—a month, six months, a year, five years later, whenever needed—unafraid, unbored, on the lookout for all kinds of excitements, pleasures, searches.

Index